A World Elsewhere

A World Elsewhere

BERNARD LEVIN

JONATHAN CAPE
LONDON

First published 1994

1 3 5 7 9 10 8 6 4 2

First published in the United Kingdom in 1994 by
Jonathan Cape
Random House, 20 Vauxhall Bridge Road, London SW1V 2SA

Random House Australia (Pty) Limited
20 Alfred Street, Milsons Point, Sydney,
New South Wales 2061, Australia

Random House New Zealand Limited
18 Poland Road, Glenfield,
Auckland 10, New Zealand

Random House South Africa (Pty) Limited
PO Box 337, Bergvlei, South Africa

Random House UK Limited Reg. No. 954009

A CIP catalogue record for this book
is available from the British Library

ISBN 0-224-03331-X

Set from the author's discs by
SX Composing Ltd, Rayleigh, Essex

Printed in Great Britain by
Mackays of Chatham PLC, Chatham, Kent

for Barbara Carey

so far
and yet so near

The cloud-capp'd towers, the gorgeous palaces,
The solemn temples, the great globe itself,
Yea, all which it inherit, shall dissolve,
And, like this insubstantial pageant faded,
Leave not a rack behind. We are such stuff
As dreams are made on; and our little life
Is rounded with a sleep.

William Shakespeare
The Tempest, Act IV, Scene I

Contents

Preface

THE WORD "utopian" has acquired a generally pejorative tone; a utopian project is one that is built without foundations, chimerical, innocent of reality, fit only for dreamers. We must bow to the way words are used; yet the genealogy of Utopia is immensely long; for sixty centuries (long before the word Utopia was coined) human beings have dreamed of a perfect world.

To a great extent, that is Utopia's fault. The nature of the world has, again and again, been such as to compel great numbers of mankind – most of mankind, indeed – to live in conditions that are unbearable; slavery, oppression, cruelty, starvation, rapine, slaughter – these could not be endured unless the sufferers, who had nothing to hope for from the real world, could find solace in a world elsewhere. When food is scanty, mankind dreams of a miraculous banquet; when the slavers come, the dreams are of a noble kingdom; when the war-clouds gather, the dreams turn peaceful. In the simplest form of the dream, from the very earliest springs of what ultimately became a giant torrent, mankind has believed in a world after death, which really meant a world after the afflictions of life.

How could it be otherwise? The first stirring of human consciousness would have asked the questions that are today still being asked: how did the world start, and why? What are we doing in it? What *should* we be doing in it? The first answers to those first questions must have been utopian ones; that is why Utopia must blame itself for the insubstantiality of the dreams that have warded off the truth.

Nevertheless, a wholly realistic world would be, quite apart from the starkness of the sufferings that Utopia soothes, unlikely to survive; but the flight to Utopia, which has so often been the only response to the necessity of action, has soaked mankind, again and again, in the dream.

Yet we cannot do without Utopia, for all the traps it lures us into. Surely, nothing could be more innocently utopian than the young people, in almost every western nation, who, shedding life-styles with contempt, sought a perfect world that they were convinced they could find, even if they had to go as far as Katmandu to find it. But no one seeking Utopia needs to look so far. Until the cinema turned sour and pessimistic, what else was it but the shadow of Utopia? *Does* love always endure? *Are* all women beautiful and men handsome? *Do* all villains eventually come to a bad end? And if a "no" comes into that catalogue, be sure that there will be not so much as the trace of negative when we get to the pages of the romantic novel.

Once upon a time... Such words, unable to do any utopian harm, yet do not realise what utopian pasts are conjured up. If we cannot find a perfect world in the present, and are rightly suspicious of one in the future, we can find any number in the past. Golden Ages abound; mythical and semi-mythical figures stalk through time gone by, all carrying banners inscribed with the perfection which the past has hidden, but which, the past tells us, is still there for the seeking.

This hunger can never be slaked; we search for real worlds that we can turn, by our own utopian conjuror's wand, into utopianised ones. Not many years ago, we were told that nuclear fission, though hideously dangerous in a world of rival, suspicious, watchful armies, was going to solve all our energy problems. Only a few years had to pass, it was said, whereupon no miner would ever need to get his hands dirty, no fumbling do-it-yourself householder would ever again get an electric shock, no gasometers would raise their round and ugly heads upon the landscape, for nuclear fission would replace every other kind of heating, lighting, travelling.

The years passed, and then decades; nuclear fission today produces a wretchedly small quantity of energy at a very high cost, and another utopian delusion is fading into the sunset. But do we learn? The next claim was that with the aid of modern technology (particularly the computer) normal industrial labour would shortly be finished for ever; if the factory does not work entirely by the hands of robots, there will be no need to do anything more than inspect the robots' running from time to time. Yet there is no sign indicating the permanent "down tools", except, perhaps, in the form of unemployment, which was presumably not what was meant.

We must remember those broken promises, and we must reject the cowardly claim that in any scheme of things there will be mistakes. Instead, we must always remind ourselves that Utopia is a shadow, and although it can help us, it cannot make our lives for us. We must make our own; we keep the utopian emblem in view always, and follow it, though it is a jack-o'-lantern leading us an exhausting dance, into a quicksand. Perhaps it cannot be trusted; but we must live our own Utopias, and we shall find, if we do so, that we need Utopia less and less. And perhaps that is the greatest lesson that Utopia teaches us.

There are many teachers, though. On the whole, utopians do not insist that their form of it is the only true one; a remarkable tolerance seems to reign, and only the more political versions demand a sole allegiance. Inside a Utopia, however, certainty is the general rule, and schism is unknown, or should be. That is how the brutal, even criminal, forms of Utopia can arise and thrive, while the followers suffer in silence, or – worse – persuade themselves that they are not suffering; how otherwise could men like Jim Jones and David Koresh attain and keep mastery of their followers?

There are softer choices. The utopians who cling to naturalism, living as close as possible to nature, have spawned a considerable literature of utopian simple-life; the nineteenth century was prolific with its imagined, but gentle, other worlds. Even the supposedly hard-headed twentieth century has had its turn at Utopia, and the utopians of the mind – men like Jung, Wilhelm Reich and R.D. Laing – played their part and offered their utopian conclusions.

Having got this far, it is time to take cognisance of the fact that there is another player in this mighty game, and one that every utopian must take account of. In the Garden of Eden, there were three figures, not two; Adam and Eve, walking in their Paradise, heard another voice than God's. The serpent had been introduced into Utopia, and from that day to this it has been a struggle between utopian man and the most un-utopian intruder.

Communities whose utopian plan of living has been admirable and set fair for the future have found that serpent has wriggled through the bars and stirred up conflict. Utopia-mongers have come and gone, leaving nothing behind, the utopian certainty never accomplished. The most detailed and complex plans for a Utopia have been studied endlessly with no success in building it. Fourier, perhaps the greatest monomaniac of all utopian thinkers, rubs shoulders with Robert Owen, the maker of the most buildable utopian village; both failed with the greatest ignominy. The serpent, somehow, had got in.

But the serpent, somehow, will always get in. That is because Utopia is perfection, and there is no such thing as perfection. What, after all, caused the enormous success of *Close Encounters* and the even greater applause of *E.T.*? It was, surely, that they provided a tiny promise, the kind that God gave the world with the rainbow, that "all shall be well, and all shall be well, and all manner of thing shall be well".

We can hold two things in our minds at the same time; that there is no Utopia, and that we can live as though there is. For Utopia did not come into the world on chance; it reflects mankind's various longings and the condition that mankind is in. Utopia, in the end, means that even though we can never reach perfection, we can strive for it, and in striving come closer and closer to the tantalising yet soothing and loving goal. And as we strive, we imagine perfect worlds, perfect communities, perfect societies, and we long to enter. We *can* enter, but there is an immense entry fee; it is called disillusion, and only those who are wealthy enough to pay the impost in Fool's Gold (for ordinary money does not suffice) may cross the threshold of certain disappointment, and perhaps even never find the way out.

★

I cannot remember how I first became fascinated by Utopia, this strange but touching belief, a belief so deeply embedded in the thoughts and feelings of mankind that it seems to be bred into the very genes. I read More's version as a schoolboy, and thought it very dull (which it is, incidentally); it was clear that the bug had not yet bitten. I grew up in the Second World War, hardly a time for thinking about perfect worlds inhabited by perfect beings. As a student, naturally, my time was taken up by putting the immediate world to rights. I distinctly recall taking part in a student march round and round the Savoy Hotel, though what the Savoy had done to offend us I cannot for the life of me now remember; it is very unlikely indeed that even I, romantic as I was then, thought that the perfect world would emerge from the Savoy if we denounced it loudly enough.

I think what drew me to Utopia was a combination of science fiction, which I devoured in my leisure time, and Plato, whom I had discovered in my thirst for the glories of ancient Athens. Plato horrified me with the severity of *his* perfect world, but at least it was an attempt to see how mankind could live, and I know that by the time I had thoroughly familiarised myself with the Funeral Oration of Pericles my fervour for the immediate institution of socialism (accompanied with the nationalisation of the Savoy Hotel) had somehow got mixed up with that most wonderful epoch; to put it bluntly, even with my young eye I could see the difference between the Royal Festival Hall and the Parthenon.

The next step was something much stranger and more personal.

The psychologists rub their hands with glee when they see a perfectionist coming. I had, and have, nothing to be perfect about, but built into me was and is (that "is" has dogged me all my life, and so far from subsiding as I grow older, it has become more intense) a truly dangerous demand of myself for tidiness. This tidiness has gone to lengths that I shiver, not just blush, to recall, for this obsession goes further; the demands of tidiness are pursued into a life of symmetry as well. (I even doodle symmetrically.)

It was, of course, a long time before I saw the connections, but when I did it was all I could do to restrain myself from announcing that the perfect world had arrived, in the shape of a square, an equilateral triangle, a rhomboid or, best of all, a circle. It would, of course, be absurd to claim that my interest in the idea of a world elsewhere, a world without pain, selfishness, power, quarrels, money or anger, grew from my obsession (though a significant number of perfect worlds do require symmetry, and one of the most horrific yet heartening anti-Utopias, its tyranny destroyed by a river, turns perfectly rigid order into disorderly perfect harmony).

Gradually, some twenty years ago, I began to collect, and then annotate, books about Utopias, or stories with a utopian theme. (Very many of these showed no sign of realising that they *were* utopian; no matter.) I also fished in the rich waters of theory; for every dozen

Utopias it seemed there were almost as many studies of the genre itself. The more I read of and about Utopias, the more I realised that there was not, and could not be, any end to the outpouring of Utopias (for, of course, the idea of Utopia is not confined to Britain or even the English-speaking world), but that only stimulated my appetite.

By then I had realised – and if I had not, I would have been singularly obtuse – that the idea of a perfect world had, through the ages, embedded itself inextricably in the feelings of the human race. The more I searched for examples, definitions and hopes, the more all-enveloping did the idea become. The range of Utopias was, as far as I could see, infinite, and any kind of catalogue would have been impossible, if only because Utopias are, amoeba-like, capable of indefinitely dividing themselves in half.

There was, and is, a vast variety of Utopias, but most of them can be subsumed under two headings. There are those which must really be classified as imaginary or science-fictional: even today, utopian worlds are created beneath the seas or above the skies. The other strain remains theoretically within reality; say, the abandonment of all military activity and the destruction of all weapons. In practice, of course, both are nothing more than yearnings; but then, why are we surprised when the word "Utopia" is treated with a patronising smile or as a useless irritant?

A reader of this book will, of course, be confronted with almost every kind of Utopia. This, in itself, delineates the nature of the quest, for there is nothing in the real world that cannot be improved by the believers in the unreal one. We find gentle communities, sharing, in every sense, their lives – the more modest, the more likely that the impetus will ultimately die, amid bewilderment. We find more sophisticated ones in our modern, hurrying world; egalitarian themes abound. There are those who believe that the nation-state has had its day, and that Charlemagne will sooner or later rise again to make all Europe one, heedless of the truth that the EC has done just that, and made a monumental mess of it, too.

Where are King Arthur and his knights? Here they are, in the Utopia story, bringing another hope of a perfect world; for King Arthur swore that he would come again, and King Arthur could not lie. (Alas, even in his pure band, there was the hiss of the serpent as Lancelot betrayed his king.)

Great nations have striven to be utopian; perhaps the Athens of

Pericles is the only one that fits the word. And yet, the voters of Athens exiled him. Smaller nations have tried even harder; the leaders of the Paris Commune believed that all France would come to their aid. But no; when the Commune was overrun, a rough and ready test for sniffing out the *communards* was for the soldiers to order a suspect to turn his hands palms up; if they were horny workers' hands, they were shot where they stood.

"Do what you will is the whole of the law"; that was the motto on the gates of the Abbey of Thelema, and gloriously did Rabelais' creations live up to that most happy charge. Does it matter that it was all in a book? After all, most Utopias have existed only in books, and how could they be real elsewhere? They *could* be real, say the utopians: that is the very flag under which they march. For Utopia is everywhere – at least while human beings exist. I have just mentioned a few instances of mankind's eternal yearning; I could have mentioned a hundred, and in the book they topple out of every page. Great ideologies have proclaimed themselves utopian, and slaughtered their people by the million to prove it, while beautiful utopian pictures of heaven give other millions hope of the happiness after death which eluded them before it.

I whisper here the truth that I declare in the book. In every human heart there is a Utopia, a belief in perfection; so there is, but the serpent is there as well. After all, I know that neither kind of Utopia will ever come about. But as the pity of it grew stronger, I found myself more and more deeply engaged in the huge tradition of Utopia, and ultimately found myself yearning, as all those thousands of utopianisers yearned, to make it happen.

I was not so far gone as to believe that I could bring about the perfect world. But at least I could write a book about it, despite the fact that giant libraries all over the world had shelves bursting with the outpouring of utopian visions. What could I add?

If anything, it would be this. The heartbreak of chimerical beliefs in Utopia has pained millions and still pains more; it pains my heart too. I believed, and still do, that I could empathise with those who want perfection and believe that it is achievable, while at the same time making clear that there is no such thing, and that to seek it in Utopia is not only to be disappointed, but to have added something to the danger that lurks always in Utopia.

When I began writing the book, all those years ago, I promised myself to keep that danger in mind. For of course there is danger in Utopia, though most utopians would deny the charge, and many would be unable to understand the meaning of such an alarming threat. No one can, with or without human or divine help, make the world perfect, and those who believe that they can are not only mistaken, but are running a great risk; moreover, the risk is not just to themselves.

It is twofold: the first part is the risk that, frustrated in their longing for Utopia, they will waste their energy – energy that could be used modestly, simply, easily, to achieve something that is not Utopia, but can be recognised as modest, simple, easy – and achievable.

The other risk is far greater. In this book I dwell at length on the terrible results when, between the wars, so many dupes, and a dreadful number of knaves, threw their minds, their eyes, their understanding, their very souls, into the greatest evil in all history. Stalin was their Utopia, and there was no need to wait for it: it was available at once. Before and after that monstrous misapprehension there have been many similar, though smaller, such aberrations; yet still the beacons beckon, and for the countless millions who died the bill has to be paid by Utopia.

As I wrote, my feelings began to change. I started with the belief that, as I said, I could hold in my mind and my heart the infinitely touching dream of Utopia, while at the same time insisting that it was indeed a dream. Gradually, as I wrestled with these two adversaries, which are also two helpmeets, my feelings tilted. Thomas Molnar (whom I quote in the book) argues that even an attempt, a trivial nod, towards friendly relations with Utopia, is dangerous; for him (his stand is a Christian one) the very idea of a Utopia is a blasphemy. I cannot go as far as that; but when I was struggling to keep my promise – my promise to keep Utopia in my heart – I found it more and more painful and difficult to do so.

This has been the most difficult to write of all my books to date, and I do not believe that that is a coincidence. True, the vast quantity of matter I had to digest made things uniquely difficult. Moreover, the story of Utopia being boundless, I found myself fighting the hydra – indeed, I was surrounded by hydras on every side; everything led to more, and the more led to yet more. I am quite sure that I could have written a book thrice as long, *absit omen*, and I am sure that these ostensibly technical problems were, unconsciously, the marks of my struggle against the seductions and delights of Utopia.

My readers will, inevitably, find themselves going along the path that

I walked. At the beginning, as the smiling utopians set off with the greatest confidence and the march gets into its stride, the bells in the valley will sound peacefully. Towards the end there will be heard a different sound, a sound composed of reality, of adjusted understanding, of real maturity: the sound is now carried on the wind, and the reader who listens closely will realise that the sound now says "Beware!"

Beware, indeed. Because, hard by the starting-place, there stands a sentinel. The sentinel turns no one back, he threatens no one, he does not even shake his head. But as each traveller passes him, he points to a signpost that stands beside the beginning of the march to Utopia, and it says: "There are no stopping-places on the route".

I

Atlantis awakens

IN EMBARKING upon the infinite sea of Utopia it is appallingly appropriate to discover that it begins at the wrong end. Golden Ages abound in history, some of them very recent, but the story of mankind's unending search for a perfect world – a world without pain, without loss, without hunger, without unhappiness, without oppression, without anger, without ugliness, perhaps even without death – surely recognises its origins in the oldest account of such an elysium. Hear Homer, the first voice in western literature, describing the eternal life of Olympos.

> Outside the courtyard, near the door is a large
> four-acre orchard, with a fence on either side.
> Here trees grow tall in rich profusion,
> pears, pomegranates, glowing apples,
> luscious figs, olives in profusion.
> Their fruit never goes rotten, never runs short,
> winter or summer, all through the year. Always
> the west wind's breath is bringing growth or ripeness.
> Pear after pear, apple after apple, grape
> after grape, fig after fig grow ripe.
> There his fruitful vineyard is planted.
> In one part currants are drying in the sun
> on a level exposed patch, in another they are gathering
> or treading the grapes. Close by is young fruit

with freshly-shed blossom, or the first tinge of purple.
Beyond the farthest row are neat beds
of various vegetables, green all through the year.
There are two springs. One irrigates the whole
garden; its fellow gives water to the citizens,
then gushes under the gate to the great house.
These were the gods' glorious gifts to Alcinous.

Now only one more century has passed, yet a shadow has already
fallen over the story. Homer's dythyrambs were not perfection-tight, and
darkness, from now on in the story, must accompany the light wherever
it goes. In biblical terms the serpent has beguiled Adam and Eve – the
serpent that will now run through this story to its end. As for the second
Greek voice, it is saying that the darkness has galloped away with the sun:
the First Pessimist has made his appearance. Significantly, what is more,
he tells his story as a tale of decline. Has the story of Utopia died before
it has had a chance to live?

It is better to read Hesiod backwards. When he wrote his *Works and
Days*, he was in despair of the human race. His five ages of man had
finished in the time of iron, and all around he could see nothing but
brutality, corruption, hunger, selfishness, hatred and emptiness. It is
worth listening first to his cry of anguish:

> And I wish that I were not any part
> > of the fifth generation
> of men, but had died before it came,
> > or been born afterward.
> For here now is the age of iron. Never by daytime
> will there be an end to hard work and pain,
> > nor in the night
> to weariness, when the gods will send anxieties
> > to trouble us.
> Yet here also there shall be some good things
> > mixed with the evils.
> But Zeus will destroy this generation of mortals
> > also,
> in the time when children, as they are born,
> > grow gray on the temples,

2

when the father no longer agrees with the children,
    nor children with their father,
when guest is no longer at one with host,
    nor companion to companion,
when your brother is no longer your friend,
    as he was in the old days.

This lament was all the more tragic and hopeless by comparison with what had gone before. "Never by daytime will there be an end to hard work and pain, nor in the night to weariness…" implies that this barren world was not the only one the earth had seen, and that it would have been better for him if he had died before hope did. This is a characteristic of utopianism, the harking back to prelapsarian perfection, corrupted as time passes. But from how steeply had Hesiod's Utopia fallen!

In the beginning, the immortals
    who have their homes on Olympos
created the golden generation of mortal people.
These lived in Kronos' time, when he
    was the king in heaven.
They lived as if they were gods,
    their hearts free from all sorrow,
by themselves, and without hard work or pain;
    no miserable
old age came their way; their hands, their feet,
    did not alter.
They took their pleasure in festivals,
    and lived without troubles.
When they died, it was as if they fell asleep.
    All goods
were theirs. The fruitful grainland
    yielded its harvest to them
of its own accord; this was great and abundant,
    while they at their pleasure
quietly looked after their works,
    in the midst of good things
prosperous in flocks, on friendly terms
    with the blessed immortals.

The yearning for what had once been (in fact, of course, had never been) is the hallmark of one variety of utopianism; whether the world had been getting better (a question urgently asked, again and again, in our time) or getting worse, some utopianisers will always opt for the pessimistic alternative. Less than two centuries later, Greek literature had taken a turn for the worse, or at any rate for the darker; *Oedipus Rex* symbolises the blackness in the heart of man, together with the heart of the implacable gods. Once the stone was kicked aside, the avalanche was inevitable; Oedipus was inexorably sentenced to pace out every inch of his *via crucis*.

No Golden Age there; but one man was determined to mock gods and men alike. Aristophanes harks neither back nor forward; his Utopias are as contemporary as they are satirical, where there is a feminist state and the gods are fit for nothing but being baited.

History moves on, and so have the Romans. Horace has restored confidence to those who want to believe that happiness can be found:

You, who have manhood, stop moping like women,
    speed past Etruria's coasts.
Encircling Ocean is awaiting us. Let us make for
    the Fields of the Blest, the Isles of Prosperity,
where each year the land unploughed produces corn,
    unpruned the vine blossoms,
the shoots of the olive unfailingly burst into bud,
    the dark fig graces its native tree,
honey oozes from the hollow oak, on the high hills
    the water lightly leaps with sounding step.
There the she-goats come to the milk-pail unherded,
    the flock is happy to bring its swelling udders home.
No bear growls round the sheepfold in the evenings,
    the ground does not swell high with snakes.
There will be more for us to marvel at in our fortune. No east wind
    rain-laden drowns the fields with showers.
The seeds swell and do not wither and parch in the baking earth.
    The king of the gods keeps heat and cold under control.
No pestilence attacks the flocks, no planet's
    torrid fury burns up the herds...
Jupiter set these shores apart for a people of righteousness.

Let us look rather more closely at that idea of a Golden Age.

Why does every fairy-story begin "Once upon a time..."? The time is very far away, so far, indeed, that it was old when the world had just been created; as early as the sixth chapter of Genesis we learn that "There were giants in the earth in those days", and the implication is that they are there no longer; indeed, it is not really fanciful to think that the Lord's words here take on a wistful tone.

A yearning for the past can be as domestic as an elderly man looking back at his life, or as colourful as an expedition to seek Prester John; inevitably, the past has taken on qualities that have now disappeared from mankind. It can be seen in the most trivial forms, as well as the most important; any middle-aged music-lover, for instance, will insist to any young one that the players and singers of today are greatly inferior to those of the speaker's youth, and when the young ones thus addressed have themselves moved into middle age, they will say the same. Now if each generation of music-lovers is correct in its respective estimation of the past and the present, it must follow that music has been steadily deteriorating from the moment it came into existence; an unlikely hypothesis.

Why, then, do we so romanticise the past, invariably at the present's expense? It is the yearning for perfection, which appears in a thousand guises but is in essence the same thing. The real world, in which we have to live, is manifestly imperfect, but instead of accepting that obvious truth and making the best of what we have, we yearn for something that no less obviously cannot now be found. What has gone wrong?

It is unregenerate man's fault, of course. In Orson Welles' film *The Magnificent Ambersons*, which recounts the decline of a family (a kind of American *Buddenbrooks*), there is a comment not by one of the characters but by the maker of the film acting as an off-stage chorus: "The city grew", says Welles, "and as it grew, it befouled itself." He might have been speaking of the world.

Man has sullied the perfection of the past; sullied it by bloody wars, by the grime and noise and upheaval of industrialisation, by cruelty and selfishness; so much so that the original world, pure, clean and holy, has turned itself into a brave and touching dream. A very few years ago, the great nations of the world pledged themselves never to disturb the eternal snows of the Arctic Polar region, though it is known that there are rich deposits of valuable minerals beneath the Pole. There are no human settlements there, of course, and a wholly unsentimental view of the matter might conclude not only that the mining would be very useful, but that this cold and empty world would be a perfect site for a global rubbish-dump, where, for instance, nuclear waste dangerous in the occupied parts of the world could be jettisoned in safety for all.

But the ecological movement is itself a utopian concept; there are meaningless terrors such as the "hole in the ozone layer", and "global warming", yet the impulse is a benign one; if there are holes, let them be patched; if we shall find ourselves uncomfortably warm, let us search for cooling devices, though not ones that emit warming gases or make holes in the ozone layer.

It has often been argued, not only by Welles, that the city itself is the destroyer of utopian possibilities; the quality of life is diminished by the inhuman demands the city exacts. That, of course, is the romantic-utopian belief that only in unsullied nature can the long-sought perfection be found, and it follows that before the cities came that is exactly what the world was like, and could be once more.

These repeated attempts to build Utopia retrospectively have an extra dimension. The utopianisers have thrown in their lot with real cities which, their time on earth being up, have vanished. Pompeii was destroyed by an earthquake, and the archaeologists are still arguing about what destroyed Knossos, but it is the abruptness with which they both died which gives them their eternally haunting nature, and which has led to their utopification. It is almost necessary for such places to be cut off in a moment, for if they had lingered for years or centuries they would have run the risk of becoming ordinary cities with no mysterious or symbolic ends, and thus losing their passports to Utopia.

But it must be remembered that the Golden Age, although a metaphor, also existed in a later reality. Whatever the Golden Age was, it was an age of belief, even if only because *all* ages for many centuries back were ages of belief; they accepted without questioning the truths of the gods, or even one god. From that position it was not difficult for anyone to know his place, and even, in time, to know also what he must do to find salvation. There are quieter and less dramatic Golden Ages, it seems, and at times through the ages – golden or base metal – a simple life could be truly utopian.

That simple life goes back to the earliest and most demotic forms of Utopia; the touching theme of Cockaigne inevitably augmented the utopian ranks, for it was the turn of the poor. A thirteenth-century picture of the golden world portrayed the innocent ease and plenty that they did not have; shops supplied goods without wanting payment, and even nature joined in the bonanza; the streets were made of marzipan, and birds cooked themselves and flew about inviting themselves on to the plate.

The theme of contrast is obvious; mankind has always invented counter-weights. When worlds are at war, the vision of a land free of strife is urgently needed, and the need calls it into existence; for every battle-scene, art provides not just warriors laying down their arms but allegories of peace herself. In an age of conspicuous consumption, simplicity and frugality are the utopian rejoinders; most powerful of all, perhaps, is the reply to an era of exploitation of the voiceless. The notion of bringing down the oppressor and elevating the oppressed has powerful support from the Bible, in which the mighty are overthrown in the interests of the humble.

This leads to the idea of something like entropy in the universe; perhaps the contrasts are not only dreams of the downtrodden (after all, most if not all of the responses to such unfair imbalances exist in pictures, songs, poems, ecstatic visions and above all utopian visions, but not in any kind of reality), but harbingers of a sea-change. For what is the most powerful metaphor for restitution, recognised much wider than its biblical form, if not the story of Dives and Lazarus? The angelic banquet at which the poor will feast, while the rich will be turned away, is a double Utopia; it hymns the poor who have come at last into their inheritance, and gives the beneficiaries the extra satisfaction of seeing the greedy ones suffering condign punishment. It is of interest to see that the second half of the inheritance is essential; the poor cannot be enthroned without vengeance being taken against the rich. Such Utopias, evidently, have no forgiveness in them.

Moreover, that powerfully symbolic form of systole-diastole in the inexorable uplifting of the downtrodden, the inheritance of the rejected, the punishing of the real sinners – this metaphor throws a huge shadow and – as is right – a no less huge light. For that, after all, is the legend of Atlantis, and the belief that it was drowned deliberately, as a punishment. (Leaving us to wonder what super-dreadful enormities must have been practised to cause the gods – presumably it was the gods – to destroy not just a city, a kingdom or a people, but an entire continent.) The belief in this drowned land, whether an accident or a punishment, may have in it traces of modern palaeontology; in the millions of years that it took to make the present earth, many upheavals of lands and seas took place. It is not without awe that we moderns contemplate, say, the Himalayas, and reflect that we are looking at one of those upheavals; the thought of watching the plain, empty earth fling itself upwards to the skies, with a groaning and crashing beyond any seismograph, must give the most prosaic among us a catch in the breath.

In the course of the millennia, then, there must have been thousands of continents submerged and new seas arising to cover them; but this cannot by itself account for the lasting belief in one special drowned world.

It is, among other things, a very powerful symbol and metaphor: "Full fathom five, thy father lies, of his bones is coral made..." Atlantis, however, is not a graveyard as is the ordinary sea; there is a world beneath the water, in which beings, half human, half aquatic, live.

In some accounts, Atlantis was drowned in the Flood, without a Noah to save man or menagerie. All the legends, however, agree that the lost land sometimes rises through the water and can be seen clearly by mortal eyes; these ghostly visitations from the sea bed presumably mean that Atlantis is allowed – once a year, once a century, once a thousand years – to leave its watery grave. (This fits with many another legend, for instance, the Flying Dutchman, who is equally doomed to roam the world without rest except for those moments – once a year, century, millennium – when those who handed down the sentence relent and temporarily allow him to find land.)

The Atlantis belief helps to perpetuate the idea of a multiplicity of worlds, all striving to attain perfection, seeking absolution for the sin that drowned their world and gradually growing nearer forgiveness through the ages.

It is noticeable that there is no general agreement as to just where Atlantis lies, beneath which earthly ocean the waters press. That, too, must be symbolic; the goal is there, but we can never be quite sure exactly where. Nor, for that matter, can we agree on whether Atlantis is a dimly-lit, wraithly empire, or an infinitely rich land, where the very table utensils are of gold and silver. Debussy's *Cathédrale Engloutie* certainly suggests that there is life in the waters, but there is another, more ethereal, form of testimony. A visitor to the island of Torcello, hard by Venice, will inevitably be drawn to the mighty church which stands on it, with its breathtaking *Last Judgement*. But the visitor will also find it difficult not to think of the building as a *cathédrale engloutie*; its strange walls, its stranger colours, the stranger still washed-looking nature of the whole building, powerfully suggest that it has lain on the sea bed for a thousand years, and may at any moment be sunk again, to rise a thousand years hence.

At which point, though, the legends of ships that have sunk with treasure aboard mingle with the legend of Atlantis. Perhaps it is better to leave the last word to Shakespeare, and moreover the Shakespeare who is in the course of laying down his magic mantle, and no less his magic pen:

> But this rough magic
> I here abjure; and, when I have requir'd
> Some heavenly music – which even now I do –
> To work mine end upon their senses that
> This airy charm is for, I'll break my staff,
> Bury it certain fathoms in the earth,
> And, deeper than did ever plummet sound,
> I'll drown my book.

2

In the beginning was the word

To More goes the palm for introducing the word into the world, and fixing it there so strongly that there cannot be a civilised country which does not have a word for Utopia; most, indeed, sensibly abandon any attempt to translate it, and merely incorporate it as it stands, with such minor amendments as are needed for the local orthography.

The Greek *Utopia* for the name seems and sounds wonderfully apt; would we have warmed to it as much if it had been – as it might – couched in Latin, *Nusquam*, and meaning "Nowhere"? More and Erasmus bandied ideas back and forth before they settled on the name that has gone down to history, though to the end there was ambiguity, and still is: should it be *ou-topos* (no-place) or *eu-topos* (good-place)? Both or neither, perhaps; at any rate More did not elucidate. But the book was written in Latin.

It is in two parts (Book One was written before Book Two, but that has no particular significance), both of which are supposed to be the account of a traveller from afar, one Raphael Hythloday. First, Hythloday describes the England he finds, and after that turns to a detailed catalogue of what he found in Utopia. For Book One, he is supposed to be giving his reflections on England at the dinner table of John Morton, Archbishop and Cardinal of Canterbury (and Lord Chancellor for good measure). Being given, or taking, licence to speak his mind, Hythloday speaks it with considerable vigour. He depicts a country in the throes of dissolution; the most powerful of the forces that are dragging her down is the contrast between bitter poverty and huge, mostly ill-gotten, riches.

As Hythloday is warming to his work, another of the Archbishop's dinner-guests, a lawyer, demurs, and does so in the terms and tones that have provided a good living for lawyers since law began:

"For first", he says, "I will rehearse in order all that you have said; then I will declare wherein you be deceived through lack of knowledge in all our fashions, manners, and customs; and last of all I will answer your arguments, and confute them every one. First therefore I will begin where I promised. Four things you seemed to me..." – but at that point the Archbishop cries "Hold your peace, for it appeareth that you will make no short answer, which make such a beginning".

Then Hythloday continues:

And, verily, one man to live in pleasure and wealth while all other weep and smart for it, that is the part, not of a king, but of a jailer. To be short, as he is a foolish physician that cannot cure his patient's disease unless he cast him in another sickness, so he that cannot amend the lives of his subjects but by taking from them the wealth and commodity of life, he must needs grant that he knoweth not the feat how to govern men. But let him rather amend his own life, renounce unhonest pleasures, and forsake pride; for these be the chief vices that cause him to run in the contempt or hatred of his people. Let him live of his own, hurting no man. Let him do cost not above his power. Let him restrain wickedness. Let him prevent vices, and take away the occasions of offences by well ordering his subjects, and not by suffering wickedness to increase, afterwards to be punished. Let him not be too hasty in calling again laws which a custom hath abrogated, specially such as long been forgotten and never lacked nor needed. And let him never, under the cloak and pretence of transgression, take such fines and forfeits as no judge will suffer a private person to take as unjust and full of guile.

This is strong language, particularly with Henry VIII on the throne, but by the time *Utopia* was published More was Henry's darling, constantly being summoned to the royal presence for conversation; not content with that, the king took to dropping in at More's house in Chelsea.

More, however, was skilled in reading men, and he could certainly read Henry; he knew that for all the pleasantries the King could not be trusted. Nor could he; which is why the roster of the saints gained another martyrdom in 1535. But by the time More's head fell to the axe, his book was safe in history.

On a first reading, Hythloday's description in Book Two of the land of Utopia (ruled over by King Utopus) is something of a disappointment. After the savaging of England, a modern reader will expect a land magical in its contrasting perfection, but he will get only a tame, strangely unimaginative picture, modest in its nature and its subfusc meritocracy, and by no means far-reaching in its transformation of England. Indeed, the most striking feature of Utopia is that it is *not* a Utopia, at least if we define Utopia as a world without blemish, pain, labour and unhappiness. In More's version, crime exists, and even war; plainly, Utopia is not Heaven, nor Eden. (A mild form of slavery exists and, more surprisingly, euthanasia.)

A second glance, however, reveals depths and subtleties which are cumulatively astonishing. For a start, Utopia is not a Christian country; the Word has not yet reached them. More, however, contrasts their ultra-Christian characters with the laxity and shallowness of so many who, having had the revelation of Christ, do not live by it. He goes much further; Hythloday finds some utopians who *have* accepted the Christian witness, but immediately begin to claim that they are, literally, holier than thou; one of these insists that any who fail to be as Christian as he is are "the children of everlasting damnation". But he runs foul of the constitution of Utopia, which includes complete freedom of religion, while proselytism is permitted only if it is carried out quietly, modestly and with no fanaticism, nor abuse of others' faiths. The zealot is deported.

Again, More surprises us with his establishment of pleasure as the highest good in Utopia; it is not voluptuous or shameful pleasure (though the remit is wide), but would be better defined as joy. Significantly, though, any pleasure that involves harming or causing pain to anyone else is forbidden, and if there are two pleasures available, the more elevated one is to be chosen over the more base.

Utopians are all literate, it seems, but we learn virtually nothing about their language. The resourceful Hythloday, however, rapidly teaches them Greek, so that they can read the classics in the original; they favour Plutarch, Lucian, Aristophanes, Homer, Euripides, Sophocles, Thucydides, Herodotus and Herodian; well-read, these utopians, and in uplifting works. But they are duly grateful for being taught how to make paper and print on it, and while the instruction is going on, More tips his hat to his beloved friend Erasmus, "For when we showed to them Aldus his print in books of paper...". The utopians would not have known that Erasmus was working for Aldus as a proof-reader, and Erasmus would have smiled when he came upon the reference as he was eagerly devouring More's book.

But the most profound characteristic of the utopians is their scorn for wealth and those who seek it, an attitude that provides the best joke in the book (truth to tell, there are few), and the best moral.

> For whereas they eat and drink in earthen and glass vessels which, indeed, be curiously and properly made and yet be of very small value, of gold and silver they make commonly chamber-pots and other vessels that serve for most vile uses not only in their common halls but in every man's private house. Furthermore, of the same metals they make great chains, fetters, and gyves wherein they tie their bondmen. Thus by all means possible they procure to have gold and silver among them in reproach and infamy. And these metals, which other nations do as grievously and sorrowfully forgo, as in a manner their own lives, if they should altogether at once be taken from the Utopians, no man there would think that he lost the worth of one farthing.

This, then, is hardly the Abbey of Thelema. Yet More's Utopia is celebrated not just because he named an entire genre. The world he creates is a transmogrified England, but it is a specific transmogrification. More could not, and would not have wished to, leave his own religion behind. In the utopians' calm religious beliefs we can see a mirror held up to More's own country. All Utopias are didactic in one way or another, or they would be meaningless; More's is simple. True faith, simple living and contempt for those who worship power and pelf; a realisable agenda. He teaches his countrymen to live like utopians, who are by no means perfect beings, living under a benign rule that is itself by no means perfect. But the utopians strive, and so could his own people. When King Utopus cut the isthmus which joined Utopia to the mainland, he was making a declaration of independence. His readers could hardly have forgotten that Britain was already an island.

Mussolini wanted to cut the causeway to Venice, so that she would be again an island. It is unlikely that he had heard even the faintest echo of King Utopus; it is most unlikely that he knew of More's book, let alone that he had read it. But Mussolini's project (he was prevailed upon to leave the Venetian causeway untouched) would have been, for More, much less strange than the extraordinary idea which was offered in 1991 as an interpretation of his book.

It should be noted that More's meaning has been treated to countless examinations through the centuries; that reasonable, sanguine figure would not have been disturbed (after all, he endured decapitation calmly enough) by even the most *outré* exegesis, which he certainly has had. Perhaps the most notable of the attempts to disturb the saint's composure is *Utopia: Fact or Fiction?*, by Mrs Lorraine Stobbart. She asks her question, and answers it immediately in the affirmative. She insists that More had in mind a real place in which to site his story, and the only mystery was whether the place was to be found in the society of the Mayas, the Aztecs or the Incas.

Mrs Stobbart starts in fine form; because More (as even she has to admit) did not visit any of the New World places, it may be that Hythlodaeus, the narrator of the story of Utopia, was a real person, and recounted to More what *he* had seen.

From that she builds a tower of hypothesis and labels it Maya; More was thinking of what is now called Mexico, and in it was the utopian civilisation that the saint was portraying. She examines the map with which More adorned his story.

At first glance there would not appear to be grounds for claiming that the Yucatan Peninsula could be the island of Utopia. Both versions of the map of Utopia included...show quite clearly a circular island totally surrounded by water with no other land close to it. An examination of the text, however, discloses that the illustrations bear no similarity to the documentary description. In fact, they are so dissimilar that one must surely question the relevance of one of the two...Hence we are left questioning the authenticity of the map anyway...

Then again:

No Utopian ever locked their doors, nor did the Maya...Both nations were keen and proud gardeners...Learning and intellectual pursuit were thought to be the most pure and high aspiration of mankind in Utopia...A thirst for all branches of learning and knowledge has always been apparent in the Maya people...The subjects taught in utopian schools included music, dialectics, arithmetic and geometry...The Maya also taught music, geometry and arithmetic...

And so on. The truth, of course, is that the utopian ideal is so deeply embedded in the culture of practically the whole world, irrespective of a knowledge of More's book, that almost any view, any interpretation, any allusion, any emulation, any parody can be fitted somewhere in the utopian spectrum. Mrs Stobbart's version (her publisher is most delicately cautious "…one such theory…seeks to argue…may find themselves disagreeing with this controversial work…") can be accommodated without difficulty beneath the vast umbrella of the utopian propensity, and she can be classified as yet another would-be utopian, yearning for a world of perfect theories.

Shakespeare essayed a play about More; the fragments that have survived have survived with stern marginal notes from the censors. (What the censors of the early seventeenth century would have said in 1935, when More was canonised, is beyond furious conjecture.) But there is an echo, and a very clear one, of More's book, an echo that Shakespeare, with his almost incredible ear, could not have missed. We must not read too much into the passage, lest we should be numbered among those who juggle Shakespeare's words into such convoluted shapes that they turn out to have been written by Bacon; but More's homespun island life under King Utopus had an extra destiny.

The Tempest is a Utopia in itself, presided over by Prospero, but it also provides a self-contained utopian prospectus, in Gonzalo's plan for such an isle of the blest. Its nature is not at all what such a placid and humble courtier would have imagined (perhaps another clue) and it does not follow the implied Utopia of Prospero's own island:

> Had I plantation of this isle, my lord…
> I'the commonwealth I would by contraries
> Execute all things; for no kind of traffic
> Would I admit; no name of magistrate;
> Letters should not be known; riches, poverty,
> And use of service, none; contract, succession,
> Bourn, bound of land, tilth, vineyard, none;
> No use of metal, corn, or wine, or oil;
> No occupation; all men idle, all;
> And women too; but innocent and pure;
> No sovereignty…
> All things in common nature should produce
> Without sweat or endeavour; treason, felony,
> Sword, pike, knife, gun, or need of any engine,

Would I not have; but nature should bring forth
Of its own kind, all foison, all abundance,
To feed my innocent people...
I would with such perfection govern, sir,
To excel the golden age.

It is worth examining this detailed map of Utopia, for the moment
forgetting the Shakespearian note, which ends in a salute to the Golden
Age. It is one to make glad the heart of any anarchist, and indeed may well
be the earliest anarchist manifesto. Magistrates and traffic are the first to be
banned, and literacy follows. Riches and poverty have been the target of
countless utopian impulses, and most have decreed the abolition of private
property. Gonzalo's haven has dispensed with magistrates, but he makes sure
that they would in any case have nothing to do, for such squabbles as break
out elsewhere over "use of service, contract, succession and bourn of land"
are unknown here.

But now Gonzalo is going much further. It seems that Gonzalia will be
teetotal; no vineyards and no imported liquor – wine goes out with corn
and oil – and no utensils for cooking, for metal itself is not allowed.

How, then, are the inhabitants to live? An unambiguous decree rejects
any kind of work: "No occupation, all men idle, all, and women too"; but
here he pauses to avoid being misunderstood, "but innocent and pure". He
reminds us that there is to be no sovereignty (though Sebastian and
Antonio, Gonzalo's tormentors, are quick to point out the fallacy – if
Gonzalo's rule is absolute, how can he dispense with sovereignty?) but in
any case no one can survive on a diet of sovereignty.

There is no need for armaments or engines of war, for this pacifist world
has no need of them. At a word, nature will provide (with no sweat or
endeavour) everything that is needed; nor will there be tight rations, for
there is (foison, abundance) enough to feed the innocent islanders.

If Shakespeare did think of More's Utopia, then, he certainly must have
abandoned such thoughts for his other two Utopias. The first of these is in
As You Like It, where the banished Duke has set up an idyllic world, so that

They say he is already in the forest of Arden, and a many merry men with
him; and there they live like the old Robin Hood of England. They say
many young gentlemen flock to him every day, and fleet the time
carelessly, as they did in the golden world.

Again, the reference to a golden age in the past; it is missing in Shakespeare's third Utopia, *Love's Labour's Lost*, but there is virtually no didactic content in that light-hearted mock-misogynist tract – a vow to eschew the company of women for a year, broken within the first week.

The theme of nature's utopian abundance recurs throughout the genre; utopians have been disappointed to learn that they must still dig and hoe if they want to eat, and it is much better to imagine the abundance as well as everything else.

But we have not finished with More. He is one of history's martyrs, and he had had progenitors and followers. These sacrificial lambs are found right through the centuries; a tyrant defied in the cause of truth. Usually, but not invariably, the truth that is defended is a religious one. The contemplative utopian is not a familiar figure, but there is one significant strain of utopianising which has had very little notice, for a very special reason. This is the utopian in adversity, indeed in prison. Bunyan is rarely thought of in the context of Utopia, but that should not occasion surprise; what could be more utopian (in its quietist mode) than *The Pilgrim's Progress*? There is no rule, after all, that would forbid us to classify a journey as a Utopia; so many are static, even rigid, that such an accession should be welcome.

Yet the utopian propensity lends itself to solitude, even the solitude of imprisonment, whether formal or metaphorical. Campanella, another utopian from the wilder shores, spent a quarter of a century in prison and was lucky to escape with his life, yet he emulated Bunyan in writing from behind bars, so powerful was his determination to give his passion to the world. As for Boethius, not only was he imprisoned for life, but he was repeatedly tortured, yet he produced the *Consolations*; he too had no hope that the work would survive.

There is a strain in humanity which sees it possible to equate ultimate deprivation with ultimate freedom; it is within the capacity of some of those who have suffered the former to take in the latter. It is not necessary to instance the members of religious orders who have vowed themselves to silence, and others who embrace poverty; there is enough evidence from the Nazi concentration-camps alone that men and women are capable of excluding the knowledge of their surroundings to such an extent that they have achieved perfect serenity. And Vasili Shipilov might have been called the Father of the Gulag, so frightful and long-endured were his sufferings. A profoundly devout Christian priest and believer, he was in prisons, madhouses and concentration-camps for a total of forty-eight years, with *one* year of freedom. His sufferings included torture and regular beatings, leading to a broken skull, for refusing to cease crossing himself in the course of his devotions. He remained steadfast and uncomplaining to the end, and to the end included his jailors and torturers in his prayers. And Alexander Solzhenitsyn has repeatedly testified to the extraordinary phenomenon of those unsung utopians who, having nothing, have everything. (Even Dostoevsky's Father Ferapont, so independent that he was unwilling to live any longer in the monastery and eat the fare provided, instead went off into the forest to live alone and survive on berries.) It is not beyond conjecture, either, that when Scott of the Antarctic reached the Pole, his famous and tragic words "Great God, this is an awful place" might have been followed not only by the thought that he had reached an ultimate point in his inhuman journey, but that he had satisfied the gods so completely that the agony he had gone through would have to be leading to his death: *nunc dimittis*.

There are, of course, self-imposed utopian silences or deprivations. The most familiar is the life of the monastery, and particularly the Trappist, though the Trappist rule of silence has been relaxed in recent years. But silence, total or partial, is so strange a thing that its meaning has been obscured by its strangeness. Properly understood, however, it is not only an inward search for peace, holiness and meaning, but a direct challenge to the world; what, the monk would say, are your mundane affairs compared to our bowing to God? The typical monastic life encompasses a vow of chastity, of poverty, of obedience, even of much silence. The outside world finds it difficult to comprehend such obedience, and much more difficult to grasp the very idea of enclosed contemplation. The monk and his vocation, the nun and hers, seem not only mediæval (which, strictly speaking, they are), but seem also to be wasting their lives, though the contemplative must believe that the waste is outside the walls.

In a sense, the life of the cloister is a symbol, for there are many other ways of seeking and even finding that inner reality that the monk and nun are seeking. Many of those who embark on that inner journey have been active in the mundane world, and come to believe that it is worthless; Siddhartha had tried every kind of living, finding them one by one unsatisfactory, until he found the contemplative fisherman and realised that he had hitherto wasted his life and only now was he to begin it. There is no need to see the fisherman as divine; for that matter there is no need to see Siddhartha's resolve to remain on the bank of the river as a token of God's wisdom; all we need to guess is that he has found peace after the years of seeking it in the wrong direction. Hermann Hesse's work comes back over and over again to that theme; the search for peace in the soul. Even in the most unlikely contexts the plea is there: *Narziss and Goldmund, The Journey to the East*, above all *The Glass Bead Game*, which is even set in a kind of monastery – seek peace inside yourself, not from the elixirs peddled in the "real" world, a world that is far more unreal than the ones to be found, often jeered at, in a world based on the practice of contemplation.

In this roster of utopians, Candide takes a prominent and well-deserved place – though only, of course, after his numberless tribulations. There are many whose *Wanderjahre* are more serious than Candide's, but in essence the same – the theme of seeking serenity through many chimerical roads to it, only to find the real thing in a quiet corner. Candide found his real thing in the cultivation of his garden, as Siddhartha finds his on the bank of an eternal river.

The theme of wandering has a long and honourable history. The journey is almost invariably a circular one – the hero comes back to the place from which he started – and he almost invariably returns to a serene old age, all passion spent, all wisdom acquired. (Even the harum-scarum Peer Gynt found peace on Solveig's breast, in the very moment of death.)

But Candide and Siddhartha are figures more important than they may seem. They are consciously seeking peace, though neither could guess in what form it would be found in the end, and it could be said, as those two certainly would say, that the whole of human life is a journey to find that peace. In our world it is desperately difficult to find, though only because we are looking in the wrong direction; as soon as Candide and Siddhartha (and Ulysses for that matter) looked in the right place, they had no doubt that their search was over.

Utopia is peace: that would make a powerful slogan. For what, after all, is Utopia, if it is not a world in which all problems have been solved, all pain assuaged, all burden lifted?

> When Israel out of Egypt came,
> Safe in the sea they trod.
> By day in cloud, by night in flame,
> Went on before them, God.

19

He brought them with an outstretched hand
Dry-footed through the foam,
Past drought and famine, rock and sand,
Lust and rebellion, home.

There is, true, some rejection of the static Utopia, though Utopia can hardly avoid being static; once the end of wandering, fear, pain, folly and need have been reached, there is nothing to do other than be happy. Some utopianisers have organised activities to stave off utopian boredom, but they are notoriously desperate to find something to entertain the utopian audience. In the end, there is comfort for Candide, who had learned the wisdom he went to seek: be contented in the cultivation of a garden.

But the search for perfection takes many roads. What else, for instance, is the mortification of the flesh? In its superficial form, it is often simply a means of subduing sexual desire, or rather, attempting to do so, for physical self-scourging is notoriously priapic in its effect, so that the feelings to be subdued are in practice greatly stimulated.

More seriously, it is argued that, because the soul is all that matters, and the body is nothing but a casing for it, the devout should despise and make little of the spirit's housing. In addition, many believers, including some of the greatest saints, have mortified the flesh – by, for instance, wearing heavy iron chains around their bodies, sleeping and waking – as a reflection of the torments suffered by Christ; if the corporeal form of the saviour of mankind was scourged, mocked and crucified, surely we should have, as a reminder, a real, not just visionary, reflection of Christ's pain.

That, however, is only one way of seeking utopian perfection; what of the hermit life, for instance? The image of the saint or aspirant is a familiar one (there is a Rembrandt etching of St Jerome praying at the mouth of his cave), and almost as well known is the figure who wants to get as far as possible from all mundane concerns; again, there are those who want to emulate Christ's forty days in the wilderness, living on locusts and wild honey.

Some will think these icons are macabre, and the attempt at emulation pitiful; perhaps they are. Nevertheless, the impulse is the same, however wide the variety of the forms it takes. But most will agree that the form taken by St Simeon Stylites must be one of the greatest manifestations of self-sacrifice. He is often – more than often – dismissed as comic, but that goes back to the belief that only the soul matters (for whatever the soul's destiny, the body's is certain), and his sacrifice was only one of the ways, albeit one of the most striking, to announce that truth. The hermit, the seeker in the desert, the mortifier of the flesh – all these are seeking the same goal; solitariness, real or as an image, in order to get closer to God.

All Stylites did was to find a different cave, a different wilderness, a different rejection of the primacy of the body. (This search is not unique to Christianity; less familiar than the Christian images, but parallels of their own, are such mortifications as the Indian *saddhu*, with his arm raised, never to be lowered until death.)

St Simeon Stylites found his cave, his stony land, and above all his strange dwelling on his pillar, in his yearning to be left alone with his soul and God. It is difficult to imagine any more powerful symbol, just as it is difficult to imagine a more complete and more longed-for withdrawal.

Perhaps St Thomas More would find it incongruous to be in such proximity of the Buddhist religion. (If, indeed, it is properly called a religion.) But if contemplative Utopias and utopians may be scrutinised, surely Buddhism must be, for Buddhism is the individual soul-seeking Utopia. It has temples, but not churches, for a temple offers contemplation, a church has a hierarchy, authorities, creeds, rules of conduct, collective actions, timetables, ritual, worship, inevitably a Supreme Being.

Buddhism, as it was conceived, had none of these trappings, and would regard them as obstacles to surmount on the "eightfold path". Buddha laid down no inviolable tenets, asked no conformity, named no book holy.

Man can free himself of the otherwise eternal round of birth, death and rebirth. Such release can be attained through, and only through, the realisation that the body, and even the personality, as well as the entire material world, are mere illusions, and must be shed if the path is to be trodden all the way. To this end, the neophyte will meditate in search of understanding, letting go more and more of the all too insubstantial substantial world.

Such a path is difficult to tread; again and again the seeker fails, and has to go round on the inevitable cycle of transmigration. Many thousands of lifetimes may be spent by the seeker until *satori* is finally achieved and the soul can go free – free, that is, to dissolve itself in the nothingness of *Nirvana*. This religion is different from almost all others, not just because of its lack of any formal structure, but because it has no Paradise, no place in which the completed soul can reap its reward. Its only reward is to get off the wheel of life and mortality, and shed the cosmic illusion that he or anything

exists. It is also one of the very few religions which dispense entirely with
a deity or any parallel figure or centre; indeed, Buddhism in its pure form
is an atheistic religion, a difficult concept to grasp.

Yet in our material, western, consciousness-bound world it is clear that
there is a recognition of so quiet and quietist a way to eternal peace, a
feeling among many who have long ago abandoned any thought of revealed
religion that the Buddhists have found a path which no other sect is
sufficiently equipped to follow. There is a strange irony in the fact that
Buddhism, the most open and giving of all religions, attracts envy, the least
likely of all un-Buddhist-like thoughts.

This, it is clear, is an entirely inward religion; no matter – Buddhism can
swallow Utopia as well as Utopia can swallow Buddhism. Perhaps, over the
centuries, the two words have fused: *Nirvana* and Utopia. They both, after
all, mean the same things – completeness and perfection. There is nothing
to stop any utopian seeker following the Buddhist purgation of desire,
having realised that desire is the block to the ultimate realisation of the
"Buddha-nature", to which all utopians, if they understand what they are
doing, can adhere.

There is a story of a dying Buddhist monk who, after thousands of turns
of the wheel, had come to the end of the path; this was to be his last
lifetime. At the very moment of death, a picture of a beautiful deer he had
seen years ago swam unbidden into his mind, and in the instant of
dissolution, he took pleasure in it, whereupon he went back on to the
wheel in the likeness of a deer.

It is also said that when Buddha himself was at the point of earthly death,
he turned back from *Nirvana*, pledging himself to remain until the last
unfree soul had completed the last cycle.

★

What might Utopia be like? Too often, utopianists ignore that question;
there is no need to describe perfection. No need, perhaps, but a clear
description must surely be interesting.

It must encompass equality for a start, but how far is the equality to go?
Shall we all wear the same clothes, if only because a difference might imply
a superiority? Or even a more costly life-style? But that surely is impossible,
for money must inevitably be outlawed; indeed, there is no need for

outlawry, for in Utopia there is no need of money. Money is not used, because money's function was to acquire, and there is nothing for us to acquire, seeing that we have everything we want or could want. (Want itself must disappear.)

Then all the goods available must be goods in common, and indeed we must all have the same share. That should not be a problem, but one problem does loom; are we identical? Clothes, food, warmth – these can be, even must be, shared as equal "rations"; but do we all see everything through the same eyes? In other words, do we all have the same feelings?

An echo from a forgotten film sounds. A man has been given, presumably by no earthly donor, the power to make anything happen. He makes mistakes, of course, once commanding the earth to stop turning; it does, but the jolt starts to bring down every building on earth, and he has rapidly to reverse his command. After more accidents he gets the hang of it, and uses his magic powers in useful and helpful ways. But there is a love-interest in the story; he had been spurned. Now, with his powers, the girl can only change her mind. "Love me", he demands, but nothing happens; it seems that such intimate feelings are proof against even the magician who can move mountains.

That suggests that there are elements in us that live on a plane even higher than the heights of Utopia, and – significantly – it is the human feelings that demonstrate as much.

But that, surely, is as it should be. Is earthly love not worthy to remain in the utopian precincts? More allows married couples to live in Utopia, and the unwed to marry there, but the conditions in which there may be marriage and giving in marriage are so frightful that most lovers would flee Utopia at once.

To start with, pre-marital intercourse (girls may not marry before they are eighteen, and boys not before they are twenty-two) is a serious offence, punishable by lifelong enforced celibacy, as is adultery. Adulterers in addition are sentenced to penal servitude, and a second extra-marital transgression is punished by execution. Nor are the unstained marriages exempt from restrictions. At every Beginning Feast and Ending Feast, which correspond to the months of the worldly year, wives are obliged to kneel down in front of their husbands, where they must confess their sins, of commission and omission, and ask for absolution. No such corresponding duty falls to the husbands.

In addition, all utopians are members of one or other of the two sects into which the country is divided (it is not clear whether there is a choice of sect, or whether their sect is laid down for them), and one of the two is strictly celibate, as well as vegetarian, and for good measure permanently insomniac. (The other sect is not much better off; they are allowed procreation – if they are married, of course – but they classify it as a duty to the country. They *are* allowed to eat meat, but because they think it helps them to work harder.) And on top of all that, priests (they are of both sexes, though the women priests must all be elderly widows) are exempt from any earthly punishment, even for crimes; they are left to God and their own consciences.

Utopia, then, is no picnic, though it would be naïve to think of More's childish, touching, moderate, appallingly colourless vision as the idea, in all its forms, of the utopian idea. In it, many of the customs and attitudes of Utopia are embedded deep in the human psyche, and it would perhaps be a mistake to take More's catalogue of utopian customs too literally. How, after all, did More's tract find such a vast audience and, more significantly, so many imitators?

Since time began, or certainly since the story of Adam and Eve, mankind has argued in terms that, however oblique, also permeate More's book. How could it not, More being a Christian? Why is man not perfect, and how can he be made so? Left alone, man will find guidance from natural reason – guidance, that is, into the paths of righteousness. If that is not enough, the same solitary thinking will inevitably lead man into the path of revealed religion, individually discoverable. But man is *not* left alone to bring himself to understanding; the imperfections in societies of all kinds obstruct and obscure the otherwise straight route to enlightenment. The parable of Adam and Eve sums it all up; is there such a thing as original sin, or not? Yes, says God (or at least the Christian one); no, says man (or at least the utopian one). The argument continues.

In H.G. Wells' *The Country of the Blind*, the people *are* blind, all of them, though they were all born blind and do not understand the condition of blindness. The man who stumbles upon this darkened community finds to his horror that he is regarded as a freak and an enemy, and that the only way to make him normal and acceptable is to remove those useless, soft excrescences below the brows and each side of the nose. He flees; in the country of the blind the one-eyed man is *not* king. Wells' metaphor is an extravagant one, but points again to the fallacy of perfection; who was perfect in the story of the blind tribe – the defective ones or the whole visitor?

Wherever we stand, we stand between vision and reality; that is what the whole utopian story means. We search endlessly for the realisation and expression of the positive instincts and their achievements – love, sensibility, honest toil, procreation, neighbourliness, generosity and the rest. How do we free man for these qualities, and what could be built on them?

3

Utopia has been delayed

THROUGHOUT the utopian consciousness, there have been utopianisers who argued that if unreformed human beings could be persuaded or commanded to live in specified numbers in specified areas in specified patterns, they would live in perfect harmony – i.e. they would have achieved Utopia. (There have been many parallel beliefs, most notable the claim that if we all took a course in semantics we would all agree.) The most extreme of these systems was what was called by its founder the "Phalanstère", anglicised as the Phalanstery. Its inventor was Charles Fourier, who may be – it is a very bold claim, savagely contested from all sides – the most extreme of all utopianisers. It is tempting to dismiss him as a madman, and there is a good deal of evidence to support such a belief, but it is certain that the impulse which drove him, and the monomaniacal application with which he worked, was single-mindedly devoted to the betterment of mankind.

Apples have played a notable role in mythology, and another in Utopia; an apple led to the expulsion from Eden, and another to Newton's celebrated discovery; it was given to Charles Fourier to make another such revelation. Seeing an apple in a shop selling very expensive goods, he was struck by the difference between the cost of this fateful piece of fruit and that of the kind he was used to at home, far from Paris. The two apples, compared as to price (the quality presumably being similar), were plainly disproportionate; but if two apples showed such startling inequality, it must follow that inequality must be built into the entire system of economics, and from that it must be true that the disparities also encompass human beings. But since there is no logical reason for that state of affairs, there must be an *il*logical reason, and the only one that fits the bill is that the rich have more than the poor. From that moment, he dedicated his life to ensuring that the gap must be closed. It was not (nor has it been to this day), but he never ceased to strive toward his hopeless Utopia of equal incomes.

He did not, of course, confine his ambitions to that noble ideal; in fact he was one of the most assiduous and prolific of Utopia-mongers, his *chef d'oeuvre* being the idea of the Phalanstery, which he approached as he approached everything – that is, in a state of total optimism which was never quenched, however many the rebuffs he had to endure. (Among these was the Tsar's failure to answer Fourier's offer to install Phalansteries throughout the Russian ruler's dominions.)

He had all the stigmata of the obsessive; letters like the one to the Tsar were a sign, another his incessant quarrelling with rival utopians, some of whom had utopian schemes similar to his, which could have been happily amalgamated; another such tell-tale was that he quarrelled not only with sympathetic workers in the field but with his very disciples, who in their reverence to the master strove to carry out his instructions to the letter, only to be rebuked rather than thanked.

His greatest obsession was the Phalanstery and all who were to live in it. He had worked out a system of mankind's passions, and by some utopian arithmetic decided that the almost finite number of permutations could be encompassed in a Phalanstery holding 1620 persons, who would presumably live happily ever after.

Many have said as much; but only Fourier is reputed to have claimed that when his Utopia was ushered in, the sea would turn to lemonade. His clusters of groups were marshalled by skills, natures, psychologies and many other indistinguishable selections; they were shifted about by the system like a monumental chessboard on which only the initiated can understand how to play. For Fourier, the optimum number of those who would fit the Phalanstery was 810, though it might as easily have been 457 or 9208; indeed, when his calculations seemed to be going awry, he coolly doubled the 810, and carried on. Yet his cogent assault on the evils of industrialisation, his distrust of the claims of reason (he was born in 1772 and was lucky to survive the Revolution), his genuine sorrow for the pain of the world, give him an honoured place in the rolls of the more tiresome, but sincere, utopians.

Fourier's Phalanstery was, inevitably, symmetrical; it is a huge concept, three stories high, and sprawling out through a central node, blissfully ignoring the question of where he could get the space to build it, let alone the money. He was forever seeking the millionaire of his dreams, whose steps had this time at last turned instinctively to Fourier. Alas, no genie escaped from the bottle to ask Fourier how he could help him, and he fared no better when he directed his magnificent begging letters to specific individuals (including Napoleon), who, not surprisingly, did not reply.

But it is his geometry that is in focus here. Utopianisers are addicted to structures, these being the framework into which utopians will or should be fitted, and their tutelary deity is Procrustes, who had the idea first, and put it into comprehensively successful practice.

In the Phalanstery all the passions could be expressed, and sin was practically impossible. Because the idea of the family had been drained of its possessiveness, there was no such thing as jealousy, and all would live in harmony. There had to be differences of income, but only if based on talent, but since the Phalansterians could move freely between professions, no inhabitant would be relegated permanently to a lowly job; in any case, when Utopia was complete, practically everybody in the world would be a genius of one kind or another.

There was method in his madness, but it needs a long spade to dig it out. He was, throughout his life, contrasting the contentment of the Phalanstery with the uncertainties of fraudulent freedom outside it. His system has all the marks of totalitarianism, but the charge fails; within the sheltering walls of the Phalanstery there would be perfect happiness in infinite variety, and it would be closer to the Abbey of Thelema than even Robert Owen's happy housing estates (he quarrelled with Owen, of course). Fourier would not be any kind of supervisor, and indeed there would be no such figure. The worst that could be said of him – and it was said frequently – was that he was mad. But it was a most benevolent madness.

Utopians must be, in one way or another, confined to their scheme of perfect happiness, as those who deny that William Shakespeare wrote the works attributed to him can think of nothing else. In a curious and ironic way, the utopian is parallel to the modern obsessive, known today as the Single Issue Fanatic, normally known by his initials. Fourier, by that test, was the most complete and unswerving SIF in all history. He never got anywhere near establishing his ideal Phalanstery, let alone covering the entire earth with them, as was his plan. As the years passed, and no massive building arose, holding 1620 perfectly happy Phalansterians, even the most devoted and tireless SIF would surely find his faith crumbling. No doubt many or most of his followers did indeed lose heart, but not the master himself. To the end (he died at a great age; it is a common experience in SIFs – their hopes keep them living), he never ceased to believe that his time and his system would come. It is perhaps the greatest example in all utopianism of the triumph of hope over experience.

But surely the runner-up is Robert Owen.

Owen is one of the few truly practical utopians, whose ideal states could have been built from experience rather than imagination and wishes; he gave solid demonstration from his own experience. Owen's is perhaps the most powerful testimony to the claim that Utopia is possible, though not as he conceived it. His business skills, and his unremitting labour, made him a substantial fortune, but he saw close-up the misery and poverty among his workers, who were in any case among the best treated. Yet, not content with his great improvements in manufacture which consistently improved the lot of the working man (he went far in reducing the amount of drunkenness among his employees, by example and encouragement rather than the more usual course of threats and dismissal), he plunged himself into a utopian world as chimerical as Fourier's, so obsessed was he with the enticing future of perfection. Owen was rightly known first for his passionate and remarkably successful assault on the conditions in the Industrial Revolution, and if he had left it at that he would have gone down in history as one of history's leading benefactors. He *was* such a figure, and recognised as such even at the time, but the clue to his ultimate failure as the utopian founder of perfect worlds lies in one inescapably utopian mistake. In Owen's factories at New Harmony, every employee, whatever his work and responsibilities, was paid exactly the same. Not surprisingly, New Harmony failed. So did New Lanark, though there were different pay-scales. Owen's longing to create a new kind of being – on the principle that "we needs love the highest when we see it" – turned him into a fanatical utopian, increasingly devoted to his militarian certainties, and repeatedly announcing the imminent Second Coming of Christ.

He could never understand why, or even how, others failed to love the highest even when they saw it. When his workmen got drunk, he remonstrated with them in the mildest terms, and he was truly astonished and dismayed when they broke their promises to abstain; if he could forswear drink, for sound reasons, why could not all mankind do the same? Nor could he claim lack of experience (most Utopias could make that claim, and not surprisingly – few have succeeded in achieving a perfect world and kept the blueprints to show the sceptical), for he had taken his utopian theories to the United States, where he had set up another Owenite colony. With that, he would teach the world how Utopia can be made to come to life, but all it taught in the end was that "men are unwise, and curiously planned", which he could have discovered from Omar Khayam as early as the eleventh century.

It failed utterly, yet although Owen squandered all his hard-headedness on impossible Utopias, he is the most hard-headed utopian ever born. After all, he set up schools for the children of his workers, an unheard-of enterprise; what better establishment of Utopia could be more practical, useful and generous? He went on from there to propose co-operatives of unemployed workers, pooling their skills to make work for them all. Even then, he could have stopped at Utopia's threshold, but like the true fanatical utopian, he must needs push the door open. Beyond it was a scheme for broadening his rational plan in which groups of workers could band together; now the number of the members in the collectives (beware a utopian bringing numbers) would be stipulated: it was 1200. Soon, these village communities would be joined by many more – a limitless number more – and after that, Owen stipulated that the villages would have to be founded in remote parts of the country, so that they would not be infected by the diseases of the old world – rotgut, immorality, laziness. Ultimately, a new race of mankind would grow from this tiny seedling.

Ultimately, all Utopias lead towards a new race of mankind, which is why they never arrive. Owen piled utopian directive upon utopian directive, each more extravagant than the last; the inhabitants of the utopian villages will do *this* at thirty, and *thus* at forty; they will have no private property; disagreement with the system would be treated as irrationality, and sympathetically cured; certainly there were no punishments. (But no rewards, either.) And the villages must be rectangular. Gradually, though gradualism was nowhere to be seen, the system would be spread; exponentially, it would grow more and more rapidly, and the end of the story would be that the whole world would be covered in these villages, all harmonious, all productive, all moral, and, of course, all rectangular.

He would have no truck with the mainstream forms of betterment, because they invariably included the acceptance of religion; the Second Coming became increasingly his own. He founded countless short-lived magazines, all preaching his increasingly bizarre views. In one of his books, this one with the ominous title of *A New View of Society*, he laid out, once and for all, the utopian fallacy, saying "Withdraw those circumstances which tend to create crime in the human character, and crime will not be created. Replace them with such as are calculated to form habits of order, regularity, temperance, industry; and these qualities will be formed".

These townships took Owen as far as he could go, or even further. The agricultural side of the business was to be communal farms; he had gone right back to the catastrophe of New Harmony, but by now he was quite unable to learn from that or anything else. As the catalogue of minutiæ rolls sonorously on, "...it will be easy...to have only one superior circumstances in every department, to the entire exclusion of all vicious, injurious, or inferior circumstances...All individuals, trained, educated and placed in conformity with the laws of their nature, must of necessity at all times think and act rationally..."

Geometry was called in again, and even sex became rectangular; prohibitions would be unnecessary, because marriages would all run perfectly, and venereal disease would be automatically abolished. The retirement age was sixty; thirty had been the point at which the citizens would all agree on everything. And, of course, there would be no private property.

The interesting qualities Owen had are not the ones that steered him into such folly, nor those which blinded him to the impossibility of what he was trying to do. What sums him up is his genuine and complete bewilderment in the face of reality. He simply could not see why his reconstruction of the world *and all who lived in it* could not come to pass. For, after all, he had laid out the methods in clear and unambiguous words; he had demonstrated conclusively that living his way would be in every sense better than the present way, including the rectangular houses; he had made provision for the rest of the world to be absorbed in the system, even if only to abolish envy; what, then, was preventing an immediate start and a rapid conclusion to the project?

No utopian has reached as far as Owen. Remember that he was a successful businessman and a genuine philanthropist in the most fundamental sense of the word. He achieved much, early on; if he had controlled his utopian fervour he would have achieved very much more. Owen – and the whole utopian universe as well – made the inevitable mistake. The mistake is not that we are, or could be, perfect beings (though that belief makes things worse); it is that we are, or could be, all the same.

Robert Owen did no harm (though he annoyed a lot of people) and did much good. Let no one believe that when more utopian plans such as his are presented, there can be any certainty that they would turn out to be Owenite, and let no one forget that they might, instead, turn out to be the monsters of utopian nightmare.

But the enclosed (and rectangular) idea of utopian harmony did not die with Fourier and Owen but was transmogrified elsewhere. What could be more Phalansterian, for instance, than the Panopticon, which was devised by Jeremy Bentham; it was to be a prison built on a many-storied radial plan which would enable the wardens to see every prisoner all the time. That device could symbolise the passion for regularity; Bentham's idea was, of course, to be symmetrical both horizontally and vertically, and a fearful symmetry has ever since infused countless designs for utopian buildings, again and again. (Even Rabelais, a most asymmetrical man, described the Abbey of Thelema as being built on a symmetrical plan, adding for good measure that it contained 9302 rooms.)

But Phalansteries and Panopticons and New Harmonies are insubstantial spectres; in the real world, realities based on principles no more hard-headed than the craziest utopian who ever drew up a programme of infinite world betterment could hardly survive. How else could the next step have been taken?

It seems, from Helen Rosenau's *The Ideal City* (a most utopian title), that it was Dürer who established the symmetrically planned cities, and she has unearthed a remarkably comprehensive number and styles of these grids. A much cruder but simpler way of testing the endurance of these patterns is to riffle through the German red Michelin Guide. The meticulous cartographer of the Michelin city-plan instantly demonstrates that the German tradition is still powerful, for almost every city of any size in Germany was utterly destroyed by the bombing of the Second World War, and for so many to be replaced not by replicas, which would at least have sentimental reasons for following the original, but newly devised maps demonstrating, in city plan after plan, a pattern rigorously symmetrical.

It is enough to make one turn to Piranesi, whose horrible nightmares at least have no physically exact mirrorings. But the modern world is full of them. Take the Seagram Building in New York; hailed as a masterpiece of modern architecture, the people who had to work in it, as opposed to admiring it from the vantage-point of another skyscraper, found that it could not be cooled when the weather was hot, nor heated when the weather was cold, and in addition they were prohibited from putting up in the windows pictures or posters which would spoil the perfect symmetry.

The search for perfection can be over-done, and in no field has it gone further in the search than in the field of planning. At times, it seems that armies of planners, equipped with the most immaculate credentials, are roving the world (in this it is not confined to the advanced nations), seeking the unplanned, to plan it. Unshakably convinced that planning is the utopian philosopher's stone that will transform everything it touches to gold, the planners dismiss the cries of the unplanned (to the effect that they feel no need for being planned) and instead extol the delights of the process itself, and the even greater boon that will be the completion of the plan.

Not long after the end of the Second World War, there began the massive rebuilding of Britain. There had been no building of houses throughout the war, much less offices, and the bombing of the big cities had obviously made the situation even more difficult. The planners, having hibernated throughout the conflict, unveiled their master plan: it was the ill-fatedly named "high rise", a tower block with anything up to 30 storeys, in which the re-housed would live, layer upon layer, like some monster ant-hill or newborn Phalansterian communal dwelling. So enthusiastic for the plan were the planners that their delight could be heard on the other side of the Atlantic, and in no time the "high-rise" was to be found throughout the United States and elsewhere.

Years later, even the planners had to admit that they had made a mistake. The high-rise had become a hideous and befouled trap, almost exclusively for the poor; vandalism and hopelessness, neurosis and polluted air, solitary confinement and post-war urban crime – these were the ultimate fruits of the great utopian dream the planners had had. They should have stayed longer in bed.

Eventually, the long prayed-for release began; one by one, the high-rises were evacuated and, amid heartfelt cheers, dynamited. Yet the lesson was not learned, and indeed the planners have grossly multiplied since those days, protected by a huge body of law. In every field – food, education, travel, shopping, the economy, the environment, child-rearing – there was and is no corner of life into which the planners do not have entry, an entry very often backed by legal force.

This is not a description of a totalitarian state, though the fact that such a disclaimer is necessary is itself alarming; it is not even, for the most part, yet another example of the way in which the appetite doth grow by what

33

it feeds on. It is the utopian belief among the planners that they know better what is good for us than we do, so that they are in a sense bringing the good news to the heathen. Invariably, the power of the planners, and the way they deploy their power, comes from a central body, run by super-planners who do not see the effects of their ukases; nevertheless, the planners insist that those effects are, if studied in the right light, always beneficial. They must be; the central body is all-wise, all-informed, all-benign, and who would be so benighted, so obtuse, as to reject what is manifestly good for him? (The growing power of the European Community has, of course, enormously multiplied the activities of the planners, who have recently given instructions that no banana may be bought or sold anywhere in the Community if it does not comply with the regulations laid down for the required length of the fruit.)

Utopia may be like this. Doing people good against their will is, to most of us, a contradiction, but it is true wisdom to the planners. And it emphasises the danger of the search for perfection. That danger runs through every attempt to make the world, or even a tiny part of it, in the image of a planner dressed as God. But it is safe to say that few if any of today's architects, however utopian, are likely to be remembered long after their death.

The effect of Utopia on architecture has almost always been malign; if we include town planning the effect is reinforced, and if it embraces novel forms of housing, interior and exterior design, and even furnishings, more weight still is given to the dismal likelihood that remedial action will sooner or later be necessary, followed by a complete reversal of the policies so trumpeted at the outset. Let utopian builders remember the famous Mies van der Rohe "Barcelona chair"; it is still every bit as striking and beautiful to look at as it was sixty years ago when it was perfected, and every bit as uncomfortable to sit in.

The most utopian architect of modern times is Le Corbusier; the least utopian Gaudi. The first registers on the mind's eye as a row of sandstone caves, doing duty for homes; with an irony that must have escaped Le Corbusier entirely, he called it the *ville contemporaine*, as brutalist and dictatorial as the even more arrogant builders who followed him. Indeed, he did not wait for followers, but followed himself, with his *cité idéale*, the very apotheosis of the ant-hill, though looking more like a particularly brutal concentration camp. And who should blame any of them, when Helen Rosenau (who holds Le Corbusier in high esteem) can say, apparently without serious qualms, that "The most static element is perhaps the rigid zoning envisaged in the four parts: a centre, urban housing, a development area and garden cities. The civic buildings with their cupolas...form a significant contrast to the high skyscrapers". No wonder that his next exercise in gigantism was to be the *Ville Radieuse*: "Here the emphasis is on the skyscraper in a park setting...and vertical garden cities...save space and allow for free circulation...The planner of ideal cities occupies a rather singular position in that he is allowed freedom of vision, but at the same time the lack of realisation limits his contribution..." The only reply is a sigh of relief.

Meanwhile, what of Gaudi?

There is a powerful symbol in his masterpiece, the Church of the Holy Family in Barcelona; unfinished at his death in 1921, it is unfinished today. Well, many a project, in architecture and other enterprises, is left abandoned, but this one has *not* been abandoned; work on it has gone on since his death, and any visit to the site will see men at work. The problem is that there seems to be no coherent plan (not surprisingly, because Gaudi did not leave one), and to watch the apparently aimless bustle raises a suspicion that each man, with his wheelbarrows, his mortar, his bricks and his hod, is pursuing a theme of his own, wholly independent not only of instructions from a central command, but of every other workman on the site, each of whom is engaged on *his* own version.

Could there be a more powerful demonstration of the truth that men can break free from the demands of Utopia, and reject the proffered perfection? The men working at the *Sagrada Familia* may never have heard of Schubert's Unfinished Symphony, but those of us who have should make a vow never again to deplore its truncated form, and if their faith in the vow wavers, let them think of Gaudi, and those wheelbarrows. It would be well, when discussing utopian architecture, to bear in mind that the truly visionary houses designed and built by Frank Lloyd Wright invariably leaked.

With this prophylactic assurance, we can start with what must be the greatest utopian suggestion in this field. Vitruvius proposed to carve Mount Olympus – the entire mountain – into a figure on one knee, with an outstretched hand through which a river would run, and in which there would be a city of 10,000 souls; the catch in the breath that the idea causes is not at all diminished by the fact that the project came to nothing. (Mount Rushmore somehow does not have the same effect.) But it emphasises what is the most salient truth about utopian architecture: most of it was never built.

Much of it never could have been built. The Sydney Opera House, designed, after all, in the second half of the twentieth century, had to wait, though the drawings were complete, until computer science was sufficiently adult to work out the enormously complex arithmetical and geometrical problems its erection demanded. Extrapolating backwards, the problems of visionary architecture were mostly doomed to remain drawings. Any amount of decoration could be easily accommodated (though it is notable that King Utopus shunned it – Utopia's own architecture has nothing that could be called by that name, strict utility being the pattern), but the structures usually required great lengths of time and great quantities of money; it was Lloyd Wright who said "there's nothing so timid as a million dollars", and although throughout the centuries there have been wise and enlightened rulers and equally understanding philanthropists (where would be Italy today if it had not been so?), lines had, and have, to be drawn somewhere.

They were drawn even in the face of Leonardo da Vinci, who designed what was destined to be literally a two-tier city; the workers would live and carry out their labours on the lower level, and the upper-class would stroll to their appointments in the sunshine of the higher storey.

But utopian architecture, like most things utopian, had little time for mere buildings; cities were the goal. The mystical qualities of the circle have throughout history been a powerful symbol for its uniquely complete nature, undisturbed by angles, and also for the impossibility of measuring its area (because it depends on *pi* – itself a symbol so powerful that it would not come as a surprise to learn that there is a sect somewhere which worships it); it was inevitable that utopian town-planners have almost always made their capitals circular.

This is not to say that their unpracticality has left them in the form of architectural drawing only; the number of radial capital cities alone is impressive. Haussman's Paris and L'Enfant's Washington are the most familiar, but Brasilia, as we shall see, stakes a more powerful claim.

Where they could not build outwards, utopians no less symbolically built upwards. The skyscrapers of America may jib at being told that they are in reality phallic dreams, but what are phallic dreams but utopian visions? But the entire skyscraper culture (many countries have emulated it, but none has such concentrated areas of these amazing buildings) was invented virtually overnight, and it is astonishing that its unique success has not been more extolled or dissected for examination.

The fate of Brasilia, the capital of Brazil, is instructive. A huge city was erected in the heart of the Brazilian jungle interior (the men who cleared the ground slept in their trucks until they had made room enough for planes to land bringing the necessities of civilisation, starting presumably with beds), and the planners had thought of everything; for instance, there are no traffic-lights – lanes have been built in the form of tunnels and flyovers. A substantial number of environmental living-spaces, truly handsome and all self-contained – each has its own shopping precincts, entertainment and possibly even schools – and only buildings such as Parliament, the Law Courts, and the Cathedral are together in a central area. Utopia had arrived.

The planners, those good and kind and far-seeing men, had thought of almost everything, but not quite. If you live in a Brasilia village, no matter how comfortable it is, no matter how handsome it is, no matter how convenient it is, you have no incentive to go out. Why? Because all the other villages are identical to yours, and everyone is living the identically same life.

Utopia has *not* arrived.

4

Bless relaxes

T HE ANARCHIST, through the years, has rarely been admired as a benefactor. He is more likely to be seen as a man with an enveloping cloak, a broad-brimmed hat pulled down over his eyes, a fringe beard, and clutching a round bomb, its wick already ignited, which he then proceeds to throw at any members of the governing class who happen to be passing by; his aim, traditionally, is poor, so that his carnage falls mainly or entirely upon innocent bystanders. (This part may be a calumny put about by the governing class.)

Something rather like that did truly happen, in the days when the word was newly employed, mainly in Russia towards the end of the nineteenth century, and it has been sporadically revived in that meaning throughout the following years. One identity problem anarchists face is the inability of non-anarchists to make a clear definition of them and stick to it. Were the young bomb throwers at Sarajevo, who started the First World War, anarchists? Were the members of the Baader-Meinhof gang anarchists? Are the members of the window-smashing organisation called Class War? Are the men and women who put bombs on aeroplanes, timed to go off *en route* and kill everyone aboard? Today, the word "anarchist" has become almost quaint, being replaced by "terrorist". But the image, smartened up and technologically modernised, remains the same.

Today, those who proclaim themselves anarchists (the word means nothing but "without a leader", or "without a ruler") have a good claim on our sympathies. The non-violent anarchist believes that society would get along perfectly well, or indeed better, if there was no such thing as government, law enforcement or power. The absurdity of such a proposition is manifest, though of course appealing; in any case it is clear that peaceful anarchists are no threat to society. (What would happen if their cause triumphed is another matter; those who most loudly denounce restraint are, as history goes, very likely to enjoy even greater restraint when they are wielding it.)

But if anyone wants a definition of "utopian", applied in its fullest pejorative sense, he need look no further than to the anarchists. Impossibilism, the science of crying for the moon, comes in many shapes, but surely none more strange than anarchism. Nevertheless, its overwhelming utopian nature demands to be considered, not least because many of the leading utopians have been proud to categorise themselves as anarchists also. Proudhon, whose utopian credentials cannot be impugned, was probably the first self-declared anarchist. If so, he cannot be accused of breaking the ground gently:

> To be governed is to be watched over, inspected, spied upon, directed, legislated, regimented, closed in, indoctrinated, preached at, controlled, assessed, evaluated, censored, commanded; all by creatures that have neither the right, nor wisdom, nor virtue...To be governed means that at every move, operation, or transaction one is noted, registered, entered in a census, taxed, stamped, priced, assessed, patented, licensed, authorised, recommended, admonished, prevented, reformed, set right, corrected. Government means to be subjected to tribute, trained, ransomed, exploited, monopolised, extorted, pressured, mystified, robbed; all in the name of public utility and the general good. Then, at the first sign of resistance or word of complaint, one is repressed, fined, despised, vexed, pursued, hustled, beaten, garrotted, imprisoned, shot, machine-gunned, judged, sentenced, deported, sacrificed, sold, betrayed, and to cap it all, ridiculed, mocked, outraged, and dishonoured. *That* is government, *that* is its justice and its morality!...O human personality! How can it be that you have cowered in such subjection for sixty centuries?

Proudhon had clearly been getting at the Thesaurus, a heady drink at the best of times, but however hypnotic his oratory, he is one of those utopians with a cloven hoof; indeed, he had two. His attitude to women would get him ejected from any well-run Utopia; he proclaimed that "The female is a diminutive of man", and practised what he preached – his perfect world would be one in which women would be an entirely lower order, with no rights except those generously permitted by their husbands, naturally subject to good behaviour, and revocable at any moment. And on top of that, Proudhon was an anti-semite of considerable virulence; indeed, he may be the first sane one in modern times to advocate seriously the extermination of the Jews. Utopia, it seems, is flawed; but how can that be if Utopia is perfection? More problems.

The border between Utopia and Anarchy is not clearly delineated; the bridge may be egalitarianism. "When Adam digged and Eve span, Who was then the gentleman?" John Ball, whose couplet it is, was not content to hear it chanted wherever he went; he outlined a coherent idea of equality, and proclaimed it:

Things cannot go well in England, nor ever shall, till everything be made common, and there are neither villeins nor gentlemen, but we shall be all united together, and the lords shall be no greater masters than ourselves. What have we deserved that we should be kept thus enslaved? We are all descended from one father and mother, Adam and Eve. What reason can they give to show that they are greater lords than we, save by making us toil and labour, so that they can spend?

In the aftermath of the Peasants' Revolt, Ball was hanged along with the ringleaders, but the utopian ideal of complete equality grew stronger, and when Wycliffe, who initially set out only to reform the Church, mingled social reform with ecclesiastical, the result is this rickety but powerful tower of syllogisms, which forwarded the growing utopian movement:

All God's bounty should be in common. This is proved thus: every man should be in a state of grace, and if he is in a state of grace, why then, he is lord of all the world and everything in it. Therefore, every man must be lord of all the world and everything in it. But this is now impossible, because there are so many men, so they must hold all things in common. Therefore, everything should be in common.

QED. But the history of Utopia is strewn with unsubstantiated QEDs, to say nothing of the utopians' unrepaid IOUs. The Peasants' Revolt, though it shook the country, had no chance of ultimate success, any more than did the Drummer of Niklashausen, with his "Princes, ecclesiastical and secular alike, and counts and knights, should only possess as much as common folk, then everyone will have enough. The time will have to come when princes and lords will work for their daily bread".

Only two serious figures, both Russian, could be taken seriously as utopian anarchists. Bakunin would have had to be taken seriously, if only because he advocated and promoted violence; in him the comic stereotype of the anarchist with a round, smoking bomb came to life, so those at whom Bakunin's troop were throwing the bombs were not inclined to laugh. The other serious anarchist, however, was Prince Kropotkin, who eschewed all violence. In between and in the United States, Emma Goldman praised the bomb, though probably did not throw it. She argued, as not only anarchists always have insisted, that the state is the greatest dispenser of violence; all the bomb-thrower can do is to throw a feather in the other scale. She was difficult to place, not least because she had no great love for consistency, but because she had a residual honesty which would not let her hopes take precedence over the truth; born in Tsarist Russia, she emigrated to the United States, rejoiced at the news of the Russian Revolution, and hastened to see for herself the old order giving way to Utopia. What she saw, however, was a long way from Utopia, and after leaving Russia she wrote two books on her experiences, called respectively *My Disillusionment in Russia* and *My Further Disillusionment in Russia*; her prescience is remarkable, for she saw at once what the nascent Soviet Union was, and what it would become. She figures here, of course, not for her fierceness, but for her high place in the tiny roster of utopians who have admitted that King Utopus has feet of clay. (The higher they go, the harder they fall: some years ago, six British leading figures from politics and literature published a collection of essays, each baring his breast for having trusted to the Soviet deity, and each describing his road to Canossa. The title of the book was *The God that Failed*.)

It is not universally recognised that the anarchist strain in Utopia is, and must be, antithetical to Marxism as well as the state as we know it. Whatever Marxism was supposed to be, and whatever it has come to be, anarchism must be its enemy, as it must be the enemy of all static, regulated systems, bred from the loins of closed societies. True, Marx proclaimed "the withering away of the state", but it was to happen a considerable time in the future, while anarchists as well as anybody else who had had the misfortune actually to live under Marxist rule can testify that the walls are high and there are spikes on the top. Bakunin and Kropotkin alike were destined to remain on the fringe of politics, of revolution, of Utopia itself. But that is not because of their lack of a significant following, nor for the want of a coherent philosophy. It was the inherent absurdity of anarchy, which has dogged the savage Bakunin and the gentle Kropotkin alike, and all their followers. Anarchy, it might be thought, should be most welcome to the table of Utopia; in reality, it is allowed to join in on sufferance, and only below the salt.

The self-delusion of utopians is one of the most touching strains in history; there are countless declarations based on nothing but wishes. In *Demanding the Impossible* there is an epitome of such hopes, in the momentary seizure of Lyons, in the wake of the Franco-Prussian War, by insurrectionists. They put up placards carrying the details of the new order; this was the kind of thing that the Lyonnais (of all cities to choose, the most placid and money-oriented one!) read when they woke up:

> The administrative and governmental machinery of the state, having become impotent, is abolished.
> All criminal and civil courts are hereby suspended and replaced by the People's justice.
> Payment of taxes and mortgages is suspended.
> All existing municipal administrative bodies are hereby abolished.
> This convention will meet immediately at the town hall...Since it will be supported by the People this convention will save France.

But what is the difference between that and the famous Children's Crusade of America in the 1960s, summed up by Jerry Rubin, whose own decrees ran like this:

> There will be no more jails, no courts or police.
> The White House will become a crash pad for anybody without a place to stay in Washington.
> The world will be one big commune with free food and housing, everything shared.
> Barbers will go to rehabilitation camps where they will grow their hair long.
> There will be no more schools or churches because the entire world will become one church and school.

The modern version does have the virtue of humour, but the yearning in the passages that are to be taken seriously can be clearly heard. What a Nirvana awaits us all when Utopia arrives! No jails, no courts, no police, no schools, no churches; but mark the significance of the reason for such liberation. It is not because schools and churches are to be burnt down, not that jails and courts will be sacked by the liberators, not that the policeman will be beaten to his knees with his own truncheon. It is "because the entire world will become one church and school".

Sancta simplicitas! But again, the benign instinct rises to the surface; again, men and women strive to find the bridge over the torrent of reality, from wishes to fulfilment. So far, the bridge has not been found.

It comes as something of a surprise to find Oscar Wilde numbered among the utopians. But here, the immovable object of his cynicism meets the irresistible force of his sentimentality.

A map of the world that does not include Utopia is not worth even glancing at, for it leaves out the one country at which Humanity is always landing. And when Humanity lands there, it looks out, and, seeing a better country, sets sail. Progress is the realisation of Utopia.

His own realisation of Utopia landed him in Reading Gaol, but in any case human love was not to be the instrument; his *The Soul of Man Under Socialism* makes clear that the dusty fabianism of municipal politics is not for him, lest socialism should stifle opportunity in its own bureaucracy. His socialism is a purely utopian–libertarian form:

All modes of government are wrong. They are unscientific, because they seek to alter the natural environment of man; they are immoral because, by interfering with the individual, they produce the most aggressive forms of egotism; they are ignorant, because they try to spread education; they are self-destructive, because they engender anarchy.

This is about as far as he can go in describing an ideal society, but the heart of his argument is the need for beauty, and the conditions in which art can flourish. Nevertheless, he too treads the path to absurdity, insisting that private property must be ended, that there should be no authority, that crime will disappear if punishment is abolished, that sickness will turn to health, and even selfishness will wither and die. Above all, beauty will flourish as never before in history, once the artist is freed to create it.

Wilde is one of the best examples of the duality of utopian mankind; the question we must put to him, begging him as we do so not to take refuge in paradox, is: how much of all that was metaphor, and how much did he believe could be achieved? Libertarianism is all very well, but dusty municipal bureaucracy does, after all, get the streets swept, and the policeman, after all, would be in a sorry plight if he waited until crime withered away of its own accord, before he set out on the beat.

The same question, of course, can be asked of every utopian; dreams can be beautiful, and beauty can be real. But the danger lies in the utopians' propensity for confusing the two. A question even blunter can be asked of Wilde: did not his dreams, and his advocacy of them, probably help to delay the modest betterments that could have been – they always can be – achieved? But it is likely that the question will in the end be answered with a paradox, after all.

The idea of equality, it might be thought, would be found in practically every utopian plan, but it has been absent from a surprisingly large number of Utopias. There have been many attempts at egalitarian systems in real history, however, as against Utopia. We only have to think of the revolts against poverty and oppression; such upheavals were almost always infused with egalitarian beliefs, which is not surprising: the movements themselves were seeking a state in which the poor were less poor and the rich less rich. But on second thoughts, it is not really surprising to find a lack of egalitarianism in Utopia; if everybody is perfectly happy, as they must be in a perfect world, there is no need for complete levelling; there are no complaints against King Utopus, after all.

The anarchists have no problem; if there is no overall power or law, no ruler however benign, everyone is equal to everyone else, and no formal system of egalitarianism is necessary. In more structured Utopias, it must be latent in the whole utopian idea. Rousseau preached equality; he could hardly have failed to do so, given his ideal "natural man", for how could such a man oppress or be oppressed: "Man was born free..." But more detailed egalitarian theory was required, and it was found in that romantic, heroic, tragic figure, Gracchus Babeuf.

Babeuf (he was not christened Gracchus, but took the name as a *nom de guerre*, after the democrat of Ancient Rome) must have read Rousseau, wherein he found the seeds of his own egalitarian prospectus, *The Manifesto of the Equals*. When the French Revolution broke out, he came at last into his own, whipping the dogs of vengeance; he founded a newspaper, inevitably called the *Tribun du Peuple*, and outdid even the most fervent revolutionists with his call for the utter destruction of the old order.

His own revolutionary plan was made of the most egalitarian stuff. Necessities such as food must be free, and all property will be in common; no one may have dominion over the production of goods and services; no one can be luckier than anyone else; all will labour, but equally those not doing their bit will be punished; and if anything cannot, by its nature, be equally distributed, it will be abolished. Babeuf was lucky to survive the Revolution, particularly because he denounced it as fraudulent in its promised equality.

He survived the Revolution, but not many years after it. His Conspiracy of the Equals hardly existed except in its *Manifesto*; a handful of conspirators were to stage a *coup d'état*, and mete out justice, severe but legitimate, to those who have hampered the egalitarian dawn. His absurd (but touching) conspiracy naturally failed, and he and his equal conspirators died by the guillotine in 1796. But he has inevitably entered the utopian Pantheon, if only because of the extreme lengths he and his followers (though leaders and followers alike would be banned in his new world) went to in their ironclad certainty that total equality and nothing else would make mankind happy: equally happy, of course.

Equality stands high in the roster of utopian lost causes. Dr Johnson polished it off in a paragraph, pointing out that in earthly terms, "no group of men can be together half an hour than a natural propensity will show that one among them is superior", and he might well have gone on to say that it would take not much longer to arrange the entire party in a hierarchy. There are, obviously, certain immediate tests – in athletics, for instance, where he who runs faster than the others has shown himself superior. But if we remove to matters of character, mind, quality and leadership, inequalities will show themselves very quickly, and however much they are resented, they cannot be denied.

They have been denied, of course; many a small utopian group has resolved to live without precedence, and some have managed to do so. (There is usually a rehearsal, in the form of equality of income, where many of the disciples fall at the first hurdle.) There have been businesses without a managing director, orchestras without a conductor, teachers who put themselves on a footing with their charges. (There are also tribes and clans for whom the women are shared in common, though few of our present-

45

day egalitarians, particularly the female ones, would approve.)

"We hold these truths to be self-evident; that all men are created equal…" But they are manifestly not. Was Jefferson, when he wrote those words, equal to the most ignorant recruit in the army that Washington was assembling? And if he was, were his slaves?

We cannot blame the Declaration of Independence; this is a very modern plague, but in Utopia it is acclaimed everywhere. Almost all Utopias are grounded in equality, with the additional advantage that the inhabitants fully share the doctrine. The reality is inescapable, and if it does not seem so, there is a forgotten play, by James Barrie, which should bring it home to any but the most ideological utopian egalitarian, *The Admirable Crichton*. In this, a wealthy middle-class family is wrecked on an otherwise uninhabited island. There are no savage animals, the island is rich with produce; starvation and attack are no threat. But the members of the family, accustomed to have the meat at dinner brought in by the servants, having been roasted by the cook, are wholly ignorant of what has been happening in the kitchen. On the island, only the admirable Crichton, their butler, has any ability of any kind that is useful to the family. Though lush plenty is available, if Crichton were not there they *would* starve to death.

They come, naturally, to depend on him entirely and their gratitude is real. While they are on the island, he is the uncrowned king of it, but in the end, a rescue ship comes in sight, and they are all saved sound. But the chains of normality are too hard to break; once they are in the boat taking them to the ship the admirable Crichton is once more their servant, not – as he has been – their master. The moral, however, remains; the helpless businessman and his even more helpless family had to bow to the pre-eminent man, and under whatever title he went, he was that man.

The truth is that true egalitarianism demands the suppression of individuality, and individuality is essential to meaningful life. In Utopia there is no need for individuality; but then, that is why it is called Utopia.

*

There are Utopias in politics, too, and alas, there are politics in Utopias, further evidence that the serpent has been on the prowl. But the utopian political programme is the more familiar and the more pathetic; more tiresome for the bystanders, too, if only for the noise. But the strength of the conviction, examined in detachment, is astonishing, considering the almost total lack of any kind of success, however meagre.

For years on end, the *groupuscules* (the word came from France, but was rapidly naturalised) toiled in the vineyard in the heat of the day, though the merest glance would have sufficed to show them that there were no grapes on the vine. The most remarkable of these was a body, founded before the Second World War, called the Socialist Party of Great Britain; its single-minded devotion to the cause can be gauged from the members' attitude to voting. At every General Election in Britain they managed to scrape up enough money to pay the deposit for half a dozen or so candidatures, but their pamphlets and speeches insisted, with great vehemence, that no one should vote for them unless the voter was entirely in accord with every item of the party's programme, down to the smallest detail. To reinforce their decree, they handed out leaflets on the very steps of the polling station, headed "Don't Vote", repeating their insistence on the need of absolute conformity before a voter could mark his ballot for the party. There could be no doubt that if the party had come to power it would have promptly enacted legislation not to suppress dissent as totalitarian states do, but the very reverse.

With such an outlook, it might be thought that the SPGB would be a bank of harsh fanatics, thirsting for blood and determined to build tumbrils and guillotines in every city in the land the moment they came to power. Not a bit of it; they were the gentlest and most gentlemanly of campaigners, eschewing criticism, let alone abuse and denunciation, of rival *groupuscules*. Patience and politeness would pay, they believed, sooner or later (they did not seem to mind which), the nation would see the light and storm the polling stations to cast a unanimous vote for the party: after passing, of course, the test of total sympathy and agreement.

Very different from the courteous SPGB was and is the Socialist Workers Party. Compared to the SPGB, it was relatively rich, its newspapers, its leaflets and its activities being well organised and publicised. There was not a strike in the land but that the SWP banners were raised above the picket lines, not a confrontation with the police but that was led by the SWP, not a square foot of pavement outside a supermarket but that a SWP member would be found trying to sell the SWP newspaper. Denunciations of rival revolutionary bodies were rife (at one time, research revealed, there were no fewer than *fourteen* such bodies all contending for the honour of leading the nation into the heaven of permanent socialism), and the numbers the SWP could field were substantial.

Yet the gates of political Utopia remain irritatingly shut. The nation does not rise as one man and woman and take power; on the contrary, though the pavements outside the supermarkets are indeed thick with members trying to sell the party's paper, it is noted that few but the faithful were buying it.

Much the same fate befell a *groupuscule* fiercely called the Workers' Revolutionary Party, commanded, in effect, by an actress of very considerable talent, Vanessa Redgrave. Although she tried to keep her acting separate from her political activities, the former was inevitably clouded by the latter, though no one ignorant of her revolutionary aims and practices could have guessed at them while watching her powerful and enchanting performances. Matters came to a head in a most unlikely fashion; the formal head of the organisation (Miss Redgrave was the most prominent member, but not the leader) turned out to have established something like a *jus prima nocte* among the younger and more attractive female members, and indeed he went very much further than the *prima*, and was to be found at his sport virtually every *nocte*.

The organisation, which had already split more times than an amoeba, split yet again; this time, however, not because of ideological differences, but of a far more earthy quarrel. (Presumably, though it was not reported, there must have been a group within the Workers' Revolutionary Party which insisted that serious revolutionaries should not bow to the shibboleths of bourgeois morality.) As for Miss Redgrave, she continued her activities in the rump led by the erring member; not on the ground that she approved such behaviour, but because she refused to believe that any such behaviour had, or could have, taken place.

These shenanigans hardly disturbed the country, which indeed hardly noticed them, and it may be thought that they are unworthy of so substantial an account. But there is a very significant utopian kernel in that basket of nuts. Ignoring the members of the *groupuscules* who were entirely beyond sanity (for some reason the smaller the organisation the more odd the adherents), there remains a mystery which has not been explained, or even noticed. How did the members remain adamantly loyal to their beliefs, when it was inescapably obvious that they were never going to win, or even get their feet on the bottom rung of the ladder of victory?

This question must be answered, so remarkable is the fact that asks it. The members could see, they could count, they could hear. They could see that their participation in strikes made no difference, they could count the meagre numbers seeking membership, they could hear no reference made to their organisations by anyone outside them. There were no oppressed or persecuted crowds on which they could feed, there was no hunger, no despair, no hopelessness.

How then did they stay faithful to their cause, and not just faithful to it, but active in promoting it? Surely, it is yet another manifestation of the utopian propensity, the world made new and perfect. So powerful is the pull of that far-off Nirvana that these self-deceived figures – so self-deceived that they did not even seem forlorn or yearning – were willing to sacrifice at least their youth (most of them, of course, were young), and in some cases even their lives. And as far as the evidence goes, there were no awakenings: no one woke up and realised that the whole thing had been a dream, to be dispensed with now that the sleep was over.

And that does not take into account the much smaller but apparently no less determined utopian standfasts of the Right. For if the Left could be admired for its fruitless devotion, how much more intense was the devotion of the Right! There they were, mostly *not* young, dreaming of a world with no blacks, no Jews, discipline at every level, the country great again, corporal punishment everywhere, capital punishment almost as ubiquitous, the Golden Age come again – what steely resolve to go on believing that one day it will all come true!

Yet what are Marxist revolutionaries on the one hand, and neo-fascist empire-builders on the other (there was a fascistic organisation called The League of Empire Loyalists, its members apparently living in ignorance of the sad truth that the Empire had disappeared long before), but modern versions of the Great Charter? That movement too dreamed of a world without blemish, for all that it comprised nothing but a vast number of signatories. Somehow, that muster had turned into a golden coach which was to transport the people, particularly the poor, to a heaven where not even a signature would be required for a withdrawal of infinite size from the Bank of Eternal Happiness.

But if there was no Great Charter for them, there were some striking equivalents. In 1968, the *annus mirabilis* of the young and disaffected people, all over the advanced world the young had a wonderful time, seizing academic and other buildings, smashing windows and cars, demanding the impossible.

The students called upon the peoples of their countries to join them and overthrow their rulers; in America, Britain, Germany and elsewhere such exhortations were ignored. The French rising was the most thrilling, but in the end there was no need for much force; the police broke a few heads (and the young people broke a few more windows), and Paris returned to an uneasy normality.

This Children's Crusade was a touching demonstration of an innocent utopianism. They had no real hope of overthrowing anything or anybody, let alone the state; and even if the state collapsed, what would replace it would have been nothing like the Utopia of which they dreamed. But the episode showed that the young had not lost their ideals, even if they never knew what power they would have to face with their pea-shooters if their rising had been taken seriously.

The British *groupuscules* were greatly heartened in their own resolve when they heard the first exciting news from Paris. By a touching coincidence there was at the time a play running at the National Theatre (it was Laurence Olivier's theatre farewell), in which the events on the theatre stage matched very closely those on the wider one. One line sums up the hopes and their dashing; a character playing a young but ardent girl cries out "It's started!", and makes for the door, as if to swim the Channel if there is no other way of getting to the "it" that had started.

★

It sometimes comes as a surprise, though it should not, that in real Utopias, those which are wholly benign in intention, the politics (in the widest definition, that is) are on the left. This is true of Utopias founded long before terms such as left or right designated a political view and position, or indeed before the terms themselves had any meaning in a political context. Those which are, or turn out to be, despotic and oppressive, almost always fit exactly into the template of the right.

There are reasons for this categorisation, most of them obvious. For centuries, the weak faced the strong, the poor the rich, the ruled the rulers, the have-nots the haves. Long before the word "capitalism" was coined (it dates from 1854), there was such a divide in almost all societies in which wealth played any part. It was largely because of these disparities and the impossibility of ending or changing them that so many Utopias came into being. Some hundred years after the Peasants' Revolt, led by Wat Tyler, a very similar figure, Jack Cade, set out on a very similar errand. Cade went on to declare "I charge and command that, of the city's cost, the pissing conduit run nothing but claret wine this first year, of our reign". (But the loudest cheer from the crowd must surely have come from Dick the Butcher, one of Cade's leading, though sceptical supporters. "The first thing we do, let's kill all the lawyers." More than six hundred years have passed since that heart-warming cry rang out, according to Shakespeare, at Blackheath, but its resonance is still clear, its meaning still plain, its capacity to stir the blood still unweakened.)

Cade, like Tyler before him, and Bohm before *him*, thought he could succeed by force, a utopian belief if ever there was one. The centuries passed and as more sophistication seeped into the hopes of change, relief could be had by *imagining* success. This was in the genre of William Morris, whose Utopia was cumbersomely but meaningfully entitled *News from Nowhere; or, An Epoch of Rest, Being Some Chapters from a Utopian Romance* (Morris is one of the few utopians who include the word in his title). Morris was not only an artist of considerable quality, but a man who had thought much about labour and made a distinction between "work" or "toil". His utopian dream honestly tackled the problem, coming up with his work/toil distinction. First, we must decide what work is necessary (and if it is necessary it must be pleasurable, or certainly ought to be), and then it must be distributed. Morris was no Luddite, but he wanted to use machines as sparingly as possible, mostly to do such work as no one wants to do but needs to be done. Evidently, Morris was no logician, either. He ruled out the possibility that some of his people would refuse to work at all; there must be *something* useful and ornamental that would fit. Anyway, this is a dream, and strange things happen in dreams.

Naturally, so gentle a Utopia would have dispensed with government, law and its enforcement (because crime, too, has automatically disappeared), private property and, *a fortiori*, money. Less obviously, marriage seems to have disappeared, though not love. Echoing More's contempt for gold, Morris despised politics; he reveals that parliament has been pulled down and the cleared space is in use only as a dung market.

Morris practised what he preached. He painted and wove and made and wrote to increase the amount of beauty in the world and to urge others to make more of it. Dreams are all very well, but waking, too, there is work to be done. Much the same could be said of Gandhi towards the end of his life. He argued ultimately that each family should weave its own clothes by hand and grow its own produce. "If all men sweep before their doors", says the proverb, "the village will be clean." But the more hard-headed Nehru saw before him a country wallowing in penury and backwardness, desperate for modernisation, and Gandhi died by an assassin's bullet before he became disillusioned.

Morris was not alone. One of the most persistent of all utopian phenomena is the outbreak of the obviously utopian-oriented unrest on the part of the poorest classes. This may take the form of the revolts of the poor or the messianic attacks on authority led by charismatic figures and the millennarian hordes who believed in them. Such upheavals are not confined to the Middle Ages; there was a revolutionary Icarian organisation in France in the middle of the nineteenth century, led by Etienne Cabet, a socialist, whose book *Voyage en Icarie* provided the basis of the Icarian campaign, and he attracted a very substantial following. The title of his book and the name of his organisation were rather unfortunate, at any rate in the eyes of anyone who knew who Icarus was, and what happened to him. But although the Chartist movement in nineteenth-century Britain has not been thought of as a utopian cause, it surely should be, and can be classed with Icarianism; even the dates of the two were very close. It certainly had all the outward signs of a mass utopian movement: huge numbers, little or no violence, ingenious promotion, a forlorn hope for a modest proposal, and a legacy that seeded more successful enterprises long after it had been forgotten.

The Great Charter was a landmark in British utopianism, as Icarianism was in French, but if they were unrecognised as utopian, our contemporary movements are even less likely to be numbered in the utopian ranks. Even in France, who now recalls Pierre Poujade? Yet his movement, though it lacked substance (a clue to its mass-utopian nature), had an enormous *réclame* in its day largely among the same proletarian circles. (A similar movement, with a similar fate, waxed notable for a time in Denmark, of all placid, well-governed and prosperous lands.) In Britain, the mass utopian rallies were grounded in one of the country's oldest grievances going back at least to Elizabethan times: the ill-fated poll-tax.

If big was not beautiful, or at any rate, not successful, can we gain something of value from the small – the communities, some, but not all, grounded in religious form. Whatever these designate, they cannot be classified in the mass movement, with all its dangers, however utopian. Many of these have had surprisingly long-lasting success, almost always by shutting themselves away in remote parts of the world, whether in the

United States, Scotland or India. One of the best-known American ones was Oneida, which flourished from halfway through the nineteenth century for some thirty years later; it was based on a strict Christian rule. But the Shakers are the most remarkable of all the communitarian Utopias; founded at the end of the eighteenth century, they are still flourishing (and, it must be said, making and selling a very wide variety of useful and beautiful things, most of the beautiful ones also useful and all the useful ones beautiful).

These silver stones, set in a silver sea, are a testimony to the determination of the participants and the strength of the utopian ideal. In India, such communities are almost invariably based on a sage or holy man, but it seems that elsewhere no such central figure is needed – and indeed a leader of any kind jars with the pure essence of Utopia. The more ethereal and abstract ideas of Utopia constitute the bulk of its career, and must do so, but there are many simple and prosaic aspects of our theme, and two particularly, though they have in common only their utopian simplicity. Who ever thought of the Co-operative Movement in Britain as a utopian form? Yet it is one.

The Movement (it spawned much progeny elsewhere) shows, sadly, one of the limitations of Utopia. It was founded in the form of a chain of stores selling food, clothing and other necessities. But its unique nature lay in its total rejection of the profit motive. Any trading surplus was to be returned to the customers in the form of a dividend (invariably named the "divi"). The system was simplicity itself. Shoppers registered at the "Co-op", and retained their receipts, or had their purchases recorded in a book. When divi-day came, whatever profit the stores had made in the previous quarter, the customer received the bonus due, according to the amount spent. ("From each to his capacity, to each…" – Marx's rule could hardly be more apposite, and it is no coincidence that the Co-op had very close ties with the Labour Party. There were "Labour-Co-operative" members of parliament.)

But there was a serpent even in this touching Eden, this demonstration of mutual beliefs leading to reward. The Co-op was, of course, in competition with other, more capitalistic, chain stores. For the Co-op customer to receive a divi, there had to be a profit in the first place, redistribute it as the Co-op most selflessly might. And as the years went by, competition from more profit-conscious stores (to say nothing of smarter ones – the Co-op seemed to have a policy of making their premises uninviting) bit into the Co-op's margin, from which it followed that the Co-op's margin could sustain only a smaller and smaller divi.

It was clear that the days of the divi were past and that the Co-op could not survive on the purity of its motives. The system had to be abandoned and the Co-op had to come down into the abhorred marketplace and fight capitalistically for its existence. Unfortunately, so pure in heart had the movement been when it was founded, that it had not only given back its profits, it had given the system, from the start, to the customers; they *owned* the Co-op, and it took years – fatal ones, it turned out – to change the constitution, accept that the divi was a thing of the past, and behave as all other shops behaved if they wanted to continue trading. By the time these precepts had been fully accepted, the Co-op and its ideals – worthy ones, remember – had failed completely, and only years later did it turn itself into a modern organisation, mostly in the wholesale trade, where the word divi would not have been understood except by the oldest and most misty-eyed employee. Selling and buying – the real kind, not the chimerical – clearly has no place in Utopia; more to the point, Utopia has no place in selling and buying. And nations which have spurned the profit-motive have invariably been, for their ordinary citizens at least, the poorest.

And so said Georges Sorel; what is more, he was not content to speak, as so many of his kind did – he acted as well.

They had plainly never heard of Georges Sorel; if they had, they would have abandoned Marcuse and all their other exemplars for him and would have been just as disappointed.

After leading a blameless career in the French civil service as an inspector of roads and bridges for twenty-two years, Sorel resigned his post and spent the rest of his life in the fruitless pursuit of the socialist revolution. His heroes and models were Marx and Nietzsche, uncomfortable bedfellows, one might think. He was one of the earliest advocates of public violence in the cause, and he was also ahead of his time in classifying everything said by his opponents as "violence" (a concept now rife in western countries, though few who practise it are likely to know the identity of their progenitor). Violence, for Sorel, meant, in addition to the more conventional kind, the laws of the state, the public institutions, religious teaching and the ruling moral principles; he insisted that socialism would come only through violent revolution.

He did not, it must be said, lead his followers in the uprising on which he had pinned his hopes; Sorel's trump card was to be the General Strike.

When this took place, it would be followed by immediate surrender on the part of the authorities, but he no more had a chance of testing his belief in this matter than he had had in the matter of revolution.

For so fiery a figure, it comes as a pleasant surprise that he lived to be seventy-five, no doubt dreaming to the last of taking to the streets, leading the people into a savage fight for the revolution, sweeping away the enemy, capturing the heights of the state, and then absent-mindedly calling a General Strike when he was firmly established in power. Perhaps he would have done better to go on inspecting the roads and bridges of France.

Yet the catalogue of touching experiences in those fateful days is still not exhausted. Apart from the anarchists, who would have nothing to do with rules, laws or society itself, the *groupuscules* spent a great deal of time drawing up new constitutions for the new world they thought they were bringing. It was plain that the present French Constitution (the British avoided the problem by not having a Constitution) would not do, nor could any amount of tinkering make it do. The young constitution-makers would have to make their own from foundations to roof. They set to with a will, and of course virtually all of the results were pure Utopia, beautiful but utterly unreal – unreal, that is, until we all get to Utopia and stay there. It was plain that they had never before looked closely at *any* Constitution, certainly not theirs, whence the bewilderment when they realised that they had to start afresh. Yet there was much guidance available to them, if they had only looked for it.

Constitution-makers are all utopians, and they must get a considerable thrill out of it. Imagine: to be given the task of ordering an entire society, drawing up a complete schedule of laws, laying down a system of voting, constructing a parliament or its equivalent, appointing hierarchies of judges, remembering to establish a police force, a civil service, an educational system, prisons, even a fire brigade – bliss would it be indeed to be entrusted with such godlike power.

In practice, the opportunity rarely offers itself. The utopian maker of societies has yet another problem, which indeed runs right through the entire utopian philosophy, though not often acknowledged or even noticed, and if noticed as like as not to be indignantly denied. It is the weakness of prediction: many a system of government (and almost any system of anything) is subject to the iron law which lays down that there is no such thing as an iron law. Intentions may be of the best, and in Utopia they almost invariably are; but to ensure that they stay the way for which they are legislated is beyond human control, for the very good reason that human control is beyond human control.

There are countless of these chimerical constitutions, existing only in printed words; many more have come and gone, and yet more will spring up in the future. It is a phenomenon surprisingly little studied; it is not easy to understand why tyrants immovable on their thrones (until a greater tyranny arises) feel the need to have a formal legitimacy by which they are understood to rule. The only explanation that might serve is the effect of the utopian propensity on the tyrant's thinking. Not only is his power complete, he must also be seen to rule over a notionally contented people, and from that position he itches for the ultimate accolade of the centuries: his rule was not just awesome in the completeness of its power, but it must be – what no other society in history has been – perfect.

Thus it is with such hopeful orderings of entire nations. Except, perhaps, one.

The Constitution of the United States reached its two hundredth birthday a few years ago, and it was only a few years before the bicentenary that serious complaints about its inadequacy could be heard. For such a document – which *was* created out of nothing – to serve so well for two centuries suggests that Utopia had been discovered and had been made to work perfectly. Inspection of the Constitution, from its original form to its latest amendment, will find otherwise; to the perpetual astonishment of history, the American Constitution is the most pragmatic, the least utopian, of all such charters. Hard-headed men, who would have no truck with fancy, built the work, clause by clause, out of simple materials that would take almost any amount of wear, and their faith in the construction has been amply borne out. It is all the more astonishing that such a text could be created, when it is remembered that the entire labour of constitution-making had sprung from what may well be the most extravagantly utopian document in all commerce between the nations: the preamble of the Declaration of Independence. Starting as it clearly meant to go on, and did, it began with those amazing words "We hold these truths to be self-evident...", and every word that followed was no less utopian, no less insecurely based, than the fanfare of the start. When they got down to the hard work it was far otherwise. It is difficult, perhaps impossible, to think of any such somersault that has infused so much wisdom when landing on its feet. It is heartening to know that men *can* defy the rush to judgement, and build a temple of laws that will stand for generations to come.

5

Heaven is above

INEVITABLY, the idea of Heaven was the first Utopia. From the earliest man, perhaps earlier still, down among the pre-men, the sky above has been a place, and a place, moreover, in which the painful life on earth is radically changed, into a world without toil, fear, hunger and cold; and finite, especially finite. So familiar is the idea of life elsewhere, almost invariably sited in the sky, that it has ceased to be remarkable. But it is remarkable, very much so. After all, though over the thousands of millennia the stars have shifted their courses, such changes were noticed only, astronomically speaking, the other day; as far as the earlier centuries went, every heavenly body had its fixed and unchanging path.

"Every heavenly body"; but who said it was heavenly? How did the idea of *celestial* bliss come about? Since records have existed (and obviously long before that), the belief that the sky above is inhabited, and inhabited, moreover, by most welcoming beings, is immovably held by practically every culture in history and pre-history. There have been arguments as to who these beings are, and many more (and fiercer) arguments about what is required for entry, but the idea of literal pie in a literal sky has taken root everywhere.

As soon as primitive man understood death, he began to wonder what followed it. He would have been helped by the mystery of the heavenly bodies; Caliban could recall the time when Prospero was willing "to teach me how To name the bigger light, and how the less, That burn by day and night". Until Anaxagoras, mankind believed that the sun, the moon and the stars were close enough to earth for the birds to visit them, from which it could be deduced, with no great leap of the imagination, that there was a world there, waiting for the dead.

In all history, then, there has been no more powerful utopian myth than that of an afterworld of perfection and eternal happiness. The idea long antedates Christianity, though the Judaeo-Christian tradition has been the most deep-rooted form, intertwined with heaven's first cousin, the millennium.

All sorts of explanations of the meaning of heaven have been offered; even Jung joined in. So powerful is the belief in a world after death that it has spawned a huge range of obsequies, rituals and customs. In William Golding's *The Inheritors*, such funerary practices are seen through the eyes even of sub-men, not yet *homo sapiens*, but there is no sense of incongruity, so deep-rooted is the thought of an after-life. Some cultures, indeed, put food and drink in the graves of the departed, to sustain them on their journey. Others mummify their dead, presumably awaiting a general resurrection; still others embalm them, and today some even freeze them, awaiting a heavenly thaw.

By then, two new aspects of death had arisen. First, the yearning for a glorious life after death was no longer a compensation for a wretched life on earth; the belief in another world had become universal, and the rich, too, look forward to what lies beyond death. Second, the ceremony of death had been incorporated into religion. And with religion, there came a sharp and dismaying division; no longer do the dead, rich or poor, automatically go to Paradise. The concept, first of Hell, and then of Purgatory, had been devised. True, the parable of Lazarus and the rich man sounds a warning; Lazarus was in heaven because of his sufferings, and the rich man was burning in everlasting fire, begging in vain for one drop of cool water to cool his tongue – not because of his riches but because he gave no alms from those riches to the poor.

Nevertheless, the demands of religion grew fiercer; it all began, presumably, with Adam and Eve. Adam's attempt to put the blame on Eve ("...the woman thou gavest to be with me, she gave me of the fruit...") inevitably failed, and the unhappy pair were expelled from Paradise for ever. From then on, the human race has been trying to find the way back, trying to outwit the angel with the fiery sword who bars their return. Only those who have not transgressed may hope for Paradise, and Adam and Eve symbolise the imperfections in humanity that keep the sinners out. (Remember what was their sin: self-consciousness. Only innocence, which took no account of nakedness, could stay.)

The symbol of the garden is a powerful one; as early as the second chapter of Genesis "The Lord God planted a garden eastward in Eden", not forgetting a river to water it, and sowing the earth with precious metals and stones to be had for the digging. But the digging in the garden must be done; Adam was strictly enjoined "to dress it and to keep it".

Ever since, the idea of a garden has had associations much wider and deeper than their beauty. There are countless poems written about gardens, and the dominant tone of them is peace. That is why, presumably, the most terrible punishment the Lord could devise was their ejection from the perfect garden and into the imperfect world outside. (Many of the apostrophes of the garden contrast it with the workaday world.) And, significantly, it was when Adam and Eve lost their innocence through the serpent's beguilings that the punishment fell upon them: perfection equals innocence, imperfection understanding. No wonder that "forbidden fruit" has become a deeply embedded phrase, and the angels with fiery swords a similarly meaningful image.

Nevertheless, there were now dues to pay for those who wanted to enter it. There was, of course, for those with sufficient patience, the coming of the Messiah to the Jews. He would gather up the righteous and take them to heaven, pausing only to destroy the evil-doers. Jews today still believe that the Messiah is to come; Christians, of course, believe that he has already been, in the person of Jesus, but will come again. These waitings are yet more obstacles before the feet of those who seek the ever-receding Paradise, though there are countless encouragements to persuade them to wait another moment.

Art took up the theme. Innumerable depictions of the life of heaven, with the martyrs reaping their just reward, reinforced both the delights of heaven and the price of the ticket – a life of holiness. Again and again the same template shows the Holy Family, with God at the top and Christ at his right hand, while the faithful are entering into their hard-won inheritance. Augustine was right to call death the last enemy.

But if the faithful dead are to be gathered into heaven from one or other of the two Messianic promises, a problem arises. What about the body? In what form would it ascend into heaven?

Augustine declares that bodily resurrection takes the shape of the living image, with all blemishes removed, along with clothing; there is an exception to the perfect body, for the martyrs, who retain the stigmata of the wounds they received for their testimony. St Thomas Aquinas says that the saints will regain their bodies, though not until the Last Judgement; but that still does not answer the question, or rather questions. There might be no marriage in heaven, but are there lovers, and can these continue to love? Do we eat and drink? Play? Work? For that matter, shall we recognise our loved ones in heaven? More to the point, what do we *do* there that we did not do in life? And what do our souls do?

These questions have been answered in an astonishing number of ways. (Perhaps the most striking was that offered by Swedenborg, who had a significant advantage when it came to describe heaven, because he had been there, examined it, and talked with the angels.) It could be, and was, left to the theologians to decide the question of what happens to the soul between death and the ultimate fate. But that would not do for the more earthy problems. Terrified humans, fearing the loss of identity, of self-knowledge (the alternative being death with only oblivion to follow), demanded an assurance that *something* survives, and then, becoming greedy, insisted on corporeal bodies, total memory recall, even sexual activity; and of course visits to the illustrious long-dead sages, wits and the saints and patriarchs themselves. From that, it was but a step to constructing heavenly resources for children cut off before they could grow into adults. By now, heaven must be crowded to bursting.

Utopias galore are strewn about the world of religion, and the sound of the yearnings they provoke is painful to hear, and more painful to understand. A utopian longing for eternal life, in whatever form (we have by now wholly dismissed the possibility of eternal punishment for sinners, and if we are wrong to dismiss it we are in for a severe shock) pervades all our thoughts about these universal – literally universal – questions. Inevitably, we fetch up ignoring them. And who shall blame us?

It might be thought that Christians, and particularly Christian writers, would have no need of Utopias. They have God's promise, delivered through his Son, that an eternity of bliss awaits those who have heeded the Christian message. And no one, whatever his standing and however thin the cord on which the believer is to mount into Heaven, is excluded – as indeed Christ promised the thief beside whom he was crucified.

But it is not so much the appearance and nature of Heaven that is the subject of enquiry, nor the nature of the tests that aspirants will have to pass if they are to be held worthy, but the simulacrum of heaven on earth in Christian enclaves on the one hand, and the vast variety of paths to goal on the other, that can confuse the humble seeker after revealed truth.

It has to be said that a reading of St Augustine's *City of God* followed by a detailed examination of Calvin's Geneva and its history, pose almost insuperable problems for a seeker after a sign. Put Geneva beside a constructed Utopia such as Johann Andreae's *Christianopolis*; few, surely, would recognise them as examples of the same religion; yet Calvin's enclave was sternly shown to the world as a paradigm of what Christ meant.

If there are many heavens, can there be more than one Christ? How can any poor devil of a utopian find his bearings in such contradiction? Yet the utopian in the case cannot go to live in More's Utopia, or Cockaigne, or the Big Rock Candy Mountain, because even the most Utopia-soaked believer knows that these are imaginary places. But when he turns to the Christian promise, and the Christian God who made it, and stretches out his arms in humble suppliance, asking to be made worthy for God's kingdom, he finds such dispute as must make him despair of the one Utopia that throughout the ages seemed, and still seems, to be no man-made construction, but the living truth.

*

If the picture of the Christian heaven is the most familiar, there are many other claims on the heavenly territory. The most vivid and three-dimensional of all these places is surely the Norse and Teutonic Valhalla, where fallen heroes, temporarily killed in battle (battle of any kind, it seems) are picked up from the field and carried by maidens whose duty it is to put the slain warrior on his horse and guide him and horse together into a new life. They have to be bravest of the brave; no coward who runs from the fight can hope to enter Valhalla. The sagas and the Niebelungenlied see death in battle as the finest end, though it is not altogether clear whether they go on fighting when they have entered the portals, and if so, against whom. (Jousting would presumably be felt beneath such fierce battlers; at any rate, there is no reference to it in the heroic poems of the northern lands.)

This is again one of the problems of Utopia, perhaps second only to that of boredom, to which it is obviously linked. Eternity is a long time; is there enough variety in the activities of those who have spent vigorous lives, and wish to continue doing so? Where is a fit utopian abode for such figures? If there is one, it must be in the sky, which brings us back to the phenomenon of a perfect world above, physically above, the earth. The mythology here is almost childishly open; we know the earth, because we live on it, and our sorrows and wearinesses and deprivations are all around us. How could we fail to turn our eyes away from the earth of pain to the sky of bliss? There have been Utopias *beneath* the earth, but very few have made any mark; Wagner's subterranean world is far worse, in its slavery and savagery, than any real land on the real globe.

But this may be the point at which one of the most remarkable ideas of Utopia should take a bow. For this story is set in a truly subterranean land, very strange indeed, its strangeness lying not only in what happens there, though that is strange enough, but by the identity of the author.

It is widely believed that Casanova wrote nothing but his remarkable memoirs (of which work Lorenzo da Ponte, Mozart's librettist, said, in his own memoirs, "I knew that extraordinary man as well as anybody ever did, and I can assure my readers that love of truth was not the principal excellence of his writings"), but that belief is very wide of the mark – so wide, indeed, that he is likely to have spent more time in writing than in pursuit of the activity for which he is more usually known. After all, he wrote 42 works, 24 of them published in his lifetime, and at his death his possessions included 8000 pages of manuscript.

Casanova's Utopia (his only novel) is a gigantic work in five massive volumes comprising in all 1745 pages; the title is *Icosameron* (which is the Greek for "twenty days" – the story the narrator tells in the book takes that time to finish it). It is likely that no one has ever read it right through; certainly, it has never been published in its entirety since he published it in 1788 by subscription, in an edition of 350 copies. He wrote it in French, and it was first republished (abridged) in German in the twentieth century. Other abridgments have been made in other languages, but it had to wait until 1986 for it to be published (heavily abridged) in English, and in America, by the heroic Rachel Zurer.

Casanova's narrator, together with the narrator's wife, find themselves, after an earthquake, in the centre of the earth, where they stay for eighty-one years; the wife remains fecund for forty years and bears 40 pairs of twins (one pair every October the first). They find themselves in the land of the Megamicres, which is divided into 80 kingdoms and 10 republics, each comprising 1,210,000 acres. The Megamicres are androgynes, they have no navels and one nipple each, they go naked except for shoes, and live on milk, which is red. They are rarely more than 18 inches high, and their horror of drunkenness is such that a sleeping drunkard may be robbed with impunity. They have a vocabulary of 30,000 words, they venerate serpents, and there are penalties for lying, yawning and immoderate laughter.

But perhaps the most significant aspect of Casanova's subterranean voyage – even more striking that he descends into a full-fledged Utopia – is that throughout his eighty-one years in the earth he is sensing and exhibiting the true scientific spirit, which was then being born on the surface of the earth, as Casanova's version was beneath it.

There are flying horses, for instance; there is beautiful, sublime music, there are wonderful gardens, electric fire made from the disturbance of the air, a working telegraph, and a heavy fine for judges who find themselves holding the minority opinion. The narrators find that they have come to the most benign of the 80 kingdoms and 10 republics, and love is supreme. Though they all die at the age of forty-eight, this does not greatly trouble them. What tips the balance into Utopia is this:

> ...at all the crossroads, in all the public parks and even in the royal courtyard, there were story tellers who gathered people around them. These sages told tales which seemed meant for children and were so understood by the uninformed. But for those listeners who penetrated their inner meaning, they conveyed profound truths in the guise of fables. Ingeniously created as simple stories they interested and amused those who did not grasp their subtleties. These sages would disguise themselves...to attract and amuse the crowds. Our friend the Chief Gardener went daily to the most renowned of these circles.

★

Utopia is hardly a children's concept; a sufficiency of sweets and cakes, treats and pleasant visits, happy days in the sun – these, it would be thought, constitute a perfect world, not least because children are largely ignorant of other, less agreeable worlds. The idea of a world (to say nothing of countless worlds) is virtually impossible for a child to comprehend. Children's literature has taken cognisance of this fact; to widen horizons is one thing, to puzzle is another.

Yet the effort has been made, and with remarkable success. Lionel

Davidson, a writer of thrillers and of children's books, has turned his hand to a true child's Utopia – that is, a Utopia that is recognisable as a serious contribution to the genre while at the same time making it comprehensible to a child. *Under Plum Lake* takes the theme and offers a child a wide variety of pleasures – taste, games, beauty – but grounds the story in a serious imaginary reality.

A boy, Barry, at the seaside in the family's holiday bungalow, goes exploring in the nearby caves, and encounters a boy apparently of much the same age. But it transpires that Egon comes from another world, and a world, moreover, beneath ours as well as above it.

Egon presses a button (his world is, of course, thousands of times more advanced than ours) and Barry sees

...a vast winding valley...Immense terraced cliffs rose from the foothills...There were canyons between the cliffs, and swarming in and out of them were millions of fish. There was an unbelievable multitude, of every colour...Ahead was a mountain range, and the nearest peak was shining turquoise...Beyond the turquoise mountain, far in the distance soared three slender peaks...Everywhere the sun glinted...

Barry begins to learn of this wonderful civilisation. He is told that

...the land above the sea used to be one continent. There was no Asia, Europe, Africa, America, Australia. They were joined. And the climate was good and everything grew bigger in it...Thousands of different forms came later, and passed out of existence...science had become so advanced that they needed a better power source than the sun. The idea was to pick one with a suitable planet and move there...Earth was the finest and most beautiful planet anywhere...

Barry sees the utopian cities. "Some of the buildings are like twists of striped candy; others like flowers or mushrooms. One had a pear-shaped dome, the colour of a pearl." Inevitably, there are wonderful things to eat and drink, and Barry comes upon "tigra".

It's silver. It's the colour of a silver cachou, with maroon stripes inside like raspberry ripple, except they move the whole time inside the silver. The drink swirls in the glass and it swirls in your mouth, and it tastes like a tigra forest smells. It's delicate, silvery, but better than that. You can't stop drinking it. It coats your stomach silver, and acts on your brain. It makes you want to do things.

Barry does indeed do things. There is power tobogganing, spring floats worn on the feet to jump about on the water, ice-cream "a hundred times better", and an assurance that "All life's fun".

But even the fecund imagination of Lionel Davidson would be incomplete if it did not encompass something that could indeed be a true utopian civilisation. Happily, the author is well equipped with the extra creative thought that lifts *Under Plum Lake* out of a child's garden of delights and makes it something far deeper and wider.

His guide takes Barry into the abyss, where there is nothing but blackness; Barry shouts in terror, but makes no sound; reassured by Egon, he must turn away his head when the final miracle takes place: the world creating itself. But Barry, for a moment, turns his head back and sees it, just for the fraction of a second...

A gigantic pillar, shining like an iceberg, broad as a river, made of light. It was all of light, but it gave no light. It kept its light. All around was blackness. In the boat was blackness. The iceberg of light moved majestically upward, a great molten mass, brighter than a furnace, brighter than the sun. Bits of it had crumbled off, and the bits moved upwards with it. Behind closed lids, I felt my eyes searing. I felt my brain coming apart. I knew I was screaming, but no sound came out...The terrible light went, and the blackness.

"I remember what I'm not supposed to remember", says Barry..."I know the future is wonderful, and the idea behind it is, and life is. But I want to get on with my own!"

Many adult Utopias have located themselves beneath the sea or above the clouds. This one, which starts with a boy's adventurings among seaside caves, and culminates in "the world creating itself", takes that familiar location into a realm (for, of course, there is much more to the boy's adventures, many of them by no means mere pleasant indulgences like the ice-cream) which seems naturally utopian. The reader of *Under Plum Lake* will be caught, willy-nilly, in a profound yearning for such a world, not because "All life's fun", but because of the depth of meaning the book reveals. To do that within the framework of a true children's book is a remarkable achievement.

★

The twentieth century has but a few years to run; there will be fierce arguments over the question: does the millennium begin on the 31st December 1999 (those who say yes, argue that the Christian era started on day nought, not January 1st), or on the 1st January 2000 (those who say no, argue that the Christian era started on day one). But there will be a much fiercer battle than the one over the calendar. We think ourselves far superior to those touchingly benighted tens or thousands or even millions who, as the year 1000 came closer (ignoring the problem of which day), were convinced that the end of the world was nigh; Christ would be sent again by his Father to gather up the righteous and destroy everything else.

Yet our supposedly much superior modern intellects will – given modern technology – devise any number of terrifying fates that we may or · will suffer as the new millennium rises over the millennial horizon. A forest of latter-day eschatological beliefs will spring up to meet it, some of them indistinguishable from the theories, warnings, expectations and readinesses that accompanied the previous thousand years.

But what if we broaden the definition of millennarianism? Surely, then, it provides something like an exact definition of Utopia. Again and again throughout history, but coming into full flood in the Middle Ages, huge crowds have been persuaded, with no great difficulty, to believe that a righteous judge is coming to break the power of unrighteous earthly rulers and elevate the poor to joy and plenty. Sometimes it has been no more than a proclaimed miracle-man or woman (some of the latter claiming to be gravid with the Holy Ghost) who sets off a wave of tenaciously held belief.

People in unbearable conditions who can see no hope of amelioration in their lot will turn to an imaginary happiness, conjuring up a world that treats them to infinities of perfection. From there, it is a short step to action, and only one thing is lacking: a leader.

Professor Norman Cohn's illuminating book *The Pursuit of the Millennium* demonstrates how, through the ages, the poor have followed, almost always to their own destruction, the great gallimaufry of prophets, holy men, Second Comings, magicians, sorcerers, reincarnations, madmen and plain rogues who have promised the poor untold riches and untold bliss. The catalogue is as lurid as it is plentiful (Thomas Müntzer assured his unarmed followers, when they confronted the fire-power of the forces of order, that he would catch the enemy's cannon-balls in the sleeves of his cloak), but perhaps the most extravagant of all these pitiful crusades of the poor was the story of the Drummer of Niklashausen, one Hans Bohm. No one could improve on Professor Cohn's account, or his prose:

Bohm declared that the Virgin Mary had given him a message...In the parish church of Niklashausen there stood a statue of the Virgin Mary...now men must go in their multitudes on pilgrimage to the Virgin of Niklashausen or else punishment would...descend upon the world...Whoever made the pilgrimage would be absolved from all his sins...whoever died there would go immediately to heaven.

The former shepherd...was suddenly able to command astonishing eloquence...crowds streamed to hear him...At first he merely preached repentance...But before long the *propheta* was claiming for himself miraculous powers...he swore that he could lead any soul out of hell with his own hand...The day of reckoning was at hand, when the clergy would be happy to cover up their tonsures...for to kill a cleric would then be seen as a most meritorious act...All would live together as brothers...The emperor is a scoundrel and the Pope is useless...

News of the wonderful happenings...passed rapidly from village to village...vast hordes...were streaming towards Niklashausen...all parts of southern and central Germany were in commotion...Artisans deserted their workshops and peasants their fields...Paradise had literally descended upon the earth...

Meanwhile the hordes...advanced...singing songs of their own composition...one became particularly popular:

> To God in Heaven we complain
> *Kyrie eleison*
> That the priests cannot be slain
> *Kyrie eleison.*

As the pilgrims arrived...they...crowded about him...Articles of his clothing were seized and cut into minute pieces...it was reported that he had...cured people who had been blind or dumb from birth; that he had raised the dead; and that he had made a spring gush from a rock...the authorities...decided that Bohm's propaganda was a serious menace...a squad of horsemen...carried him off to Würtzburg...next day a peasant took up the prophet role...They were to march boldly to the castle...where Bohm was imprisoned...As they approached it the walls would crumble like those of Jericho...thousands of men, women and children marched through the night until they arrived at dawn beneath the castle walls...shots were fired in earnest and followed by a cavalry-charge. Some forty pilgrims were killed, and the rest at once fled in helpless panic...But before fresh disturbances could occur Bohm had been tried...and found guilty of heresy and sorcery...he was burnt at the stake, singing hymns to the Virgin...

So much for the Utopias of the poor, and how they end. Yet in that inevitably somewhat ribald account, the tragedy of the yearning poor is laid bare. No doubt the crowds that pressed around the Holy Youth, and followed him to disaster, were convinced of the religious beliefs that Bohm preached, including the claims of his raising the dead. But the mass must have been drawn to the upheaval by the simple forces of hunger, labour and pennilessness. And why should they not grasp at such straws? Embedded in Bohm's short and violent story there was another theme altogether: it was the cry of the dispossessed when they saw a rainbow and remembered God's promise. Once again, the promise had been broken; those artisans who had deserted their workshops, those peasants their fields, limped home (unless they were among the 40 dead), to take up their wretched lives anew, and to dream the dream that comes to all those who have nothing: that some day they will have everything. Assuredly, those who survived the cavalry-charge, went on dreaming the dream.

On much more solid ground – at least as they believe with fanatic certainty – are the Jehovah's Witnesses, with their street-corner magazine *The Watchtower*. These are in flight from the corruption and false religion of the world; their twin tasks are to find and convince as many more believers as possible Armageddon is nigh; from then on there is nothing but utter destruction for all but the elect. When the whole world has been swept clean of those who did not see the light in time, the chosen ones will enter into their Kingdom.

We have come some considerable distance from the idea of heaven as Utopia. But surely the yearnings which surround the picture are profoundly utopian. What could be more so than the naïve but touching belief that severed families will be united in heaven, never to mourn again? This, you may say, is the last gasp of the Romantic Movement, or the first step into childish anthropomorphism and the sickly-sweet taste of a heaven consisting of the beatified sitting on clouds all day. But if so, there is a long and distinguished pedigree behind the notion: Luther believed that the beasts of the field, both wild and domesticated, will be found in heaven, together with insects, their stings drawn for good measure. Well, there was something of a precedent; St Francis of Assisi, bitten by a flea, pardoned the creature rather than swatting it.

Whatever the churches say about the Pathetic Fallacy – that is, that animals, such as pets and watchdogs, however dear to their owners' hearts, will not be found in Heaven – Utopia has no such severe exclusion policy. Indeed, the in-gathering of the dead with their four-footed companions is an essentially utopian picture. Men like Fabre and Maeterlinck hovered between serious animal research and the countless legends and fairy-tales which surround the animal kingdom – a phrase full of meaning, though only one among a great range of metaphors with animals at the heart of them. ("Hive" and "ant-hill", to denote human natures or activities, are by now hardly metaphors at all.)

The animal kingdom, of course, goes back much further than the human one. *When Dinosaurs ruled the Earth* may denote only an unpretentious film, but it is the literal truth; more to the point, we are fascinated by the thought of these mighty creatures, and fascinated even more when we compare them to the human race, with their vastness of body and minimal brain. If it is absurd to talk of a dinosaur "civilisation", we should not talk of "the elephants' graveyard", though serious anthropologists do so. Utopianisers, particularly the ones with the most ordered society, are attracted to the animals and the insects: "Go to the ant, thou sluggard, consider her ways, and be wise".

Meanwhile, a drastic revolution has been going on in the utopian spirit; animals have been promoted to leadership in the field of ecology. Claims, not all of them grossly inflated, have been made about the rate in which certain species are dying out, or will be soon. The concerned humans have done good work in this field, but an interestingly utopian theme has been running through the campaign. There has long been a tradition of thinking of animals as repositories of wisdom (they have, after all, been worshipped in some cultures), and it was the whale and the elephant that were supposed to shame man. A change in the hierarchy has been made; today, it is the dolphin that reigns. Meanwhile, there can be little slackening in the sales of the miniature sculptures in the form of three wise monkeys ("Hear no evil, see no evil, speak no evil"), though on the other hand he would be a bold man who today would let it be known that he keeps in his pocket, for luck, a mummified monkey's paw. But at least the argument of the monkeys at the typewriter (could a thousand of them, hitting the keys at random, ultimately find that they had typed, word perfect, the complete works of Shakespeare?) has now been settled; expert mathematicians have recently deigned to examine the problem, and unanimously report that it would be impossible.

But the entire relationship between human beings and animals is far more complex, studied through the binoculars of utopianism, than has until recently been realised. There has been a blurring of the boundaries; there is serious argument to be heard, insisting that there is no such boundary, that a human being is only a different kind of animal. The American pestilence called Political Correctness has invaded even this field; to refer to a dog or cat (or, as far as is known, even a tarantula) as "my pet", is almost dangerous. No, it is – must be – "my companion".

In some areas, it is reported, the reserves of charitable donations and activities to help human beings (or human animals, as PC might prescribe) have become seriously depleted, the eleemosynary instinct having been transferred to the other animals. Elsewhere, a fashion for breaking the windows of butchers' shops has sprung up, in the wake of the earlier taste for throwing paint at ladies wearing fur coats. "Greenpeace"; "One World"; "Planet Earth"; these rubrics were once ideals, far from any substantial existence. Now, they are mighty organisations, inter-continentally entwined, and none dare question them.

Meanwhile, the utopian propensity embraces more and more of the animal kingdom, and voices have even been raised in anxiety on behalf of beings that might be found in the exploration of other heavenly bodies (a utopian phrase if ever there was one). What else was *E. T.*? The cold-hearted scientists wanted the extra-terrestrial creature to question and study (and perhaps even dissect), while the children – again, the utopian theme of the innocents – wanted only to get him safely on his way home.

Amid the many kinds of jungle – mysterious, threatening, pathless, savage, poisonous – it comes as a pleasant surprise to find a truly utopian one. It is the one inhabited by the creatures – creatures emphatically embracing trees, bushes, flowers and human beings – depicted by the Douanier Rousseau.

The figure of the neglected genius has dogged the pages of history, particularly art history, and Rousseau, though he was not one of the worst sufferers, attracted very little notice other than in the shape of scorn. His very name was transmogrified into a contemptuous joke; he was indeed a customs officer by trade, but the soubriquet was intended to class him as childish amateur, and it remained, a thorn in his easel, to the end of his life. Well, it is an old story: "Seven great cities contend for Homer dead, Through which the living Homer begged his bread".

Rousseau was of a placid disposition; a glance at his pictures would confirm as much. His genius (it stirs yet again the long and incomprehensible history of unrecognised greatness) leaps from the canvas, full of loving mystery, unearthly deserts and jungles, lions that can at once be seen to be no threat, figures asleep and dreaming of more beauty, high fronds waving in a breeze that will bring more beauty still, more mystery within which "nothing is here for tears, nothing to weep and knock the breast". This is a world above which floats a heavenly orb, not certain whether it is the sun or the moon, nor does it matter, for we are in a world that is recognisable though it has never been seen before, a world that fits Schiller's *Seid umschlungen, Millionen, diesen Kuss die ganzen Welt!*, a world made not just of innocence, but of purity. It can be seen everywhere in his work; every shape is clean-cut, there is nothing at all of Impressionism. Where did he find such peace, where did he find the light he threw on his figures, his landscapes, his friends of the jungle?

There can be only one answer: deep in his soul the Douanier Rousseau had stumbled upon the Garden of Eden, and the angels with the fiery swords, forever on guard at the gate against Adam and Eve, threw it wide open when he, in all his gentleness, humility and mighty gift, tapped gently on the gate. It is tempting to stretch the analogy a little further and classify Adam and Eve as those who jeered at his work, forever shut out from being taken seriously, but it is not necessary: his triumph is recorded in every bush, every tree, every animal, every human being asleep or awake, which he painted, and which is to be found in Eden. It was typical of his generosity that he left us – we who can never find the gate, and would not be worthy of entrance even if we could – so many of his neglected masterpieces.

6

And cry to dream again

WE SMILE superciliously at our own cost, or even danger, if we reject that most utopian search for the longing to hear that the stars in their courses are on our side. Those who deride astrology entirely would deny that there are two kinds of the practice. Those who have an open mind on the subject would distinguish between vulgar astrology and the serious kind. The latter has claimed some results worth further investigation; the brothers Gaucquelin in France have ably defended their work and its fruits against both scientists and lay-people who would reject it altogether. The latter category would not be expected to examine evidence on the subject, but to the deep distress of those who believe that scientists are scientific, it is clear that many of them have taken no more notice of the evidence than have the other party.

It is, however, the vulgar form of astrology that touches the idea of Utopia. The seaside fortune-teller is a familiar figure, almost an archetype, at any rate the picture of her never changes. She wears a floor-length skirt, an embracing blouse, a scarf on her head, and she is peering into a crystal ball which sits in a wooden cradle. When she has peered enough, she delivers her verdict.

This normally begins with an account of the customer's present condition and recent experiences; these are couched in terms sufficiently wide to be almost certain to match something in the life of the patient, eliciting a cry of "That's right!" and cementing the belief in the accuracy of the wise woman. ("Wise woman", of course, is truly an archetype; lines can easily become crossed in this ill-defined world.)

Confidence established, the fortune is told. The more sophisticated of the mystery will hint at forthcoming misfortune; it is invariably mild, and almost always in a form easy to avoid. What follows, however, is the utopian nature of the enterprise at its most obvious. The familiar words – almost, but not quite, established forever outside the fortune-teller's booth as a joke – are employed when a glance at the customer's left hand reveals no marriage ring; "I see a dark stranger".

Money, love, work: these are the staples of the fortune-teller's trade. If you have been unfortunate in these, "luck" is about to turn and give you a cornucopia of at least one of them, with sufficiently propitious encouragement from the infallible crystal ball, two, or even all three. There then follow the equally familiar words (sometimes they are pronounced before the consultation begins), "Cross the gypsy's palm with silver". Real gypsies, the Romany folk, are distressed at the theft and debasement of their name, but that very reasonable complaint contains another clue to the utopian propensity revealed in this harmless trade; the gypsy, in folklore, is supposed to have psychic powers denied to others, and it is therefore fitting that the wise woman in her booth should imply that she holds the concealed keys of knowledge.

An even more vulgar form of bastard astrology is to be found in newspapers of mass circulation; the reader turns to his or her "star-sign", under which is printed the day's good and bad (but never seriously bad) fortune. It is said by experts that the removal of this feature would inevitably lead to a catastrophic fall in the newspaper's readership, and by the extraordinary surge of new interest in such "horoscopes", which are now appearing even in the glossiest of magazines, it seems that the experts are right.

These absurdities cover, as well as much well-believed harmless nonsense, a great unrecognised yearning. Fortune-tellers are sought out not only by the lonely, the fearful, the unfortunate, desperate to find hope. There are many others, leading comfortable and satisfactory lives, who are willing to cross the gypsy's palm with silver, whether literally or metaphorically. The yearning for more by those who already have much that can be measured by a money standard, does not always, and probably not even frequently, take the form of wanting more, or more expensive goods. The yearning leaps over material gains and seeks something beyond the mundane. That something comes in many guises and is pursued in many ways, but it always means the same thing: there is a world elsewhere. That world is a perfect one, and the yearning is a measure of our inability to find it on earth, and of our fear that we may be shut out from it. Surely no amount of silver on the gypsy's palm would be too much for a promise of certainty that we shall inherit – if not here, then perhaps beyond the grave – the utopian perfection we seek.

But reality is the death-knell of Utopia; that is why we shun reality. We do so in a vast variety of ways, some of them grand and tempestuous, some quiet and domestic. There is a childish strain in Utopia, but it is not to be jeered at. Indeed, it is in one important sense almost a definition of a perfect world. For what *is* a perfect world? It is one in which there is no unhappiness, no sorrow, no hate, no ugliness, no poverty, no loss, no envy, no deceit, no folly, no worry, no crime, no disappointment, no disease, no cruelty, no quarrels, no treachery, and no failure – perhaps above all, no failure.

Moreover, it exists, which is more than most Utopias do. It can be found and acquired with no difficulty, and at only a trivial price. It is harmless, comfortable, and very easily replenished when it runs out.

Where, then, is this true Utopia to be found? We must be told at once, so that we can run to the gates and give the password (but no password is needed and the gates are never shut). At last our dream has come true. A dream indeed, for there are no fewer than three perfectly utopian worlds at hand, in respectively Hollywood, the romantic novel, and the nursery.

Very early on in the days of the cinema, those who made the films and sold them got hold of a tremendous truth; it was that most human beings, and most particularly the people who enjoyed the cinema, led lives that were at best dull, and at worst full of pain. The cinema realised, perhaps through the advocacy of a prophet whose name must now be forever lost, that their new enterprise would thrive, expand and be enriched if they deliberately made films in which there would be nothing dull, nothing painful, and nothing in between. Outside that banned spectrum, there was nothing but beauty, happiness, comfort, laughter, wealth, goodness and enduring love. In the real world, and among the real people who are confined to it, those qualities are very rarely all found together, and in any case are never unadulterated by pain, unhappiness, dissatisfaction, anger and – if all else fails to disturb the equilibrium – death.

The cinema boasted, and rightly, that ordinary life cannot evade these negativities, but the cinema could; more, it went to the furthest lengths of enticement by claiming, quite truthfully, that it had also abolished death.

"One short sleep past, we wake eternally, and death shall be no more; death thou shalt die." Who would have thought of those hard-headed men echoing John Donne? But they made good their claim in the darkness – that artificial darkness which is brighter than the sun itself.

Early in its career, the cinema coined for itself the phrase "the dream factory". What else could it have been called? For where else in all the world could anyone find a society in which all the women were beautiful, all the men handsome, and all the children small, golden-haired and well-behaved? This is no exaggeration. In the early days of the talkies, the five-year-old Shirley Temple took by storm every land that had cinemas, and it could only have happened thus if the audiences were using the golden-haired moppet as an ideal. For a couple of hours, a perfect child pranced and sang and shook her curls, and for those hours there were no real children in the world in which the audiences lived, real children who were not perfectly behaved, not perfectly beautiful, not perfectly cherubic, not the product of a dream.

The adult characters offered an exactly parallel escape into the dream. The only figure in the films who was permitted to be ugly was the villain; though for a long time, a villain of any kind was excluded, even if the film ended with his complete failure, brought about by the hero. And of course, no plain woman, let alone an ugly one, could be tolerated, not even for the second female lead when she was playing a comic part. (A "homely" man could be accepted, though not as the lead, and he had to be portrayed as a faithful and unselfish friend, preferably of the hero.)

Utopia-in-the-darkness thrived; inevitably, it had to become more sophisticated. It did so; yet still it made sure that no one could emerge from the film feeling unhappy, or even not positively happy. Why, after all, was the building in which the films were shown called – the exact equivalent to "the dream factory" – "the picture palace"? Of course it was elevated to a palace, for if the audience had a dream from the dream factory, the dream could easily encompass a real palace, built to order in the dream.

Very slowly, the cinema grew up; the old image (it was exquisitely encapsulated by the rule that if the hero and heroine were embracing on a bed or a couch, the hero was obliged to keep one foot on the ground) of a utopian world began to adulterate perfection. Pain slipped in; unhappy endings were allowed; even failure, that unspeakable and unspoken word, was faced. Of course, the majority of films displayed no such heterodox qualities. To this day, there must be ten happy endings to one shadowed by sorrow. But the key which opened the door to cinematic reality was held in a hand that knew what it was doing; the cinema was allowed to come of age because television had been born. Television inevitably closed an enormous proportion of the picture palaces; if you can sit comfortably at home, why go out of doors? But television did more than whittle down the cinema; it took on the role of provider – provider, that is, of the dreams which put the factories out of business. With television, the last bastion of sophistication was overthrown; it revisited the earliest days of the cinema, with its childish beliefs and requirements. It went further, in that it actually sank beneath the lowest level the cinema had ever reached; the pap of game shows, soap operas (so called because the first substantial body of television advertising was for washing-powders), "sitcoms" and things even less demanding, so weakened the demand for the mature films (they cannot be called "adult", because by a fine irony the word has been adopted for use solely to indicate that the matter on offer is pornographic) that any attempt at discernment in the television fare would inevitably lead to failure by the implacable test of the "ratings".

Television, then, came clothed in the mantle of the dream factory, and its abiding rule was to ensure that the mantle should always be made of cheaper, thinner, and less weather-proof cloth, in which endeavour the governors of television have succeeded handsomely. Did St Thomas More die on the scaffold for this?

The romantic novelist long antedated the cinema, but there was no hostility between the old and the new utopian story-telling; both, it seems, were easily accommodated under the rule – it must have been carved on some triumphal arch – that was enshrined in the rubric "and they lived happily ever after", perhaps the most utopian words ever written.

What is striking about the romantic novel is that it has continued to flourish, and indeed has gained huge numbers of adherents; true, the modern romantic novel is less naïve than the earlier ones, but its essence has not changed at all. Handsome men and beautiful women abound, and despite all sorts of vicissitudes, the last chapter will have paired off the handsome men and the beautiful women, who will then proceed to live happily ever after. The *locus classicus* is Dame Barbara Cartland, who apart from writing, so far, some 600 romantic novels (she writes six at a time, dictating from a *chaise-longue* to relays of secretaries), spiritedly defends the *genre* on most realistic grounds: she says that the world is strewn with unkindness, ugliness, bad habits and rudeness (to mention but a few of the world's disappointments) so should there not be a corner in which beauty, honour, purity, courage and many more pleasing qualities can thrive? Taxed with the claim that the world she depicts is a false one, because not all men are handsome, honest, and invariably true to their marriage vows, she replies that not all men are ugly, villainous and unfaithful, though very many modern unromantic novels imply or baldly state that they are, and why should she not try to redress the balance somewhat? (She has one powerful weapon, though she rarely uses it, which is that her romantic and happy novels almost always greatly outsell the unromantic and gloomy ones.)

The ingenuity of the writers must be very great. It is widely believed that such writing is very easy, because the characters are for the most part stereotypes, and so they are, but that makes the work harder, not easier, because the narrow range of figures with their predictable endings, demand, from an ever-shrinking pool, new predicaments, new misunderstandings, new locations. But the technique is not the most interesting thing about them, nor is it the authors; in truth, it isn't even the books. It is the readers, who drive away reality, and replace it with Utopia. Millions of women (practically all the books are bought by women) devour these works, the only stipulation made by the buyers being a demand that nothing should be found in the pages that could also be found in the real world.

True, yet it is not widely recognised that the romantic novel contains the last refuge of true chivalry; the men, in addition to being handsome, are always chivalrous. If chivalry is dying out, as some insist, then Roland's horn will one day fall silent, but it has not done so yet. There are men – true, few of them are young – who remain chivalrous, however old-fashioned, and who would remain so whether their self-imposed rules commanded them to give up their only hope of survival in a shipwreck by giving a lady – any lady – their seat in the lifeboat, or – less dramatic – invariably opening a door for a lady – any lady. And there is a curiously recondite test for recognising chivalry. In Abel Gant's monumental film *Napoleon* there is a scene in which the *ci-devant* nobles, having been condemned to death, are in prison awaiting the tumbrils. The rabble are gleefully watching their last moments, and one such moment stands out. As the prison officer reads out the list of the condemned, each named man or woman goes out to the carriage of death. One devoted couple are called by name; the husband is first. He bows solemnly to his wife and apologises for going before her through a door, a solecism that he never committed in all the years of their

77

marriage. The rabble laugh and jeer, caricaturing his bow, but he ignores them, bows again, and leaves, his wife following. As a definition of chivalry, it can hardly be improved upon.

The third element in the childlike Utopia is the literally childlike one. In the nursery, Utopia has arrived; there are toys, picture books, sweets – gifts of every kind, their supply infinite. For history there is the fairy story, for travel there is *Alice in Wonderland*, for sweet dreams *Alice Through the Looking-Glass*, for comedy the pantomime, for drama Punch and Judy, for art Al Capp, for the utopian dream itself the Schmo. This is Utopia indeed, a world in which nothing is lacking, and if we say that growing up will bring disillusion, so much the worse for growing up.

But the serpent has crept in through the nursery window, quite properly left open for the requirements of fresh air. No adult can live entirely on a diet of one-dimensional films (and non-dimensional television), nor on desperately shallow novels and nostalgic dreams of childhood. We have to remind ourselves that Utopia is an imaginary place, however close we can come to making it a real one. It is good – indeed, necessary – for us to steep ourselves from time to time in a world without difficulties, inadequacies, impossibilities. But it is not good, indeed disastrous, to try to remain in such a world. The beguiling call of Utopia is immensely powerful, as Adam and Eve discovered to their eternal sorrow.

People do seek a perfect world and can die of disappointment when they cannot find it. The wiser ones, of course, know from the start that if Utopia exists, it exists only inside of us among the invisible, intangible, inaudible qualities that we are all given, to make or mar. The others, cheated out of their prize, give up.

There is a danger here. We can smile patronisingly at the absurdities of the cinema, despise those of television, and even begin to be angry at those of romantic fiction. But who would claim a ruler so straight, so long and so fierce that it can be sure to mark, with the greatest exactitude, the line dividing romantic fiction, whether in book form or on a screen, from art?

*

Stern critics argue that the pabulum of today's reading and viewing is empty, meretricious, a blurring of reality. But what is the exact difference between such shallow stuff and the shallow stuff that the eighteenth century created to lay at the feet of Marie Antoinette? After all, it is unreal, it is incapable of reaching the depths of true art, it is made very much to measure – all the charges brought against the pabulum so despised.

The contribution of art to Utopia must not be neglected. We might as well start with France, where, after all, real utopianism flourished as nowhere else. The hour brings forth the man; three men, in this case, Watteau, Boucher and Fragonard. The world they painted was the world that the French court believed it lived in, and indeed the succession of French courts continued in much the same belief until its head was cut off. It was a ravishingly beautiful utopian dream that the court painters created, and the luscious beauty that all three painted (fortunately all three had enormous genius) captivated the court.

Watteau was the precursor; it would be an exaggeration to say that he invented the painting of the *Fête Galante*, but he certainly established it. And it was with a delicious irony that his admission into the Academy was gained by his first significant departure from the work he had been doing: the majestic *L'Embarquement pour l'Ile de Cythère*, a utopian scene if ever one was painted. But Watteau's full flowering was cut short. He died of tuberculosis at the age of thirty-seven. When Watteau died, Boucher was eighteen, but was quick to take up the fallen torch, indeed, his earliest serious work was the engraving of some of Watteau's paintings. This salute to the older master was not just an obeisance; again, he did not invent the Rococo, but the use he made of it rivalled any painter alive or dead. The ripeness of Boucher's women, not forgetting the scenery, is so far beyond reality, while remaining utterly true to the artist's truth, that Madame de Pompadour must have thought Utopia had arrived. It hadn't, but he painted her repeatedly and waxed rich on her commissions, so perhaps *he* thought that the perfect world was at hand.

Boucher was no dilettante; he was, among other things, a director of the Gobelin tapestry factory. He took up the post in 1755 – an omen, for Marie Antoinette was born in that year. But he had the good sense to die well before the Revolution, at sixty-seven, leaving his most successful pupil to bridge the terrible gap between the court of Madame de Pompadour and that of Madame du Barry.

Fragonard survived, though many artists no more frivolous than he, no more a court painter either, died in the Terror. He outlived Robespierre by twelve years, but for years past, there was no call for the things he did so well – so well, indeed, that he even surpasses the wonderfully caught frivolity of his teacher, Boucher. Just as Watteau's first great success (the *Embarquement*) was a symbol of the beautiful unreality he would create, so it could be said that Fragonard's final salute (the *Bacchante endormie*) demonstrated that whatever was to happen with the Revolution, he would not be part of it. (He was safe with Napoleon, but Napoleon had no use for him.)

To be a painter of Utopia can be a very rewarding experience, but there are dangers in it. Marie Antoinette used to dress up as a simple shepherdess, and play the part among her ladies-in-waiting; for her and for them, it was a perfect world, which would exist forever, and if there was outside the gates another and most imperfect world, a world in which the people had no bread to eat, the breadless could at least look through the gates and eat cake. (Utopians rarely die in bed; not necessarily by violent means, but very frequently of a sharp dose of reality.)

But it is not only the pictorial arts that sum up Utopia, it is also the musical contribution. It seems to have escaped notice that virtually the whole world of opera is a teeming utopian gallimaufry on both sides of the footlights. Opera is an essay in Utopia; the passions alone would make that clear. What utopian yearnings there are, in the opera-house, and what utopian miseries, what utopian hatreds, what utopian love, what utopian comicality, what utopian wickedness, self-sacrifice, treachery, amazement, ruthlessness, vengeance, contempt, laughter, tears – what utopian musical instruments, what utopian voices, what utopian off-stage jealousies to rival the on-stage ones, what utopian failures, so often emphasised by utopian boos.

It is here, surely, and in the darkness for safety, that the utopian world lives, and those who live in it would not change their imaginary lives for real ones, at any rate until the curtain falls and the lights come up. There is no other artificial experience to touch the opera for unreality, an unreality that is made in the workshops of Utopia.

Let us look at the tiny list of operas which have escaped the utopian contagion, and survived. What distinguishes them from the rest? Not their tunefulness, not their happy endings, not their avoidance of operatic improbabilities, not even the depths they sound. What they offer is the truth, the whole truth and nothing but the truth.

Examined dispassionately, Utopia is a lie, and in the opera-house there is almost nothing *but* lies. Of course, these are harmless lies; no one goes home after *Tosca* and stabs an unjust civil servant. But those operas whose composers remained wedded to the truth are there, in the darkness, whispering the truth of music, and imploring us never to accept a utopian lie, but to hold fast to the un-utopian truth.

And what of the written word? What, necessarily, of the utopian novel? These sell by the millions, as we have just seen, and they sell on the promise of a utopian journey to perfection. This ought to be the most powerful utopian force upon reality; the written word must take precedence even over the sounds of music – that is what the written word was made for.

Yes, but the sword of the printed page cuts both ways. No other weapon in all history can be so easily wielded, but the ease and power with which it strikes takes no cognisance of which way it falls. The sword itself is neutral, it has no sentient understanding, it is nothing unless it is wielded by a human being. It may speak of good or of evil, and it can deliberately confuse the one with the other. No other art can touch it for the force it can bring to bear. How can it be constrained to cut only on the side of truth, and be held from using the other edge of the blade?

It cannot. Nor can we – though thousands of times the expedient has been tried – falsify the truth in what is declared to be a higher truth than the truth. There is no lie so wicked that someone will believe it, and act on it. There is our utopian danger; if we want perfection we must tread the path of the word, but the path of the word can be a crooked one. We do not have to go as far as the great ideological lies, for all around us the sword of the word is being swung, and until it comes to rest it is impossible to see where it struck. Utopia is, or at least can be, the conduit for the lie to seep into the world. Fallible we are and must be, but we yearn for infallibility, and the only way we can get it is to be utopians. *But we cannot be utopians, because there is no such thing*, and the simulacrum is the greatest danger we run.

The art of painting is the most innocent, it might cause the artist to suffer, but he is in no danger of causing others to suffer. The art of music is more dangerous, and we have to police it with those operas which stand sentinel between the utopian work and the reality. But the art of the word is the most dangerous of all, and many have died because a utopian ideal was thought to be incomplete. There are Utopias of the mind, too, and these are mostly harmless. The simplest form, which practically the whole world employs, is the daydream. This may be a mere twinge of wishing things were other than they are, to a mighty scenario in which our enemies are vanquished, our hopeless loves are consummated, everything that money can buy is ours for a cheque, and of course we live happily ever after and probably turn out to be immortal.

★

The most familiar form of the utopian naïve dream in Britain is the winning of the Pools, which can now shell out to a jackpot winner more than two million pounds. (Other countries have their equivalents in public lotteries, in which sums far greater than the biggest Pools win are paid out to the winners.) The utopian attraction for the Pools is that somebody always wins; not often a huge fortune, but substantial sums nonetheless. Indeed, a very large number of winners, be their winnings only a few pounds, refresh the hope that next week it will be a jackpot and the dreamer will win it. Experts have estimated the chance of a full jackpot win at about one in roughly three-hundred million, but Pools betters do not enquire of experts and the Pools companies do not advertise the arithmetic.

This is the dream of instant riches, which most of us have been tempted to dwell on, nobly deciding that we would give large sums to our nearest and dearest, and largesse to needy causes. Like so many dreams, nightmare is not far away. There are too many authenticated stories of instant riches leading to utter disaster (including suicides) to reject them as coincidence. If wishes were horses, beggars would ride, but wishes are not horses and the beggars therefore do not ride. But no one can be prevented from wishing.

Imagination can carry us far, but not as far as we would like. Daydreams with no monetary strings attached can also be dangerous, if only because the daydreamer can waste more time in dreaming than he can afford. Nevertheless, it is a poor heart that never rejoices, and a poorer one that never muses, half awake and half asleep, for things not really attainable.

There is another form of internal utopian activity. It is, almost literally, a meeting of minds. There have always been groups with similar ideas and feelings; what more is needed to make a group and a group which (this is almost invariable) excludes outsiders. If we wish, we can trace such conclaves back to the fourth and fifth centuries BC when the Peripatetics and other groups offered their doctrines to anyone who would follow them, and Socrates was willing to teach anyone who wanted to learn. Covens, societies, sodalities, single-issue preachers – all these have started in their own minds, and gathered around themselves any likely disciples.

But there have been more specific groups, proud of their learning, their understanding, their exclusive arcana of knowledge. France has many such groups, starting from the *Philosophes* (actually much further back); the *salons*, presided over by the *grandes dames*, not necessarily blue-stockings, led the way.

A couple of centuries on, one weird utopian world of pure mind, or rather pure minds, came together and flourished. Exclusivity was their watchword, though they would have denied it. It was English to the core, and could not have been mistaken for any such coterie elsewhere, or at any other time. It was the Bloomsbury Group.

They were following in earlier footsteps; before the First World War there was a similar group calling themselves the Apostles; these, however, were a largely political grouping, and in addition sought no public fame – indeed, they craved circumspection, if not real secrecy. The Bloomsbury Group (the name was foisted upon them, but they showed no great longing to erase it) began its life not long after the end of the First World War.

These were no dilettantes, though they strove to behave as such. The group included some artists and encouragers of art who had considerable talent. It included painters (e.g. Roger Fry) and men of affairs (e.g. Maynard Keynes). For no discoverable reason, most of them were homosexuals of one kind or another, but it is unlikely that had drawn them together, though it might have played a part in keeping them close-knit. But they laid down the artistic law, and, with few exceptions, lived in the mind and were proud to be thought so.

The life of the mind is usually thought lonely; the Bloomsbury Group would have none of it, for they were gregarious one and all; they were, or liked to think they were, in revolt against the Victorians and their attitudes. They would probably not have thought themselves a utopian world, but that was what they were nonetheless. The image of the circumscribed patch of land – whether in the desert island or a well-kept lawn, or even a drawing-room, arises at the first glance. In any literate and artistic century, they would have got together, to spread their own enlightenment, quite gently, to exclude those whose standards did not match the group's standards and above all to get on with their work. Much of that has faded, or at least ceased to be in the forefront of art, but a good deal of what they did remains. The life of the mind in the Bloomsbury Group was real as well as absurd, productive as well as stifling, sincere as well as comical. And anyway, this little utopian coterie has been retrospectively revived. There is a publishing house called Bloomsbury, and when last heard from, it seemed to be doing well.

7

Crime and Banditry,
Distress and Perplexity

THE BIBLE, both the Old Testament and (very much more) the New, is full of perfection. Of the New Testament, indeed, it could be said that it is one sustained statement of perfection and the way to find it. After all, "Gospel" means "God's tidings", and both Testaments proclaim precisely that. Wherever the seeker (or common reader) looks, the same message is given him, telling him what he must do to be saved, and what glorious reward awaits him, if he will do it. And it is not enwrapped in mystery, for he who runs may read: "In the beginning was the Word, and the Word was with God, and the Word was God".

A reading of almost any part of the Bible, by devout believer and complete sceptic alike, will point inevitably to a form of Utopia that is many magnitudes greater than any man-made final happiness could aspire to. Nor is it very difficult to believe and be saved; it could not be, since the message goes out not only to the learned but even more so to the unlettered, to the convinced and the doubtful, the strong and the weak, the old and the young, certainly to both the rich and the poor, the brave and the fearful, the happy and the wretched, the sinner (though we are all sinners) and the godly.

The price of admission, moreover, is trifling, as Pascal's famous wager pointed out; a beautifully crafted utopian image. Forget, he said, for the moment, the troublesome question of whether God exists or does not. Put your wager on the side of God's existence, and live as though he does indeed exist. Then, if you have wagered correctly, you will inherit eternal life. But if God does not exist, and there is nothing beyond death, you will

85

not be disappointed; you will not even know that you lost the wager. What could be more utopian?

The great monotheistic religions have in common many things, but the most important and powerful is their clear instructions as to what must be done by any individual seeking salvation, and what must be eschewed lest that salvation should be refused. This, of course, has been derided by sceptics, who argue that such a pair of scales so plausibly convenient for keeping the believers obedient and the unbelievers frightened, and in either case the priestly power untouched. It may be so (though Pascal's Wager will take care of truth and falsehood alike), yet the Bible, at least, argues its case so tremendously and convincingly that the sceptics are hard put to it to keep a foothold. The 23rd Psalm, among the most well-loved passages in the book, puts it beautifully, second only to some of Christ's own words (the Beatitudes, for instance). Other versions of the biblical perfect world spring to mind among the hundreds the Bible contains; one – calm, gentle, sure – from the Old Testament, the other – heightened, visionary, passionate – from the New:

Hear Isaiah:

And the wolf shall dwell with the lamb, and the leopard shall lie down with the kid; and the calf and the young lion and the fatling together; and the little child shall lead them. And the cow and the bear shall feed; their young ones shall lie down together; and the lion shall eat straw like the ox. And the sucking child shall play on the hole of the asp, and the weaned child shall put his hand on the basilisk's den. They shall not hurt or destroy in all my holy mountain; for the earth shall be full of the knowledge of the Lord, as the waters cover the sea.

And now hear St John the Divine:

And I saw a new heaven and a new earth: for the first heaven and the first earth were passed away; and there was no more sea. And I John saw the holy city, new Jerusalem, coming down from God out of heaven, prepared as a bride adorned for her husband. And I heard a great voice out of heaven saying, Behold, the tabernacle of God is with men, and he will dwell with them, and be their God. And God shall wipe away all tears from their eyes; there shall be no more death, neither sorrow, nor crying, neither shall there be any more pain: for the former things are passed away.

Isaiah's imagery is very powerful; the theme of savage beasts being transformed into peaceable creatures is a great metaphor for God's grace. Again and again, in the passage, a child can play happily with deadly enemies to the human race; at the same time, the animals facing each other for ever in similar enmity will be similarly transformed, so that the wolf shall dwell with the lamb, and the lion eat straw like the ox. This, by God's deliverance, will one day come to pass, though not until the earth shall be full of the knowledge of the Lord, as the waters cover the sea.

But Isaiah did not know (until a few years ago, nobody knew) that this miraculous transformation has already taken place on earth, nor is this a metaphor, though it will, as the news of it spreads, spawn hundreds. The new Isaiah is to be found in the Galapagos Islands, off the shore of Colombia. In *Hamlet*, Marcellus says that at Christmas-time,

> The bird of dawning singeth all night long;
> And then, they say, no spirit can walk abroad;
> The nights are wholesome; then no planets strike,
> No fairy takes, nor witch hath power to charm,
> So hallow'd and so gracious is the time.

The more sceptical Horatio replies "So I have heard, and do in part believe it".

The sceptic is wrong; and even the believer falls far short of the truth, as Isaiah had no inkling of it. For in that group of tiny islands, the thing has happened. Bathers may play happily in and out of a shoal of sharks; walkers may encounter an orang-utan and pass the day with it, in no fear that it will turn savage. The very snakes never launch their poison, and there is no animal, however fearsome, and however untamed, that has not signed the peace treaty between mankind and the animal kingdom.

Why it happened there, and in no other place, no one knows. *How* it happened no one knows either. It was at first thought that the animals had never encountered man for so many years that they had lost their fear of him, or more likely never acquired it. But happily, the experts have put paid to that theory, and we can bask in pure magic, a magic that Isaiah would have wept to see, his tear being shed for God's promise, which he had never doubted through all the years.

Perhaps the most perfect, concise and beautiful definition of Utopia according to scripture is from Isaiah. His image of the wolf lying down with the lamb is a wistful one, looking forward to the wonderful day when it will have come to pass. In an earlier chapter, however, Isaiah paints a joyous version, and one that seems almost imminent.

> The wilderness and the solitary place shall be glad for them; and the desert shall rejoice, and blossom as the rose. It shall blossom abundantly, and rejoice even with joy and singing; the glory of Lebanon shall be given unto it, the excellency of Carmel and Sharon, they shall see the glory of the Lord, and the excellency of our God. Strengthen ye the weak hands, and confirm the feeble knees. Say to them that are of a fearful heart, be strong, fear not: behold, your God will come with vengeance, even God with a recompense; he will come and save you. Then the eyes of the blind shall be opened, and the ears of the deaf shall be unstopped. Then shall the lame man leap as an hart, and the tongue of the dumb sing; for in the wilderness shall waters break out, and streams in the desert. And the parched ground shall become a pool, and the thirsty land springs of water: in the habitation of dragons, where each lay, shall be grass with reeds and rushes. And an highway shall be there, and a way, and it shall be called the way of holiness; the unclean shall not pass over it; but it shall be for those: the wayfaring men, though fools, shall not err therein. No lion shall be there, nor any ravenous beast shall go up thereon, it shall not be found there; but the redeemed shall walk there: And the ransomed of the Lord shall return, and come to Zion with songs and everlasting joy upon their heads; they shall obtain joy and gladness, and sorrow and sighing shall flee away.

Would that that picture of eternal bliss might close the argument for ever! Alas, it has been said that there are as many interpretations of Scripture as there are readers of it. It would be presumptuous to claim Isaiah's blessing in any reading, but the temptation is at its greatest height when it faces the rock of fundamentalism.

*

Any rock that stands the crashing of the seas has an open invitation to Utopia, no matter what the rock is made of. And one of the most solidly seated rocks is the fundamentalist nature of the Christian and/or Jewish

Bible. The fundamentalists' argument is simple and hard to dismiss by logic; but in matters like these logic really has no place.

Fundamentalists take their stand on the authenticity of the Bible. If, they argue, this book is the word of God, it cannot be mistaken. So far so good; many a modern cleric will stir uneasily at the claim, but he is hard put to it to demur. Very well; if there can be no mistake, it follows that every word must be the word God intended to be read. When God, through his Book, wants to say something, what he says must be what he means, and *a fortiori* it must be true.

Methuselah lived 969 years. That is what God says, and who shall dare to say that God got it wrong? Exegesis is unnecessary; indeed to a fundamentalist it is blasphemous. In any case, when a statement like that is made by God, there is nothing more to say on the subject.

The rest of the world puzzles over the passage, and many another passage, too. Methuselah did *not* live 969 years; nobody does. The table of the kings is given differently in two places, and in any case modern historians and archaeologists know that it is inaccurate more or less throughout.

The fundamentalists deny the lot of it; there was a man called Adam, and a woman called Eve; God put them in the Garden of Eden, and subsequently turned them out, at His pleasure. In any case they were the couple from whom the entire human race is directly descended.

And so on. At every crux, every contradiction, every obviously garbled passage, the fundamentalist appears to insist that God meant it, and it is we who have got it impiously wrong. Were all the Pauline Epistles written by St Paul, word for word, and was every recipient thereof the individual or collective named? Certainly.

This must have been like the original idea of Utopia, and certainly has been the guiding principle for many religious utopian retreats. They stand their ground like the rock, and they are very difficult indeed to dislodge.

The dispute, however, has a core of importance, foolish though it must seem to most people. Let dogs delight to bark and bite...the step from a lack of religion to a belief in it is a difficult one; many hover over the decision for years, and some never come to the waiting conclusion. The ditherer, dipping his toe nervously in the unaccustomed coldness of the stream, may be frightened off for ever by the sight of this struggle and what it implies in the way that great religions can spend their time swallowing at camels or straining at gnats, or – as is all too likely – both.

When dealing with matters spiritual or exegetical (to say nothing of dealing with both at once) there are, of course, an infinite number of fragments; some, as we have seen, are substantial, most are tiny, very many so small as to be seen only under the microscope, many more visible only to the eye of faith; one of the very oddest concerns Joanna Southcott.

Joanna Southcott was a prophetess in England in the late nineteenth century. Her prophecies were largely incomprehensible, and she was thought of as a harmless wandering woman, probably deranged, of which there have been, over the ages, no lack. She did, however, attract a not insubstantial following, and when she died, she gave careful instructions to the still living acolytes. Her stipulation was not to be easily carried out, since it involved the attendance of the entire body of the bishops of the Church of England. What the bishops were called upon to certify was that her prophetic papers had revealed all truths of all religion, so that there could be no more disputation.

These papers were in a locked and sealed box, which was to be opened when, and only when, the bishops had gathered round. The lack of bishops continued, but since the prophetess had left a modest sum of money for the promotion of the cause, and her living followers also contributed, it was possible for the group to continue – continue, that is, demanding the bishops' attendance. After many years of fruitless appeals, one bishop consented to stand in for the entire bench. The remaining acolytes, presumably feeling that, inadequate though one bishop might be, he was probably the only one they would ever be able to persuade, settled for a compromise. The box was duly opened, and the papers examined by the faithful followers and the bishop alike. The latter politely made clear that there was nothing of interest or meaning in the prophetess's words, and took his leave.

Nothing daunted, the faithful declared that the box had not been the real one, nor the papers in it the real papers; the real treasure had been felt to be too important to entrust to one fallible bishop, and they continued in their touching beliefs. There used to be posters in London and elsewhere, declaiming the order's regular and by now familiar charge: "Crime and Banditry, Distress and Perplexity, will continue until the bishops open Joanna Southcott's box of Sealed Writings". The bishops never did.

Yet this utopian doggedness is worthy of admiration; they believed, though no one else did; they campaigned though no one took any notice; they demanded dozens of bishops and got but one. Joanna Southcott's words may have been meaningless, indeed almost certainly were, and even if they were not, they were most unlikely to end Crime and Banditry, Distress and Perplexity. No matter; belief has sustained every utopian movement, cause, hope and patience, and this gallant band was in essence much the same as the mightiest ideals of the whole story of Utopia.

No one knows where Joanna's box is now.

★

The Crusades constituted one of the most utopian enterprises of history. They have been analysed in a score of ways, from the most lofty (the professed reason – reclaiming the Holy Land and its sacred sites for Christendom) to the most base (booty), and the degree of scepticism held by those contemplating them will fix the place they choose on the spectrum. For our purpose, however, it does not much matter; the very idea of the Crusades shines a powerful light on our subject.

The very name of the project – "Holy Land" – removes the argument to a utopian meaning. The places where Christ was born, where he lived, taught, made miracles, was betrayed and crucified – the Holy Land – were not in Christian possession. Moreover, some seven centuries after Christ another great religion disputed the eternal truth: though Islam and its founder respected Christianity and *its* founder, it made clear that there would not be room for both religions. Such ecclesiastical differences, no less than secular ones, are inevitably subjected, sooner or later, to the arbitrament of force; whence the Crusades and their apparently unshakable place in the more mythological end of history.

The icons are powerful and memorable; it was not only the Pre-Raphaelites and their ghastly works which kept the legends alive – which indeed have kept them alive to this day. It is significantly easy to conjure up the familiar figure: shining armour with the Crusader's red cross on the breast; a white horse; an air of nobility and chivalry. Religious susceptibilities, ecumenical movements and modern good taste in these matters have combined to make Crusaders something of an embarrassment, and it is unlikely that the story of the Crusades is taught much in British schools. But so many centuries can hardly have been a mistake, and there is evidence that they were not; the word has passed into the language in all its forms, and there is a wide range of usages for it.

Political movements call themselves crusades; individuals and groups trying to right wrongs are said to be crusading, even in newspaper headlines; a popular television figure (successor to Batman) is called "the Caped Crusader", and does much the same as Batman in the way of ensuring the rout of the villains. More significantly still, the word and its cognates are invariably used in admiring terms; not only is there no pejorative form, but even the use of irony seems to be unknown in any context with "crusade" in it.

But the Pre-Raphaelites must have their hour. Dreadful as their work was and remains, it is difficult to deny the artists a kind of sincerity, and if we grant them that, only one more step is needed to reach a utopian truth. Let them have their time in the light.

The Brotherhood of the Pre-Raphaelites announced its nature with almost its first word: *brotherhood* is more than a band of brothers. It must have a collective purpose, for one thing, and an uplifting nature is also required. These tests and more the Brotherhood passed with ease, for they were dedicated to the noble cause of the purity of art. Their subjects did not always measure up to the expressed ideal, but on the whole they strove to be worthy of their certainly worthy aim. (Most of their pictures were appalling, but that does not invalidate their motives.)

All sorts of myths clustered around them; there is no doubt that many of them thought of themselves as the Knights of King Arthur (they painted him and his court countless times) come back to earth. And, just as the Grail was the symbol (the "logo" it would be called today) of the Arthurian Brotherhood, so it became also the oriflamme of the Pre-Raphaelites. True, the Grail has a less wide but much more intense symbolism in its role in the Christian religion, being the cup that Christ drank from at the Last Supper, in which form it has inspired even more quests and usages; Wagner – a most unlikely apostle – uses it to immensely powerful effect in his *Parsifal*, a work steeped in Christian symbolism and indeed telling a form of the Christian story.

One more step, then, and the Brotherhood were in a mystical-religious-artistic Utopia; the draperies of their models and their female subjects would serve perfectly as the correct dress in which to enter heaven, and their notorious artistic pallor was no less fitting for the lately dead. Thus equipped and accoutred, they were free to glide among the asphodels, which they had painted innumerable times, to all eternity or until (mixing the legends again) Arthur's return, while far away the horns of Roland and Oliver at Roncesvalle can be heard, giving yet another similar legend to stir into the brew.

But there are more citizens of love, the beloved republic. If the Pre-Raphaelite Brotherhood can be welcomed into God's truth, then surely Mozart, who spoke more of that truth than most of God's creatures ever did, has a high place.

Mozart's *Magic Flute* is the most mysterious of his operas. Without da Ponte for a libretto, several hands were pressed into service in his place, the result inevitably being a good deal of confusion. Many learned treatises have been written on the structure and meaning of the opera; all have vanished, while the sublime music remains to carry the listener over the thin ice of the symbolism. But not even masonry and muddle put together, multiplied by the feebleness of some of the words (particularly the spoken dialogue), can hide from the listener the feeling appropriate to one of the greatest and deepest musical works ever written.

Whatever else the *Magic Flute* is about, it is certainly about love; moreover, there are no fewer than three orders of love in it, or perhaps even four. The first is love of the simplest order; earthbound, procreative, naïve but real. Papageno and Papagena demonstrate love on this level; their duet in the penultimate scene speaks of happiness and children (both sexes), and they do not seek to enter into the kingdom of heaven, though in the final scene heaven's portals are opened.

The next order of love is more profound; there is no suggestion that the love between Tamino and Pamina is to be celibate (though there is no suggestion that it isn't either), but this love is pure – indeed, it has been purified before our eyes in the trials by fire and water in the second act. They come unscathed through the tests, with their love and faith to keep them, and the tremendous symbol of the flute itself to ensure that they do not waver.

Significantly, they have already endured a stern trial, in which Pamina's love *does* waver; Tamino, having been sworn not to speak, obediently remains silent when she comes to him, and his refusal of a response (though it is agony for him) persuades her that his love had died. As she grows into full enlightenment, she understands what Tamino's silence meant, and their mutual love flowers again.

The third face of love is their assumption into Sarastro's heavenly kingdom; he has asked his ranks if the loving pair are worthy to enter, and the reply is a unanimous affirmative. There are, of course, many parallels with the Christian heaven; it is not difficult to see Sarastro as God, and the ordeals the testing of an aspirant. There is even a Satan, in the Caliban-like form of Monostatos, a very feeble Satan, and a more serious element of evil, in the Queen of Night.

None of these correspondences is really necessary; quite probably the masonic references are not necessary either. The confusion in the libretto (not least the invocation of Isis and Osiris) is put in order by the music, and the most unambiguous statement of love-the-king is Sarastro's rules of harmony in his world:

> *In diesen heil'gen Hallen,*
> *Kennt man die Rache nicht;*
> *Und ist ein Mensch gefallen,*
> *Führt Liebe ihn zur Pflicht.*

(Within these sacred walls, vengeance is unknown; and if one of our number strays, it is love that brings him back to his duty.)

That, surely, is the fourth and highest love of all, and the perfection of it achieves a utopian world that mankind has always dreamed of, and will dream of to the end of time, or until such a heaven is found on earth.

There are many clues in the opera; Papageno's terrified meeting with Monostatos, for instance, is resolved by his reflecting that there are black birds in the world, so why not black men? The magic chime of bells wards off the human threat; the magic flute charms the animals to peace and love. The armed men who guard the outer wall of Sarastro's fortress of love are also symbols of the divine duty of which Sarastro sings; why would the walls themselves cry "Back!" if not to conceal the truth until it is time to be known – that the walls are chimerical and can be walked through as the flames of the ordeal can be walked through, provided that love is in attendance. As for the Queen of Night's three ladies, they must be the unawakened part of the soul; not evil, but not yet ready to understand. That is why the Queen *is* evil; because she is complete – complete but fatally flawed.

All this is made clear by listening to the music; not in the sense that the music interprets the words, like the modern surtitles of opera-houses all round the world today, but in bypassing the words and their puzzles altogether, and trusting the sublimity of the sounds Mozart received from wherever genius is engendered, and is now passing on. We must *feel* our way into Mozart, and if we throw away the synopsis, the interpretations and the theories, we shall be rewarded by having the music steal its way into our souls. In the darkness of an opera-house, when the Magic Flute is in the bill, it is not really far-fetched or blasphemous to think that a true communion is taking place, with the bread and wine of the opera's words changed into the body and blood of the music.

8

In the country of the blind

THE REPUBLIC is naturally taken for Plato's principal statement of the ideal society, and so it is; but it dwells more on the ideal man, presumably because Plato assumes that his readers would take it that the ideal man would create the ideal state in his (the ideal man's) own image. That, however, largely leaves out the mechanics of the thing. For that – a specific legislative programme, with means of enforcement – he turned to *The Laws*. An ominous title, and there are more omens to come: it is the longest of all the Socratic dialogues, longer even than *The Republic*, it is the only one in which Socrates does not appear, and it is Plato's last work. A sceptic might well think that after publication of *The Laws* the best thing Plato could do would be to fall silent for ever, since the legacy he left in this chilling constitution has the fingerprints of the grave all over it.

True, it is shot through with benevolent, indeed godly, precepts, but when we look in detail at what is proposed for the citizens of the ideal state according to Plato, we wake to nightmare. Lulled by the long disquisition on morality which precedes the details, we are the more repelled when it comes to the programme.

The first tocsin sounds when the proposed city is to have exactly 5040 landowners, and therefore 5040 households, for no better reason than that the number can be perfectly divided by every figure from one to ten, or, Plato adds, from one to twelve excluding eleven.

Then he warms to his work:

…there must be no place for poverty in any part of the population, nor yet for riches...So the legislator must lay down the limits of each. Therefore, let the limit on the side of poverty be the value of one allotment...The legislator will take it as a measure, and permit the acquisition of two, three or even four times the value. If a man acquires further possessions...in excess of this measure...it shall be open to anyone who wishes to, to lay information and claim half the property, the convicted offender also paying a fine of the same amount out of his own pocket; the other half to go to the gods. The whole property of every citizen...must already have been inscribed in public records under the scrutiny of magistrates appointed by law for the purpose...

After that, it comes as no surprise to learn that the new city should be situated as near as possible to the centre of the territory, and divided into twelve sections, the sections being of exactly equal worth, because those with poor soil will have a greater acreage than those with better soil. That done, there are to be 5040 allotments (to fit the 5040 households), and each of these must be cut in two for an even more recondite reason. After a great deal more of this, Plato says firmly "This completes the business of settlement".

Eugenics, the various orders of slaves, a uniform architecture, education (with syllabus), athletics, marriage (men must wed between the ages of thirty and thirty-five, on pain of a fine and public disgrace) – all these aspects of Platoville are laid down by the legislator, nor does he stop there:

The law of fruit shall follow these rules. If a man taste the common sort of fruit, whether grapes or figs, before the season...either on his own land or on someone else's, he shall incur a fine...As for pears, apples, pomegranates and suchlike, it shall not be a felony to take them, but if any man below 30 years of age be caught in the act, he is to be punished by a beating, which must not draw blood.

But it is in the field of the family that these fanatical directives are seen in their complete frightfulness – the frightfulness lying less in the severity of the punishments as in the mad rigidity with which the laws are laid down:

If a man, not insane, dares to strike his father or mother...the bystanders shall come to their aid...Any resident alien who intervenes shall be

97

offered a seat in the front row at the public sports, but if he fails to do his duty he shall be permanently banished. A non-resident alien giving such aid shall receive public commendation, one not giving aid shall receive public censure. A slave who helps shall have his freedom, one who does not shall suffer a hundred lashes with the scourge, to be administered by the commissioners of the market if the offence is committed in the market-place, but if committed in the city though not in the market-square, the punishment to be administered by the urban commissioner in residence, and if in some rural district, by the authorities of the rural commission. Every bystander of native birth – whether child, woman or man – shall join in the hue and cry, denouncing the assailant as a wretch and a monster, and anyone who fails to take part shall be held, by law, to be under the curse of the god of kith and kind.

Nor does that exhaust the prescriptions and proscriptions that Plato lays down; there are scores more of such rules for living, until the lineaments of the modern totalitarian state can be clearly seen in its mad detail and awfulness. Another random selection turns up these:

The number of hearth fires established by our present division must remain forever unchanged, without increase or deviation whatsoever.

(The founder) should then make a division into five thousand and forty allotments. Each of these, again, should be bisected and two half sections, a nearer and a remoter, paired together to form an allotment, one which is contiguous to the city with one on the border, one in the next degree of proximity to the city with one next most nearly on the border, and so on in all cases.

No poet shall compose anything in contravention of the public standards of law and right, honour and good, nor shall he be at liberty to display any composition to any private citizen whatsoever until he has first submitted to the appointed censors of such matters and the curators of law, and obtained their approval.

Bride and bridegroom should make it their purpose to present the city with the best and finest progeny they may...The mother shall be under the surveillance of the women we have appointed...who shall assemble daily...At these assemblies each member shall report to the board any person, male or female, among the procreants, whom she sees to be paying regard to aught else than the injunctions imposed...This period of procreation and supervision of procreants shall last ten years and no longer...

Plato's proposals for the ideal society were not put into effect at Athens; but they festered through the centuries – some twenty-three centuries – to turn up again and again in a thousand forms. Those forms were – are – in essence one: they lay out the boundaries of freedom and forbid the citizens to cross the lines. Incessantly and repetitively, when rulers who are, or aspire to being, absolute, their first action is to draw up laws, codes, obediences, salutes, threats – all to be followed scrupulously on pain of frightful punishments.

The curious nature of the rules governing absolute power has been strikingly little examined. Absolutism, after all, is what it sounds like, and *quod principe placuit habet legis vigorem*, or "What pleases the ruler has the force of law". Why, then, the parade of truly meaningless statutes and ordinances? Certainly, in the case of the most brutal of rulers, it cannot possibly be a feeling of a necessity to be seen carrying out laid-down orders, for who would or could challenge the lack of them? Yet there they are for tyrants to brandish, heedless of the absurdity of the action.

But now, Jean-Jacques Rousseau pushes in, whining and yelling, demanding to be heard, insisting that his enemies are conspiring against him and that so are his friends, bursting into tears at a rebuke, and redoubling and redoubling the weeping at proffered sympathy, only happy when being soothed, babylike, by Mme de Warens, repaying all help with treachery, backbiting and slandering: if the telephone had been invented in his lifetime, the first general use of it would have been to take the receiver off the hook, lest Jean-Jacques might be on the other end, going on for hours.

Cucullus non facit monachum; but Rousseau was everything he seemed to be, however improbable. Consistency never touched him; but he saw things that no one had seen before, and understood things that no one else had unravelled. Rousseau did have genius, however untidily, and he deserves a hearing. He left no utopian construction, but his meaning was plain – too plain, as we shall see.

"Man was born free, and everywhere he is in chains". It is his most famous sentence (for most people probably his only one), and it heralded his *Social Contract*, which crowned his substantial output. Throughout that output, the utopian strain can be clearly heard. It is there already in the book that started him off, the prizewinning essay *Discours sur les sciences et les arts*, where his "natural man" takes his bow, contrasting the artificiality of culture as it is, with its rules and shallowness. More directly, his *Discours sur l'origine de l'inégalité*, in which "man in the state of nature" figures (once more dispensing with the striving for riches); Rousseau admits that mankind cannot go back to a perfect form of such a utopian idyll. *Emile* is the children's Utopia. Astonishingly advanced for his time, he argued for what is today called "child-centred" learning; the child, in effect, defines the perimeter of the offered culture, and emerges a fully rounded being, knowing his needs and seeking no others. (It must be added that Rousseau sent all his own children to the foundling hospital, one by one.)

Rousseau used the phrase "*monde idéal*", but it is not strong enough to be called a Utopia; it is an inner ideal world. But now the serpent enters Rousseau's Eden. If we cannot return to the state of nature, when man was content to fulfil his simple needs and, significantly, kills only for food or when defending himself from attack, how can we suffer the fragmentation of mankind, each man alone in his private wilderness: if man is free, and must no longer lie in chains, how can the circle be squared?

Look here upon this picture, and on this. The individual must not, of course, be dragooned out of his individuality, but he can submerge his will – in truth he *must* do so – in the General Will, a kind of collective aye or nay. The people remain sovereign, of course, but they put their sovereignty into the trusted hands of those who are charged with determining the General Will and acting on it.

Where does the General Will end and totalitarianism begin? Nowhere; long before the respective measures can be compared, the fig-leaf of the General Will has been torn away, and man – natural and artificial alike – has given his freedom into hands that will never give it back.

It is very unlikely indeed that either Stalin or Hitler ever read *Du contrat social* (though Lenin might have done so), but whether they knew it or not they were applying Rousseau's doctrine of the General Will, and when we survey the endless columns of the martyred dead in this century alone, no plea from the progenitor should be accepted, however many tears he sheds.

Rousseau neither intended nor imagined what would be done with the weapon he forged. He was wrestling with the problem he had himself posed: how can the many be incorporated in the one? Perhaps it was the utopian propensity which allowed him to leap from the truth to the fallacy. Indeed, it is hardly possible to think of an alternative explanation; what could be more like a *monde idéal*? But if Rousseau must be condemned, even pleading truly that he had no idea of the genie he was liberating from the bottle, there are two more bottle-smashers to be reckoned with, and both of these knew well what they were doing; indeed, they proclaimed their intentions unambiguously, and were proud to put their names to every manifesto they produced. Beside Marx and Engels, Rousseau comes spotless out of the wash.

For those two were the greatest utopians of all. Not only were they in their lives utopians without compare, but – a far greater charge – they left behind, untidily, the crusts and wrapping-paper of their discarded doctrines, which were picked up and put to uses far more terrible than Marx and Engels ever dreamed of.

Can words, and words long since dead and buried, too, cause such consequences? They can, and they did. But where is the bridge from their beliefs, enshrined in dusty and unreadable books, to such lurid claims of slaughter? That is precisely the mystery; how did an economic system, with no serious substance in it, so grip the world that until only a few years ago more than half the world lived under governments which claimed to be Marxist? How, indeed, did the word enter into practically all the world's languages? How did the fusty economic system, indistinguishable from hundreds that flowered and died in weeks if not days, become an all-encompassing system which, with no logical foundations, turned this chimera into a giant and ruthless empire?

It was a propitious time to start a hare. The years up to the middle of the nineteenth century were ripe with brutal poverty; economic systems, such as they were, were failing; no one could have foreseen the unimaginable transformation of that poverty, when modern technology, allied to the apparently infinite natural resources, had shown that there was at last a place for the poor at the table. In what seemed to be a slough of despond with no way out of it, there came almost overnight an alternative, couched in words so deftly and powerfully composed, that a great wave of utopian belief and hope washed over virtually the whole of Europe. It read "Workers of the world unite! You have nothing to lose but your chains!" The echo of Rousseau was obviously intended by the authors, but when it was moved on by nearly a century, it exploded in the heart of the industrial world. Yet when the pamphlet to which it was affixed – *The Communist*

Manifesto (the echo from Babeuf would also have been heard by the authors, though they had long since rejected Babeuf's solution for equality – the abolition of private property), it was a programme as obviously utopian as Fourier's.

Can a mere slogan have such momentous power? That is to ask can Utopia have such momentous power? We shall see.

If Marx's economic theories were all he had to show, he would be numbered among the thousands of minor prophets offering nostrums in the market-place and getting few takers. Even Major Douglas and his theory of Social Credit held the stage for an astonishingly long time, despite the fact (or possibly because of it) that no one but its progenitor understood it. Marx, however, cunningly wove his economics inextricably into his politics, his sociology, his predictions, his polemics and his history. From that *olla podrida*, he created with the help of the uncomplaining Engels, upon whom Marx sponged financially and intellectually (Engels wrote most of the second volume of *Das Kapital* and all of the third and fourth), a pseudo-science, utopian from beginning to end, which held the world to ransom from the middle of the nineteenth century to almost the end of the twentieth.

What conjuring-trick enabled Marxism to flourish so long, so wide, so deep and so powerful? When it became, theoretically, the governing principle of great and less great nations, the answer is clear: Marxism was the mask behind which tyranny lived and worked, and his theories had no more effect on its conduct than did the prophecies of Nostradamus. But it will be observed that the prophecies of Nostradamus are held in awe by many simple folk to the present day, and by many far less simple ones as well.

Marxism is the high tide of Utopia; nothing prepared the world for the waves that crashed over it, and nothing could stem the flood once it had reached its unsubstantiated claims, despite the frailty of its construction, the absurdity of its premises, its useless evidence, its impenetrable jargon, its irrelevance to the real world, its fundamental flaws, intolerance, abusiveness, vanity, anti-semitism and selfishness of its creator. (Selfishness? Marx had a servant, who bore his illegitimate child, almost certainly conceived in rape; he treated the girl as badly after she gave birth as he had before. Once, he went on a picnic *en famille*; he went on ahead, while the servant-girl staggered along with the hamper.) No greater confidence trick has ever been played; exploded continuously, the fragments of Marxism invariably settled into their original shape, ready to resume their monstrous and colossally successful fraud. Any thinker and any system of thought that deviated in any way in the revealed truth was not just rebuked or corrected, but reviled in the foulest terms; though they might plead that they were on Marx's side, and were genuinely working tirelessly for him and the propagation of his gospel, they must give total allegiance or be cursed, excommunicated and scorned – frequently, with an irony that can induce shivers even today – as "utopian".

But what can be more utopian than Marxism, in theory or in practice? "From each according to his ability, to each according to his productiveness": then "From each according to his ability, to each according to his needs"; that was the schedule, and it was only a matter of time before the first stage was passed, and the second was being put in place. The student rubs his eyes; can all this imaginary world have been brought to birth by an absurd theory, based on a mistake, called "surplus labour"?

Most of mankind would like to see an end to hunger, poverty, unrewarded toil and a hopeless future. Many of mankind have devoted their lives to attempting to ameliorate such conditions, and many have succeeded, in one form or another. As they worked at the future, they realised that they were in the present, with all its limitations, and sighed for a magic wand with which they could wave themselves into a world, many, many years off, a world that would know no such deprivation. But having sighed, they have got on with making their slight but real contribution. A few, however, abandon the spade, the seed, the water and the hoe, and insist on the wand; those are the utopians, and no such extreme utopians have ever waved it more enthusiastically in the name of Marx and his ism.

Weigh the dust. It is no use Marx protesting that what has stemmed from his theories is the fruit of misunderstanding; he may not have meant it, but he *was* it. If he was proud to think, as he did, that the whole world was obliged to take him and his system seriously, he must accept the accolade and shoulder the reality. Unfortunately, Marx had no idea what reality was, the while insisting that he trafficked in nothing else. Marxism was the strangest aberration the civilised world has ever seen, and the aberration itself, together with what it led to, must be laid at Utopia's feet. The trouble with Utopia, in this context, is not that it has feet of clay; it always has had. It is that Utopia, while of course regretting the Marxist consequences, is secretly proud of enlisting so powerful, complete, ruthless and long-lasting an idea into the utopian ranks. What would Thomas More say? What *did*

Oliver Cromwell say? He said "Beseech you, gentlemen, in the bowels of Christ, think it possible you may be mistaken". Neither Marxists nor Utopia have ever heeded the advice.

The refusal of advice is perhaps the most familiar blemish on the body politic of Utopia. Again and again, warning after warning, disaster strikes when it could have been avoided. The talisman of Utopia, it seems, is enough to ward off danger, and however many times the talisman is *not* enough to ward off danger, it is invariably brought in and brandished, to demonstrate its magic powers. And in no field of rashness is there greater testimony to the utopian fallacy than the *ignis fatuus* of Utopia, because it encapsulates the greatest mistake of all utopians: their belief that it is possible, and if possible then desirable, to make sacrifices today which will bear fruit tomorrow.

The Germans should have known. Hitler promised his people a Volkswagen in every garage; there was a complicated system of paying in advance, but before the cars could be distributed the Second World War had begun. No matter, said authority; keep your documents, and as soon as the war is over, the cars would roll off the assembly-lines. Why, did not Hitler promise the finest road-network in Europe, and did he not make good his promise? So it would be with the Volkswagen, and in a sense that promise was not broken either, for when the new German state arose from the ashes of the war, one of its first industrial endeavours was the immense success of the Volkswagen, which did indeed roll off the assembly-lines in their thousands. But the scrip, which was to be redeemed with a car, had long since lost its potency, as had their Führer, and if they wanted a Volkswagen they would have to pay for it all over again.

Put not your trust in princes, and particularly those who promise utopian bliss in the future at the trifling cost of pain and poverty in the present, though almost invariably the choice is not available; the pain and poverty are real and immediate, the bliss imaginary.

There is a tiny symbolic clue to that thesis. Some years ago, when Brezhnev ruled the Soviet Union, a group of philanthropic people in West Germany got together to send food-parcels to an area in the Soviet Union populated to a significant extent by Russians of German extraction. The parcels were confiscated, and that might have been the end of the matter, were it not for the theory of Utopia-longing. The food was hungrily wanted; most Soviet citizens living otherwhere than Moscow, Leningrad and few more large cities, had not seen meat for many years, and as for the dried eggs (the parcels had included packets of them), the recipients must have been beside themselves for such wonderful delicacies that until then they could hardly have dreamt about.

The authorities, after confiscating the food, made a great public stir about it; huge quantities of indignation were summoned, to declare that this feeble and trashy bounty should have been thrown into German dustbins and would most certainly find their way into Soviet ones. The dried eggs were the target most attacked; the Soviet authorities reserved their most passionate scorn for them, acclaiming the infinitely more delicious and abundant Soviet eggs that Soviet hens were proud to lay.

Yet everyone in the country knew that an egg, even a very stale one, was a prized boon. And since everybody *did* know it, why did the authorities feel the need to tell their wretched subjects what every one of those subjects knew was a lie? Surely it was that the utopian dream would still not let the sleeper sleep in peace, but must ensure that he would toss and turn and cry out all through the night.

★

The Stalin Constitution is an amazing work, proclaiming a virtually miraculous utopian state, run by benevolent democrats in the interests of the people alone. That the people knew its reality to be a lunatic denial of everything it contained was deemed not to matter; the Word had gone out, and the Word must be heeded.

It has been argued that this Potemkin constitution was for show in countries with democratic governments, but that cannot be true; trade was not affected, nor was security, and it could not have mattered to Stalin whether people outside his *cordon insanitaire* believed that the Russian people were living in Paradise or Hell.

But, fortified by the empty words, many people *outside* did indeed believe that the Russian people were living in Paradise. And of no western figures was that more profoundly true than those two avatars of falsehood, treachery to scholarship, self-debasement, smiling on suffering, and ultimately madness: Sidney and Beatrice Webb.

The greatest delusion in all the centuries of utopianising was the belief that the Soviet Union was the pure and perfect essence of democracy, brotherhood, selflessness, benevolence, wisdom and love. A new way of living had been discovered, a new kind of human being had been engendered, a new light had shone on the world. The adulation of the Soviet system and its leaders was at its height when Stalin's murderous destruction was at *its* height, yet so powerful was the rush to believe, only a handful could see; the rest was darkness at noon.

There is a strange precedent. When, after the Spanish conquest of Peru under Pizarro, the first reinforcements and supplies from home by sea arrived, the ships hove to just off shore. The Indians literally could not see the vessels, for their inability to comprehend sights so extravagantly unlike anything they had ever seen before led not to ordinary bewilderment but to a mass outbreak of hysterical blindness; communication between eye and brain was temporarily severed, and where the Spaniards saw a flotilla, the Indians saw nothing but an empty ocean.

Something very much like that seems to have happened to the dupes. Fuelled by their yearning for a land not of this world, they sought and found paradise, blinding themselves to the manifest truth that it was hell. Malcolm Muggeridge summed up the delusion in one savage paragraph:

> Wise old Shaw, high-minded old Barbusse, the venerable Webbs, Gide the pure in heart and Picasso the impure, down to poor little teachers, crazed clergymen and millionaires, drivelling dons and very special correspondents…all resolved, come what may, to believe anything, however preposterous, to overlook anything, however villainous, to approve anything, however obscurantist and brutally authoritarian, in order to be able to preserve intact the confident expectation that one of the most thorough-going, ruthless and bloody tyrannies ever to exist on earth could be relied on to champion human freedom, the brotherhood of man, and all the other good liberal causes to which they had dedicated their lives.

It is difficult to write about this gigantic *folie en masse*, for two reasons. The first is that the catalogue of wickedness – the word is not too strong – is so enormous, so inexcusable, so ultimately vile, that it sickens any reader not gripped by the madness. After all, the millions of men and women who were killed in the Gulag, while western adulation of the killers went on, deserve a better epitaph than "I see no evil, hear no evil, speak no evil".

The second reason is that Professor Paul Hollander's magisterial, comprehensive, witty and merciless book *Political Pilgrims* has done the job for us. That is to say the *past* follies have been imperishably recorded; there is, alas, no reason to believe that such abominable behaviour will not break out again as soon as a suitable focus for it appears. (At the time of writing, the dupes have had to put up with Nicaragua, but a modest wager on Haiti could pay well, and if the Burmese tyrants were more accommodating, so that they were willing to allow visitors into "their" country, the splendours of Burmese democracy governed by a brutal military dictatorship might be just what the latter-day pilgrims want.)

Sidney and Beatrice Webb have an honoured place in the Pantheon of Folly; indeed, they are the greatest gulls of all that great galaxy who looked upon evil and saw that it was good, and not only saw that it was good, but said so, most vociferously.

But just as the Webbs may – must – stand for the farthest limits of Soviet self-deception, they must also carry off countless other prizes, effortlessly won. There must be (God protect us all from ever laying eyes on it) a comprehensive bibliography of their writings; surely, in all history there cannot be anything to touch their monstrous logorrhea, nothing to compare with their stupendous Niagara of *cacoethes scribendi*. Year after year, they poured out gigantic volumes, hundreds of thousands words thick, about the Poor Law, Local Government, Economics and kindred subjects, adorned with appendices, introductions and footnotes which doubled the length of the monstrous texts.

No one has read, no one could read, these massive doorstops, usually printed in formats and typefaces well calculated to warn off even the most foolhardy seeker after a dim enlightenment, so hideous was the result.

On those terrible grey pages, no gleam of humour was permitted, no living human creature could hope to enter, no embellishing anecdote might settle, even as fleetingly as the gentlest butterfly. Now, from the perspective of hindsight, it can be seen as inevitable that the couple who knew everything and understood nothing would sooner or later appoint themselves to their greatest and most pernicious endeavour, the writing of a book half a million words long without a single true sentence anywhere in it. Though they were to write many more thousands of pages, all still unreadable then as now, fate, for its own inscrutable purpose, had marked them out to sum up the world's greatest delusion. The Webbs had turned to a detailed examination of the nature of the Soviet Union. *Finis coronat opus.*

Stalin is not a dictator. So far as Stalin is related to the constitution of the USSR, as amended in 1936, he is the duly elected representative of one of the Moscow constituencies to the Supreme Soviet...In what manner, then, does Stalin exceed in authority over his country's destiny the British Prime Minister or the American President?...Here I will note that the Communist Party...is not an oligarchy; it is democratic in its internal structure...Nor has Stalin ever claimed the position of a dictator...Far otherwise...

But this pair of monsters, who had already flung away scholarship, truth, scrutiny, witness, scepticism, curiosity, even sight and hearing, are still nowhere near the topmost mountain of their Himalayan determination to demonstrate that black is white.

Is the USSR a political democracy? It is clear that, tested by the Constitution of the Soviet Union...the USSR is the most inclusive and equalised democracy in the world...Stalin's recent step down...to the prosaic position of Prime Minister, elected strictly according to the constitutional procedure of a political democracy has, so to speak, secularised his status and made it that of any other Prime Minister ultimately dependent on the votes of the people.

But it was the Treason Trials that brought out the Webbs' greatest and most conclusive abomination. At first, it seems that their faith has wavered at last; but it is in fact strengthened:

To many people in Great Britain and the United States the outstanding feature of the record since 1934 is the series of trials of highly placed Soviet citizens for high treason, conspiracy to assassinate, criminal intercourse with spies and other agents of foreign powers, and even the wilful wrecking of railways and industrial plants. That so many men in high official positions...should have committed such crimes...has seemed to Western observers almost incredible. That...the defendants should, one and all, have made full and detailed confessions...of the guilt not only of themselves but also of their fellow criminals, seemed to raise the tragic story to the fantastic madness of a nightmare; it seemed that the confessions must have been forced on the prisoners by torture or the threat of torture.

But wait; there is an explanation for these puzzling phenomena:

Why should a conspirator who is caught out by the Government, and who knows that he is caught out and that no denials or hypothetical fairy tales will help him to escape – why should he degrade himself uselessly by a mock defence instead of facing the facts and discussing his part in them quite candidly with his captors?...the Russian prisoners simply behave naturally and sensibly...What possible good could it do them to behave otherwise? Why should they waste the time of the court and disgrace themselves by prevaricating like pickpockets merely to employ the barristers?...some of us are so obsessed with our national routine that the candour of the Russian conspirators seems grotesque and insane. Which of the two courses, viewed by an impartial visitor from Mars, would appear the saner?

No wonder, then, that although the first edition of their Soviet study appeared in 1935 under the title *Soviet Communism: A New Civilisation?*, by the time the final edition appeared in 1941 they felt quite confident that the question-mark could be dispensed with, and they duly dispensed with it.

Undaunted, they might well have signed off their monstrous eulogy with the following truly utopian vision, a touchingly modest prediction of what would be the future of what they had just announced was its present. Unfortunately, they were debarred from doing so, because – Soviet utopianism notwithstanding – it was written by Trotsky, whose name, having been expunged by the expungers of Stalin's wonderworld, could not be mentioned.

In a society which will have thrown off the pinching and stultifying worry about one's daily bread, in which community restaurants will prepare good, wholesome and tasteful food for all to choose, in which communal laundries will wash clean everyone's good linen, in which children, all the children, will be well fed and strong and gay, and in which they will absorb the fundamental elements of science and art as they absorb albumen and air and the warmth of the sun, in a society in which electricity and the radio will not be the crafts they are today, but will come from inexhaustible sources of super-power at the call of a central button, in which there will be no "useless mouths", in which the liberated egotism of man – a mighty force – will be directed wholly towards the understanding, the transformation and the betterment of the universe – in such a society the dynamic development of culture will be incomparable with anything that went on in the past.

It is worth commenting on a few of his predictions: for instance, he was quite right about the transformation of electricity and wireless into gigantic forces; on the other hand, the liberating egotism of man might well dismay him. As for the children, albumen has probably long ago been banned. But the way things are going, they may all be well fed and strong *and* gay.

It is fitting to dwell on these two at such length because they seem so wholly and perfectly to epitomise the utopian mirage at its most profound. They yearned for the Soviet Union to be the earthly paradise that they scorned as superstition when it was portrayed as a heavenly one, and it cannot be a coincidence that of those who sailed to Moscow in the Ship of Fools, there was an overwhelming preponderance of learned men and women, intellectuals all, cold-bloodedly seeing what they had so long wanted to see, even though what they now saw was not there. And among these clever men and women – so clever that they could conjure up thought-forms, disembodied images and an infinite supply of chimeras – Sidney and Beatrice Webb were the extreme examples of a folly so great, so perverted and so inexcusable that it has to be designated as evil.

9

Revolutions devour their children

A T SOME POINT, then, ideology had muddied the pure stream of Utopia. The great tyrannies were grounded in belief-systems that to the originators, and those who applied them, consisted of conclusive, revealed truth, which might not be challenged without severe retribution. Of course, these monstrous beliefs had ancestors; the revealed truths of religion had long before claimed certainty, and burned a lot of people for disagreeing with it. There was, true, a subtle difference (though one which would presumably have escaped those who were burned) in that divine powers demanded such conformity. It is true that Communism claimed descent from Karl Marx, and Nazism from the ancient Germanic qualities, but neither of these had anything that could compare in genealogy with the Church, and indeed neither relied to any serious extent on such scriptures to establish its legitimacy; the two greatest *ipse dixits* since mankind appeared on earth drew their being from themselves alone, twin virgin births slouching to their own terrible Bethlehem to be born, and if things fall apart so much the better – it gives us more scope to usher in our forms of a world made perfect.

How did it happen? How, that is, did ideology in all the meanings of the word fail to see (or, if it saw, fail to draw the obvious conclusion) that the incompatibility of the great beliefs can only mean that there is no one great belief that is right and that all others are wrong; for so far from recognising the stupendous error into which they plunged, they insisted that the very multiplicity of incompatible views strengthened their claim to the one objective truth, in that they could now dispense with all the others, flawed and unnecessary as they were.

It is all very well to say that these people were convinced that they were right; we are all convinced that we are right, but there is something in us, something absolutely necessary to meaningful life, which tells us that our conviction, though we hold it immovably, can yet be reconciled with the equally cherished opposite opinion that is held by another disputant. That still small voice, to which the ideologues are deaf but which prevents us killing our opponent, is the recognition that great truths, with however august a lineage, may be incompatible with other great truths. The moment that thought takes root in any human being, the falsity of ideology is exposed. So where did the ideologue find the weed-killer that killed that precious root?

Here, Utopia tugs at our sleeve, to answer the question. What is the essence of Utopia? It is, surely, perfection, a perfect society, in which the inhabitants are, or have been made, perfect. All the ideologue has done is to insist that *he* has the key which unlocks perfection. That sounds absurd; who could claim that, say, Hitler was seeking perfection? But of course he was, and his greatest crime was based on precisely that search. For Hitler, Jews were not merely bad people, who should be deprived of rights or driven out of the country; they were literally inhuman, a bacillus that was poisoning the pure and perfect Aryan blood of his Germany.

It is worth pausing here to study that extraordinary phenomenon. How could such thoughts (leaving out what the thoughts led to) have entered and struck root in Hitler's mind. There is no point in saying that he was mad; of course he was, but there are a thousand forms of madness, and to understand his particular way could have meaning outside the confine of Hitler's thought.

"New"; the very word has great meaning in the utopian dictionary. The utopian impulse is to wipe away the existing world and create a flawless replacement. It is a powerful metaphor, but sometimes the powerful metaphor escapes from the language and creates havoc.

And not just havoc. When Hitler came to power, he did so under the banner of the New Order, which he had been incubating throughout his life, through the shabby rooms of his youth, the years of grown-up poverty and nonentity, the fiasco of the Putsch, the fateful time in prison where he laid the terrible egg, and promised himself that he would one day hatch it.

Nor did he fail in his promise; the New Order cleansed the state of every trace of the old; and whether he realised it or not, he was obeying the utopian propensity, scouring the vessel that is to hold the precious liquor of purity.

Among the first new orders in Hitler's state – it went understandably unnoticed in history among the terrible decrees that followed – was one imposing a fine for littering the German streets. Today, many countries demand such admirable cleanliness, but it was a novelty in those days; an exceptionally perceptive psychiatrist might have diagnosed Hitler's malady from that evidence alone. Purging, cleansing, sweeping, distilling, purifying – these were the fateful words that seethed in that dreadful furnace of his mind, and now he was going to use them not as metaphors but in reality.

There was also a powerfully utopian chileastic element in this madness. Somewhere in Hitler's mind there must have been a millennarian vision; indeed, he proclaimed the millennium in plain words: his regime was to be the "Thousand Year Reich". It fell 988 years short, but he was not to know that; all he knew was that the world must be pure before the end of the thousand years, pure, that is, for entering into kingdom come.

But who can enter into the kingdom? Only those, of course, who are worthy: "Who shall ascend into the hill of the Lord? or who shall stand in his holy place? He that hath clean hands, and a pure heart; who hath not lifted up his soul unto vanity, nor sword deceitfully". There are, however, those who are not fit to enter: "But the fearful, and unbelieving, and the abominable, and murderers, and whoremongers, and sorcerers, and idolators, and all liars, shall have their part in the lake which burneth with fire and brimstone; which is the second death".

And Jews, gypsies, homosexuals and other lesser creatures, unfit to enter into the Nazi kingdom, are to be cast into the outer darkness; and if that does not suffice they shall "have their part in the lake which burneth with fire and brimstone". So they did.

The theme that runs through all utopian visions, whether benign or evil, is completeness. Imperfection is inevitable in the ordinary world, but in the ideal world of Utopia it has been cast out, or if it has not been, it must be. The monomaniac strain in Hitler's mind led straight to the exclusion of the pure in heart – that is, the pure of blood, and of blood, moreover, certified pure for generations back.

In the Jewish and Muslim religions, when a new synagogue or mosque is built, a brick is left out, or a patch of wood unpainted, or some other tangible incompleteness is recorded. The reason is that God alone is perfect, and no mortal can aspire to Godhead. The imperfection deliberately left untouched is the reminder of this truth, and a notably vivid humility in the face of the Deity. Would that Hitler and his cohorts had heeded the profound truth in that beautiful image of imperfection. But the fanatic, most certainly including the fanatical utopian, cannot bear the thought that something has been left out. For the Hitlers of this world, and for the miniature Hitlers, as well as the harmless but too tidy innocents, there is danger to others. Although there is, of course, no conclusive evidence, it is quite certain that Procrustes was rigidly tidy, that he deplored the dropping of litter, and that he insisted that any building put up must be inspected for imperfections, which, if found, must be immediately rectified.

What all ideologues and ideological utopians always forget is that (that is how you know them) *the future has not yet happened*, and all history demonstrates that before it *has* happened, guesses at its nature are a waste of time. "Call no man happy until he is dead."

This is the greatest charge that can be levelled at Utopia, and it is a real one, not to be glossed over or ignored. If the verdict is "Guilty", then a burden of guilt, in the form of tens of millions of deaths, will crush Utopia beneath it; the Trojan Horse of ideology should have been caught and ejected from every utopian Troy.

There is a defence, and a skilled lawyer (remember Thomas More was a lawyer, and practised at the Bar) can hope for an acquittal. Look through the catalogue of Utopias, and see how overwhelming a majority are based on gentleness, loving-kindness, the curing of afflictions, the ending of poverty, the healing of the sick, the lifting of toil, the extinction of envy, hatred, war, crime, wickedness itself, the equality of possessions, the harmony between beliefs, the happiness everywhere, the peace of mind, the brotherhood and sisterhood.

A powerful plea. Yet none should imagine that perverted utopianism is confined to the states of the world, massive movements and philosophies, implacable beliefs grounded in stern religions. The truth is that so powerful is the utopian propensity, that wherever the scent of it can be tracked it will be tracked to the end, no matter how many disappointments it produces on the trail, for the faith of utopians is one of the world's most touching phenomena.

It can be seen in the countless contexts, the principal one, of course, being the very belief in Utopia, and Utopia on earth, too. We can see that faith in the promises of politicians with their grandiose and utopian projects and promises, and we can see it more spectacularly in the holy men who have worked out the date on which the world is going to end, and so far from being abashed when it continues untouched on its way, simply announce another date, with hardly any falling-off in the numbers who believed the first projection and have only just risen from their knees when they are eagerly genuflecting again.

Inevitably, such faith will be abused. It is not surprising; if crooked door-to-door salesmen can make a fat living, an even fatter living can be made by promises not of comprehensive life insurance but of comprehensive life itself. Elixirs of all kinds abound throughout the history of Utopia, and one variety returns again and again: a charismatic leader gathers around him a band of eager followers, promising them a new life, indeed often eternal life. Some of these prophets are interested only in profits, but a surprising number are perfectly genuine in their self-delusion. (There is a particularly ghastly example from Hitler; just before he shot himself in the Bunker, he dictated his will, in which he said that he had to die because the German people had been unworthy of him.)

★

In modern times (ancient times have had their fill), it would be hard to match the story of Jim Jones and his tragic band of followers in Guyana.

Jones was mad, monstrously mad, and no less monstrously criminal. He began his catastrophic career in the high society of American mainstream politics, being courted by such figures as Governor Jerry Brown of California, Vice-President Mondale, First Lady Rosalynn Carter and San Francisco Mayor Moscone. If such streetwise politicians could not see through such a dangerous charlatan, there can hardly be any blame attached to the following he gathered, led and brought to an end.

Jones was white, but he recruited mainly among uneducated and unsophisticated blacks, partly by his claims that the white, western world was planning a genocidal Armageddon on blacks, before itself disappearing in a nuclear holocaust. He set up a chain of "People's Temples" in San Francisco and elsewhere in California, mulcting his dupes, poor enough already, of their few pennies. He claimed that he was Christ risen, and at the same time (uneasy bedfellows, surely) Lenin; he could raise the dead, cure cancer by waving his hands and see the future.

His acolytes believed, and their belief was the kind that can move mountains. Having robbed them of their last cent, he ruled them with a rod of iron – almost literally, for he did indeed mete out brutal beatings to his meek and willing victims. (Presumably, the poverty eagerly shouldered came from the Christ half of his resurrection, the beatings from the Lenin part.)

They lived, apparently without complaint, working at making things to sell for the Jones' bank account; no wonder, then, that after he moved his communes to Guyana, his first action was to deposit a cheque for a third of a million dollars in a local bank.

For reality was closing in; but so was the law. The Guyanan jungle seemed a better place to rule his people. He ordered them out on the trek, something like a thousand of them; he had gone on ahead to prepare the Lord's banquet. With his stolen or hornswoggled money, he bought thousands of acres of jungle, and called the place "Jonestown".

Miles from any possible check, Jones intensified the madness and brutality of his regime. The followers worked day and night to clear the jungle for Jonestown; now they got no pay at all. The beatings, and other forms of degradation (shaven heads, denial of food) became more common; there were sessions in which the followers were made to denounce others as backsliders, and more beatings followed.

Now, even the jungle was not deep enough to be cut off entirely from the rest of the world. The parents of some of Jones's younger followers were determined to rescue their children. Led by a Congressman, they managed to prise out some 16 of the presumably disillusioned young, and were awaiting a jungle plane to take them on the first leg of their return journey. Some of them did not complete it; crazed members of the sect, armed and clearly under the direction of Jones, opened fire on the rescue party; the Congressman and four more of the party were killed, and another eight wounded.

The game was up at last, or so it would seem. But Christ/Lenin had other plans, and spectacular ones they were. There were some 900-1000 members in the community; Jones commanded all of them to drink poison, assuring them that, if they did so, all their earthly concerns would be put aside for ever (as indeed they were).

Heaven awaited; but they had to get there first. What followed had surely no precedent in modern times, and few in history. Huge bowls of poison were distributed among the faithful, and faithfully they drank at the spring of death. It seems that almost all of them went willingly into the night, convinced by Jones that they were going to heaven; the only problem was the pushing and shoving (and no doubt the dying) was being carried out in a disorderly manner; the mass suicide was taped (a very modern Christ/Lenin was Jones), and on it can be heard Jones calling for death with dignity. Jones himself, together with his wife and child, perished among the rest and in the same way; it is not known, and now can never be known unless Jones stages yet another resurrection, whether he stayed to the end, like the captain going down with his ship, and, having surveyed the bloody field, followed his followers to heaven.

There is good reason to remind us of this story, even though it was blazoned over the skies at the time it happened. It is clear that among the thousand in Jones's communes, first in California and then in Guyana, there were only a handful of dissenters and only a fleeting disappointment. It is no less clear that the denouncing-sessions and the beatings did not change the attitude to Jones, even of the denounced and the beaten. Just as certain is the fact that the poverty endured among the faithful was accepted without envy or resentment, nor would such faith have wavered if they had known (as came to light after the orgy of death) that Jones had something like five million pounds banked in Europe, Latin America and the United States.

It is no use saying that Jones was mad or evil or both, though that is all too horribly true. In California, there would have been nothing to stop any member of the People's Temple walking away from it, and although it would have been harder, or at any rate more dangerous, to walk away from Jonestown, it could have been done. Hypnotism, mysterious drugs, magic powers on Jones's part – none of these account for what happened. We shy away from the truth: these people *believed*. And they believed on the earth that their believing would carry them to heaven (and for that matter nobody can prove that it didn't). Perfect worlds – Utopias – have their own nature, their own momentum, their own circle of belief.

But it is in that circle that lies the danger. When More's King Utopus cut the isthmus joining Utopia to the mainland, he set off a chain of events which – absurd though it is to put it in such unsubtle terms – led Jones's tragic sheep to the slaughter. Self-contained beliefs are as tempting as Jones's cyanide, and just as poisonous. Again, we must remind ourselves that More's Greek pun – is Utopia good-place or no-place? – is really saying that it can be used for good and for ill, and all who seek from it solace, understanding or happiness had better know the difference. Jones's victims perished because they had come to believe that their world was *the* world, and that nothing outside it need be considered; in that belief they lived, and died. Christ knew better (though Lenin didn't): "We are members one of another".

Such manifestations have run throughout history, with an astonishing recrudescence in the last decades of the twentieth century, in the United States particularly. The pattern (it is frequent enough to be called one) usually begins with a breakaway from an established religion, usually one of a strict order, though not strangely eccentric. The breakaway group find a leader – more usually the leader finds the group – and he steadily climbs the ladder from a repository of true wisdom to the Godhead itself. Such, *mutatis mutandis*, was Jim Jones.

And such, too, a few years later, was David Koresh, who set up his standard in Waco, Texas, where his disciples believed he was God, and happily endured beatings from the very deity's own hand, and died in flames when he set his premises on fire.

But such madness can be, and has been, played out on a very much greater board; imagine a hundred thousand Jim Joneses, giving the orders to die, that the land shall be made pure.

The cleansing metaphor came to dreadful life in Kampuchea; one day, a pronouncement was made by the ruler, to the effect that the whole of the capital city, Phnom Penh, must be at once evacuated. No attempt had been made at relocating its population (some two million), nor were any instructions given as to what the city's throngs should do, or where they should go. The decree was promulgated, and came into force immediately; no time was allowed for getting food, much less transport; indeed, no time was allowed for families to gather any of their members who might be from home. Unprepared, unequipped, unprovisioned, undirected, unbelieving and unable to understand, they left their homes, and with the bayonets and clubs of the Khmer Rouge cleansers to make sure that they keep moving, made off into the uncharted jungle. A haunting image remains; in the news photographs of this terrible exodus there was one of an obviously elderly and moribund man, with a drip-feed inserted in a vein of one his arms, with the transparent bag he was holding whatever life-saving substance was entering his body fixed to a pole. He was being pushed on a barrow, by an equally frail old woman, presumably his wife.

Nor was Pol Pot at all reluctant to explain this curious event; it was done in the name of the purest ideology. The city – apparently *any* city – was sinful, pleasure-loving, unmindful of its ideological duty, and had to be emptied out and filled with matter that was to be born anew. Only then, of course, would the utopian perfection be completed, and the world made clean.

There is a hideous appeal in such diabolical purity. Do not mortals yearn for perfection based on a *tabula rasa*, where a completely new start can be made? Why can we not do what Noah did, and see all but a handful of creatures drown? Would that not enable us to make sure that the new world will be free of the evil that had corrupted the old one – nay, of the very blemishes and untidinesses that marred the otherwise acceptable (only acceptable, not worthy) world? After all, God himself later found that even the new world had slipped into the bad ways of the old one, and reminded it very sharply at Pompeii and – seeing that the portent's message had gradually been forgotten – again at Lisbon, with the same backsliding.

But it is the blemishes and untidinesses that make a civilisation, and – much more important – keep it from perfection, that terrible perfection that, when thirsty, can slake its thirst only in blood. The whole of western terrorism since it began in earnest some twenty-five years ago is attributable to that terrible belief: if enough of those who stand in the way of perfection are killed, the way to perfection will be open, and will be reached in a single step. And besides: it is pleasurable to kill, and becomes more pleasurable every time. And that was demonstrated for all time in 1789.

★

How utopian was the French Revolution? Very much so for St Just – with Robespierre and Marat he was one of the three pillars of the Terror – who put it in words that any utopian would be proud to put on his banner: "You know very well that mankind is not born wicked; it is only oppression that is wicked".

But the Revolution had started long before those chilling utopian words were spoken. When poor Louis XVI finally summoned the States General he had no idea what it would lead to; the storming of the Bastille was a symbolic gesture rather than a presage of revolution, but the gesture turned into one of the world's greatest upheavals; from that moment to Napoleon's "whiff of grapeshot" was only a decade, but it left its mark on history for ever.

And on Utopia. In France, the Terror did not last long, and although the executions (some in mere butchery but most by the essentially utopian new device, the guillotine) were frightful, the numbers who died, great enough, were hardly enough to compare with the great ideological massacres of history.

Yet no one has yet managed to draw the exact line that runs between utopianism and fanaticism, though on both sides of it there is an inevitable feeling that the right solution having been found, anyone who challenges it becomes an enemy. So it was with the Revolution; when Carlyle dubbed Robespierre "the sea-green incorruptible", he meant by the first half of the soubriquet nothing more than a reference to Robespierre's greenish pallor, which could be traced to the revolutionary's inadequate diet. But it is no coincidence that both halves of the phrase (certainly Robespierre *was* incorruptible, and would that he had not been, for many good heads would then have remained on their shoulders) together make a more resonating description; anyone can be incorruptible, but to be steeped in the eternal ocean and to resemble its implacable tides and storms, its regular ebbs and flows, its even-handed drownings and its ineradicable salt – *this* is the figure who has come to free France and the world, and nothing – nothing whatever – may be allowed to stand in the way of that achievement.

Even then, there is a place for Condorcet.

Let us contemplate him, that ideal utopian, who believed that science must be the vanguard of the army that would storm heaven and bring liberty, equality and fraternity to all mankind. Numbered among the *philosophes*, he might have been born to expound the first principles of the French Revolution, and no less certain to die at its hands, which indeed he did. He announced "the idea of the limitless perfectibility of the human species", and insisted that gunpowder was a benefactor because it meant that warriors would no longer fight hand-to-hand, and thus lose their taste for bloodshed. He was convinced that all the nations, however backward, would ultimately scale the heights of civilisation and liberty, which would include a steady biological progress. He believed that stupidity could be dissolved by a broad enough body of rights, and that as soon as the news of the Declaration of the Rights of Man had reached all the inhabitants of all the nations they would at once accept its message. As for his beloved science, the leading scientists would inevitably agree to share their work, if only because whole populations would become educated more or less overnight and would therefore wish to understand the new scientific discoveries. Moreover, since all men would be educated, there would be no need of government, because administrative decisions could be shared out haphazardly, with everyone taking a turn. As for wealth, nobody would be interested in acquiring it because, all being equal, it would no longer proclaim the owner as someone above the ordinary people, because there would be no ordinary people. (Or rather, everyone would be extraordinary.) The laws of happiness would shortly be discovered by the collectivity of scientists, and it would follow that crime would disappear, and that the dream of perfectibility would be ended; the morning of perfection had dawned.

Indeed, Condorcet calmly forecast the complete emancipation of all oppressed peoples everywhere, and was certain that his prophecy would be fulfilled. Had not the Declaration of the Rights of Man been promulgated? So who could possibly deny that the last word in the debate had therefore been spoken? And we can be sure that, even when he was proclaimed an enemy of the people, his faith in the Revolution and what followed it had not wavered for a moment.

Condorcet's tragically comic fate, and the benevolence of his nature demand, and should get, our sympathy. But he cannot be entirely absolved from blame. The certainties of the Revolution led to the death of thousands, and those certainties, like all other certainties made by man, were not to be trusted. Condorcet (and he was only the most extravagant of the believers) could not believe, indeed could not comprehend, that there could be flaws in the ruthless logic of the Enlightenment; once the truth had been demonstrated, there could be no argument. But we who live at the end of the twentieth century have bitter cause to know what is the fate of those who are thus deemed hardly human. Condorcet had one of the most beautiful of souls, but he stained his own with his vision – it was his swan-song as well as his creed – of what the world would and must become. He sums up with an apostrophe to Ideal Man, who is only waiting to be born:

In contemplating this vision he receives the reward of his efforts for the progress of reason, for the defence of liberty. Then he dares to marry his labours to the eternal chain of human destinies. He finds there the true reward of virtue; it lies in the pleasure of having achieved a lasting good, which fate will never again destroy by a sorry reversal which would restore prejudice and slavery. This contemplation is for him a hiding-place where the memory of his persecutors cannot pursue him. Living in thought with man who has regained his rights as well as the dignity of his nature, he forgets the man whom avarice, fear or envy tortures and corrupts. Then he is truly with his equals in an Elysium which he has been able, by his reason, to create, and which his love for humanity embellishes with the purest joys.

But, even in his death, there was banality. Condemned *in absentia* as an enemy of the revolutionary state, he took refuge, disguised, in an inn. It was full of his enemies looking for him, but the disguise held. Then he was asked by the inn-keeper what he wanted for supper. He ordered an omelette, and the inn-keeper asked how many eggs. Condorcet, who had probably never seen an omelette being made, let alone made one himself (indeed, he had probably never been in a kitchen), guessed, within earshot of Robespierre's spies, "Ten".

That is a far cry from Robespierre, it will be said. But it is not; Robespierre was always ready to see enemies among his friends as did the two great evil leaders, and while the *ci-devant* aristocrats filled the tumbrils, the great sniffer-out of plots was preparing his own *battue*. As Trotsky was the real maker of the Russian Revolution and therefore had to die, so the French revolutionaries had followed the hypnotic figure of Danton who in his turn went to the same death.

Here, a shadow falls on the story. We are driven, all unwilling, to the conclusion that there is *no* barrier between the true fanatic and the true utopian; depending on their particular vision, both can do terrible deeds if they are required for the safety of the state, even if the state in question is Utopia.

The key that turns the lock which will open Pandora's box was put perfectly by Shakespeare: "To do a great right do a little wrong". But Shakespeare had his own reply ready: "It must not be, there is no power in Venice Can alter a decree established".

The clue to Robespierre's utopianism is his renaming of the months. That was probably just megalomania, though it was a symbol of the destruction of the old order that as titles of nobility were swept away, everything that could remind the new-made citizen (himself an entirely utopian figure, having inherited all the wisdom and understanding that the Revolution provided) must also disappear. The summit of this reordering (the citizens, for all their hastily acquired superiority, took no notice of the months' new names) was the designation of a great Parisian thoroughfare, not with the name of an acclaimed hero, not in gratitude to a great General, not even by the awesomely justified name of Robespierre himself; but as the Avenue of the Elysian Fields. The whole story could be no more utopian: a street named in Heaven, and no doubt expected to live up to its name on earth.

★

Arguing with the past is a fruitless pastime, except in the imagination; one of the most powerful elements in the utopian propensity is the hunger for the past as well as the future. It could be said that the whole of Utopia is only a dream of putting right what had been put wrong: "O call back yesterday, bid time return". Utopians are inured to disappointment, or at least they ought to be.

If utopians continue to put hope before experience they are doomed to perpetual disappointment; perhaps that is the true moral of Utopia. But there are always fellow-utopians to throw a lifebelt to those still struggling in the water of broken promise, little knowing that the lifebelt was torn and rotten, and would not hold up the wearer for long. Just such a dangerous disappointment was – is, for it is still bought and read – *Walden Two*, by B.F. Skinner, a dream of a perfect world which gradually, very gradually, turns into a nightmare, entirely without the author's intentions.

Walden Two's history is fully as interesting as the book itself; indeed, more so if it is judged by its prose. The reader coming to it with a picture of a ruthlessly classical form and a lofty style will be astonished to find an almost nursery atmosphere; the writing is naïve, almost childish, and the plot (in so far as it has one) is threadbare almost to invisibility. And the shock is intensified for those who are familiar with the author's scientific work, and the fierce arguments it has provoked everywhere.

As Skinner reveals in an explanatory note attached to the reissue of the book almost thirty years after its first publication, it was at first, and for many years, an almost complete failure as far as sales went. For a book which later became a kind of secular (and not even entirely secular) bible, and which became a massive best-seller, an explanation of its curious fate seems essential.

It was first published in 1945, when the war in Europe had ended and the war in the Far East had only a few weeks to go; exhaustion in every form ruled, and there was no time for a mythical world of perfection. The striking thing about the book is not that it failed in 1945, but that it took some twelve years to pass into the general domain and then enjoyed an explosion of sales. What had been gestating in the minds of the reading public that only at that moment was born?

It could only be that that was the moment at which the earth became self-conscious. The first stirrings of what was to change attitudes that had been apparently immovable for centuries had fastened onto a new world being born, and Coriolanus had a word for it: "There is a world elsewhere". As we all know now, it was very much more complex than it seemed, but then there were thousands of worlds elsewhere, springing up daily, their *vade-mecum* the *Whole Earth Catalog*; one of those thousands of worlds was *Walden Two*, and it offered a world that could, it seemed, exist. The sales of the book climbed, and went on climbing, until it was left behind in the ever-growing tide of real accomplishments in the real world; Skinner artlessly summed up what was happening, saying that "...to the amazement of the American tourist, there are people in the world who are happier than we are, while possessing far less".

The amazement began to die in the Sixties, and it is still dying, but it is certainly not yet dead. There is a passage in Skinner's prefatory note that sounds a deep, but undeniable, tone of despair; remember that the note was added in the mid-Seventies:

> We boast of our short workday and week, but what we do with the free time we have to spend is nothing of which we can be very proud. The leisure classes have almost always turned to alcohol and other drugs, to gambling, and to watching other people lead exhausting or dangerous lives, and we are no exception. Thanks to television millions of Americans now lead the exciting and dangerous lives of other people...One may spend one's life in these ways and be essentially unchanged at the end of it.

Of course nothing like that happens in Walden Two, that touchingly naïve world that the troubled Skinner invented.

First to go, predictably, are the dangerous emotions: "...the meaner and more annoying – the emotions which breed unhappiness – are almost unknown here, like unhappiness itself..."

Out goes unhappiness, followed by competitiveness: "We are opposed to personal competition. We don't encourage competitive games...We never mark any member for special approbation...A triumph over another man is never a laudable act..." (It is interesting to note that in Britain, to a considerable extent, that attitude has gained much ground; many schools have banned such sports as running and jumping, lest one child should be shown to run faster or jump higher; not only do such schools practise such a rule, but some municipalities *demand* that in state schools such rules must apply. It is, however, noticeable that the local government forces which require these precepts to be kept, under law, are almost without exception the most ill-run, wasteful, spendthrift and even financially corrupt.)

In some ways, Walden Two is behind the times – a considerable feat for a utopian world; for smoking, though dying out, is still practised there, but of course not rebuked. Nothing and no one is rebuked; but there are many unspoken (because unimaginable) rules. "This is a world without heroes", the visitors to Walden Two are told, "we have got beyond all that". They have got beyond a great deal more, saying "A society which functions for the good of all cannot tolerate the emergence of individual figures...On the other hand, a society without heroes has an almost fabulous strength..." And more still: "Democracy is the spawn of despotism...Democracy is power and rule. It's not the will of the people, remember; it's the will of the majority...My heart goes out to the everlasting minority...".

Walden Two brings many echoes with it. The sterner kibbutzes in the early days of the Israeli state had something of the tone of selflessness – selflessness taken to the limit of virtual disappearance – which pervades Skinner's Paradise. The *advocatus diaboli* in the tour of Walden Two is Augustine Castle, whose every objection is met, thus causing him to fall into an impotent fury. Unfortunately, he tries to fight the Waldenites on their own ground, whereas the ordinary reader, suffocating in the dreadful perfection, would long for an outbreak of crime, or at the least of bubonic plague.

Now, however, it is necessary to cross-examine not Frazier (the man who shows the visitors the delights of Walden Two), but Skinner himself. When the book was first published, Skinner had published only one book: *Behaviour of Organisms*. It is not at all fanciful to believe that the utopian novel provided the template for the score of books that came after, or rather the ideas. From time to time in the book, the mask slips; for instance, there is a startling claim from the Waldenite, when he is told that he seems to have unbounded faith in human nature; "I have none at all", he cries, "if you mean that men are naturally good or naturally prepared to get along with each other. We have no truck with philosophies of innate goodness – or evil, for that matter. But we do have faith in our power to change human behaviour. We can *make* men adequate for group living – to the satisfaction of everybody. That was our faith, but it's now a fact".

But if the mask has slipped in this incident, it is torn off in this passage:

If it's in our power to create any of the situations which a person likes or to remove any situation he doesn't like, we can control his behaviour. When he behaves as we want him to behave, we simply create a situation he likes, or remove one he doesn't like. As a result, the probability that he will behave that way again goes up, which is what we want. Technically it's called "positive reinforcement". The old school made the amazing mistake of supposing that the reverse was true, that by removing a situation a person likes or setting up one he doesn't like – in other words by punishing him – it was possible to *reduce* the probability that he would behave in a given way again. That simply didn't hold. It has been established beyond question. What is emerging at this critical stage in the evolution of society is a behavioural and cultural technology based on positive reinforcement alone.

Having got that far, Skinner becomes the complete behaviourist; the final pages of the book (significantly, the innocent childishness of the prose falls away) are full of what in years to come would be his formidable *oeuvre*. It is strange to think that it started in a utopian science-fiction perfect world, and went on to an entire science without fiction and certainly without Utopia. How many geese marched back and forth at his behavioural behest? How many human beings would have marched back and forth if he had reigned over, say, Walden Three? How much effort and experiment went into his absurd philosophy for want of a glance at a volume of James Elroy Flecker, where he would have learned that "Men are unwise, and curiously planned", and another glance at another page of the same poet, from which he could have learned that "...it may be Beyond that last blue mountain barred with snow, Across that angry or that glimmering sea, White on a throne or guarded in a cave There lives a prophet who can understand Why men were born...".

10

News from nowhere

THE ALCHEMISTS are Utopians Extraordinary to a man, woman and
witch. They are, after all, attempting the most utopian of
transformations; it is all very well to turn the scoffers into believers,
the drunkards into total abstainers, the greedy into the selfless, all at the
threshold of Utopia. But the alchemist, as he strives to turn base metal into
gold, is dealing not with fickle human beings, with their individual
attitudes, but with the impassive ore of nature, that will make them
infinitely, utopianly rich.

The very tools of the trade, the alembics and other vessels, the cabalistic
writings consulted, deciphered and interpreted, the familiar, in the form of
a bird, a light or the devil, perched on the shoulder of the alchemist and
whispering into his ear – all these aids to striving for the explanation of the
ultimate mystery are aiming at a superutopian outcome, while the universe
looks impassively on, knowing that there can be no such consummation.

It is more than just a metaphor; the language in which the search is
couched is powerfully significant: the philosopher's stone. What could the
phrase mean? At its simplest, it means that the alchemist has discovered a
substance which, merely touched to the base metal that is to be
transmogrified, effects the momentous change. But that cannot satisfy
philologists, let alone students of magic. Surely, the "stone" is the heart of
the mystery, a mystery that only a "philosopher" can understand. But what
is the mystery?

We can seek a clue among the gulls and gull-catchers. These are, of
course, essential to the story; since there is no means in reality of turning

base metal into gold, these who yearned to find success in the endeavour are bound to be disappointed, which is where the rogues pluck the feathers of the gull, most notably in Ben Jonson's *The Alchemist*. But although every gull can be called greedy, and most of them foolish as well, not all the "philosophers" were rogues. The serious ones believed that it could be done (the scientific morning had not yet dawned), and therefore believed that not only great riches were in store, but the transformation of the world: Utopia, driven out of the front door, has returned through the back.

Nor should she be blamed; there is more than these gropings to the story. In modern times, psychologists, particularly Jung, have searched in alchemy for a subterranean understanding of man's innermost life. For such investigations alchemy is no mere metaphor; it would be a touching irony if they were to bear valuable fruit in the form of more balanced and self-understanding human beings. But we are discussing Utopia here, a never-never land, and the power of that kingdom is all too likely to encompass yet another utopian last laugh.

Yet the false alchemists must not be allowed to tar the real ones with their fakes. If there are, or were, real ones, they must surely be those who, instead of changing matter, invented it – or at least brought it to earth. That, of course, is what Prometheus did, and a fearful price he paid.

The myth of Prometheus is one of the most profound and meaningful. In essence, it is simple, even straightforward; he stole fire from heaven, and was punished by being chained to a rock, to which eagles repaired to tear and consume his liver (presumably replaced each time) for ever.

So much for the plain mythological facts; for the terrible *lèse-majesté* of his theft, he would suffer a terrible fate. But that is where the story starts rather than finishes.

First, there is nothing in the legend to suggest that Prometheus stole *all* the fire in heaven, leaving the gods cold and wretched; if he had made a great bonfire and brought it down to earth, they would not have been incommoded in any way, save perhaps by having to re-ignite their own bonfire, a trivial task. Clearly, then, it was not the theft in itself that enraged Zeus, but what would happen when earth acquired the precious substance which the gods must always have possessed.

However, there is no suggestion that fire is an attribute of the gods, so that Prometheus had assumed godhead, which would indeed have been something for the gods – the real ones – to punish with the greatest severity.

We are forced to conclude that the gods were afraid not of losing the precious substance, but of seeing the earth acquire it.

Presumably, before the fateful robbery, the earth and its inhabitants were indeed cold and wretched; imagine for a moment a world without it, tantalised by seeing the sun, but unable to benefit from it. The imagination cannot stretch so far; such a condition is meaningless. But of course the legends deal in symbols, and one of the most powerful of these is represented here. It was *knowledge* that the gods guarded so fiercely from mankind, and well they might. Again and again in history, knowledge has been contraband, starting with the nakedness of Adam and Eve, banished from Eden for knowing it. The Princess Turandot is only one of the figures in countless legends which comprise dangerous, even fatal, knowledge; her male equivalent is Lohengrin. Again and again it is, significantly, a *name* that must not be known; even Rumplestiltskin figures in such a situation. (A macabre image sidles into consciousness; after the Nuremberg Trials that followed the Second World War, those condemned to death for "crimes against humanity" were all hanged on one day, one by one. One by one they were brought into the execution chamber, and one by one they went to their well-earned death. But as each of them mounted the scaffold, they were ordered to say their names, and one by one they did so, as the room rang with the badges of infamy: Ribbentrop, Kaltenbrunner, Seyss-Inquart, Streicher and the rest.)

A little knowledge is a dangerous thing... For centuries the Bible was kept from the hands of the multitude; they were to live by its precepts, and be punished if they transgressed them, but they could not safely own a copy. On a more mundane level, governments – not just undemocratic ones – take care to seal and store documents, mostly harmless trivia, which may not be opened until many decades have passed. (Britain is the very worst in this curious practice.)

It was, then, knowledge that the legend barred, and the metaphor was perfect; fire was the most dangerous and destructive of the elements; no one could handle it safely, and anyone who tried to do so would face a terrible retribution.

There is an oblique and beautiful retelling of this legend, in a story by Ray Bradbury 'The Golden Apples of the Sun'. It is set in a space-ship, and we learn that the voyagers' destination is the sun; they are on an errand to bring back some of the sun's substance, as the earlier space-travellers – the real ones – brought back pieces of the body of the moon. A special attachment to the sun-going spacecraft is to scoop up some sun and shut it into a compartment of the vehicle; as they approach their goal, the outside of the spacecraft is kept at Absolute Zero. The last glimpse of these intrepid travellers is when they have just turned for home, the almost sacred booty (and indeed there have been and still are fire-worshippers) is safely stowed.

So there went the First Utopian, known by the unmistakable *stigmata*: an awakening from a glorious dream, followed by the fateful decision to put the dream into sound and beneficial practice, followed by inevitable catastrophe.

Must it be so? Ask Prometheus, or better still, the eagles, which are still at their dreadful meal, as the First Utopian writhes in unending torment. Yet if we go back to the legend, and interpret it correctly, so that knowledge is the forbidden fruit, would we, catastrophe included, reject "fire"? Surely not; the idea that something good, available and free is ours for the taking is no doubt a naïve belief, but it is a belief held by most of the human race, and even if they ignore Prometheus and his fate – indeed, if they are fully conscious of what it means and what follows the challenge to it – they will go marching towards that tantalising horizon.

★

If there is one aspect of Utopia that conveys its message more directly than any of the others, it is the insistence that over the next hill is the solution to the mystery, or if not the next hill, then the next but one, or perhaps the one after, or…but the infinite number of hills in the utopian landscape can be rendered down into a most magical solution.

The legend of the Conference of the Birds originated in Persia, and in a sense sums up the whole story of mankind's search for a perfect world. It tells the story of the birds' search for the same ideal life. They debate long and anxiously; should they set out to find the Simorg, a kind of avian deity, who will solve all their problems? The journey will be long, and there are many perils to face; some of the birds refuse to go because of the dangers, others do not believe that the Simorg can give them the solution to their problems, some even do not believe there is such a figure.

Eventually, a band set out, and painful is the journey; some of the birds despair and die, some turn back, quarrels arise. Over mountains and across deserts, the most determined push on, as their numbers continually decrease. At last, the survivors straggle in and seek the Simorg, the goal for all their hardships. What they learn is that they have carried the Simorg with them throughout their journey, for the Simorg is no more and no less than their own courage, resolution and faith.

There is a close analogy with Hermann Hesse's *Journey to the East*. There, a band of men travel, as the title suggests, in search of wisdom and understanding. There are quarrels over precedence; who is, who should be, their leader? They get to their goal at last, but are turned away, and have to retrace their steps from where they started. There it is revealed that the lowliest and least considered of their number was their true leader, and had they had enough enlightenment to recognise him their journey would not have been in vain.

There is an even simpler form of the story, by James Thurber. It tells of a moth which shows no interest in fluttering about lamps, and when its fellows ask it why it is so different from all of them, it says it wants to get to a star it sees in the heavens. Derision follows; this eccentric moth is jeered at and scorned, told it is wasting its time, and urged to behave like them. The eccentric moth refuses; but one by one, the realistic and sensible moths flutter into a flame and are burned; only the dreamer survives, still trying to get to the star. It survives so well, in fact, that it lives to a great age, and in its dotage it comes to believe that it did achieve its goal far away in the sky.

Even if we are not moths, so powerful are the utopian longings in almost all of us that we insist on creating habitations in which Utopia-dwellers live their utopian lives. The most notable of these is Shangri-La, a concept now so ingrained in millions of minds that it now appears in dictionaries; even the Concise Oxford Dictionary includes it as "noun, imaginary paradise on earth".

The name "Shangri-La" is so deeply embedded in the entertainment culture (and not only the entertainment end of the spectrum) of at least the western world that it is virtually impossible to convince anyone who has not read the book or seen the film based on it (James Hilton's *Lost Horizons*) that it is fiction. To start with, the name is so perfectly fitted to a remote part of the Himalayas (Tibet is not specified, but clearly suggested) that even people who have read the book *and* seen the film are convinced that there is a real place of that name, so hypnotically exact, at least to our occidental ears, are those three syllables.

A planeful of very different people are diverted (it is not entirely clear whether by accident or design) from their expected route, to land in this unique place. Its uniqueness is many-sided, but every side is benign, loving and wise, and these characteristics begin to seep into the stranded travellers. The testy businessman who demands transport out of the place becomes happily resigned to let his business look after itself; the shy girl who blossoms under the spell, the finicky figure, who would never let a hair get out of place on his head, is soon found wearing an open-necked shirt.

And so on. But the most remarkable quality of the inhabitants is that they never grow older, and it is clear that the newcomers will acquire that immortality, too. There is, however, a catch in it; to remain in a state of agelessness the inhabitants can never leave Shangri-La. That is no great problem for the inquilines, for they do not want to go, but one of the immigrants, the hero, wants to leave, because he has fallen in love with the heroine, one of the citizens of Shangri-La. They leave together; no one tries to stop them. But once they are through the city's walls a terrible ageing begins in the beautiful young girl; in a matter of moments she acquires the hundreds of years she has really lived, and she crumbles into dust as he watches, helpless and bereft.

In Shangri-La, then, King Utopus reigns. In Shangri-Utopia, the lame walk, the dumb speak, the misfit fits perfectly; no tears are shed, or only tears of joy. And most significantly, there is the one boon that western man craves above all others: no ageing. (Western man has not read Swift on the Struldbruggs, but he would not believe – he would not dare to believe – that immortality comes with a price-ticket on it, as indeed it did in *Lost Horizons*.)

The story (though the film-makers may not have had the point in mind) is another pointer to the inevitably static nature of Utopia; the tragedy of the beautiful young girl is characteristic of rigid utopian rules. The film was enormously successful, a success surely achieved through the longing for such a world among most of mankind. After all, who would not wish to live for ever, never getting older, with only one law to obey – that permanent residence is required?

The acclamation that greeted *Lost Horizons* bears eloquent testimony to the utopian yearning; once give up thoughts of leaving and nothing can trouble you again; a tempting vision indeed. How can the serpent get in now, when all the cracks in the wall have been filled, and the sentries are alert at their posts?

It is impossible to say, but he is there. More than half a century after *Lost Horizons* had had its great 1930s success, it was decided (by whom it is not clear) that a remake of the film would be likely to succeed just as completely as the original did. It was made; it even had John Gielgud in the role of the Great Lama. And it was a monumental failure, immediately and everywhere.

But a most touching tribute to mankind's insatiable appetite for romance is a massive, and beautifully printed, volume with the title of *The Dictionary of Imaginary Places*. The very idea of such a volume is so utopian that it could not exist in reality, but it does.

It is a huge and handsome book, lavishly illustrated (another utopian impossibility, but the compilers have been faithful to every hint and depiction).

There are some 1500 entries in the book, and each of them is seriously and carefully delineated; where the places are, what happens there, who are the leading or most notable inhabitants – these and other questions are copiously answered. Copiously indeed; very few of the entries are sketched with only a hundred or two words.

What startles the utopian seeker is the extraordinary number of such places from Atlantis to the Moon. Anyone seeking enlightenment in Utopias, and already fully apprised of the huge variety of forms it takes, will nevertheless be astonished at the fecundity of the utopian imagination.

The book is not, however, the creation of the compilers; the whole point of so majestic a project is that every one of the imaginary places is real – real, that is, to its creator. For this is a book of all the places which writers through the ages have conjured up and created, from Homer to Tolkien. (The scholarship is immaculate; at the end of every entry there is a detailed note of attribution.)

Maps abound, as do drawings of notable buildings, artefacts, tombs, flora and fauna; the imaginary history of these imaginary places is chronicled; religions and customs are thoroughly explored; and the reader inevitably falls into the belief that they are reading a monumental gazetteer of real places in the real world. Much of the task is lightened by the fact that very many utopianisers are eager to delineate the shape of their country, down to the details of the longitude and latitude, and only then go on to describe the nature of the place, its history and quality of life.

Utopia, naturally, has the most detailed entry, with 15 columns, but many have substantial records; C.S. Lewis's *Narnia* has 3000 words to its entry and Mervyn Peake's *Gormenghast* occupies 4000. Some of the entries have more than one place; the unassailable record is that of Tolkien's *Middle-Earth*, in which there are more than 200 named places in his 6000-word description of that mysterious land.

Some of the most powerfully real of these locations are didactic in meaning. Chelm, for instance, is a non-existent Jewish town in, probably, the Ukraine, where the Town Hall has no windows; visitors are advised to bring a bucket of sunshine when visiting it. (In Chelm, of course, the Rabbi – normally the most learned and the wisest man in the village – is the biggest fool for miles around.) Thus inverted, Chelm came to be a place whose inhabitants cannot get anything right, and many's the hapless employee or stupid schoolboy throughout the land who is told that he is fit for nothing but Chelm. But even places like Chelm play a part in the wishes of millions – those wishes which can truly be called utopian, so intense is the longing and so unlikely the success – success in finding a world without pain and without trouble. And perhaps it is to be found even in Chelm.

Again and again in this quest for a perfect life, a perfect dwelling, a perfect polity, a perfect peace, the explorer comes up against one of the most striking items in the utopian catalogue; it is the need, apparently unassuageable, for the utopian to make his own perfection. There is almost nothing in the huge number of utopian efforts to suggest that any utopian would willingly leave his own for another. That leads to yet another utopian mystery; very few of these havens are seen being built, and fewer still are engaged on a collective building plan. Almost all Utopias are fully-formed, and are discovered in some remote part of the world, or already established without any history to offer.

The roster of Utopias, as befits such a theme, is taken seriously. As any student of the subject will know, some of the minor or newer worlds, unfamiliar to the seeker, turn out to be utopian nightmares; the compilers take no sides, and are content to take the utopian country at its own face value. It will be interesting to discover whether the *Dictionary of Imaginary Places* has to go into further editions, to encompass new Utopias as they emerge from the earth, the sky or, above all, the human imagination.

But assuredly there is one legend which will endure for ever: Noah's Ark.

The legend itself is so powerful that it is one of the most well-known (and, significantly, well-loved) of all biblical stories, and as a children's toy, together with innumerable jokes, poems and songs, it has weathered astonishingly many centuries. The animals ("two by two"); the dove's fruitless journeys, and her final triumphant one; the new land, new start, new news. (How many are the lands, found by intrepid sailors, that were christened thus appropriately: *New*foundland, *New* Zealand, *New* Caledonia, indeed the New World!)

Noah's Ark, then, caps the theme of flight from corruption to a utopian purity; it is almost a definition of Utopia, and points once again to the strength of searchers and the intensity of their determination to find their utopian gold.

I I

A myth is as good as a mile

HEROES FLOURISH, naturally, in Utopia, though some of them – Roland and Oliver, for instance – have no Utopia to flourish in. On the other hand, Sancho Panza is rewarded by Don Quixote for his much-strained loyalty by the governorship of an island, no less chimerical than the windmills the Don charged.

Robin Hood is a perfectly utopian figure, spending his time robbing the rich and giving to the poor; he has the inevitable foil in the Sheriff of Nottingham, whose remit is presumably to ensure that the dangerous egalitarianism of Robin is contained. There is a huge literature of pure giving, starting with the Good Samaritan, in which the utopian theme of material equality can be heard. Many of these are concealed tests; the donor gives with no thought of return or reward, whereupon the beggar turns out to be a saint in disguise, or even Christ himself. (Abou Ben Adhem triumphantly passes the test of true humility in the face of God's messenger.)

Defoe's *Robinson Crusoe* was the first (or the first successful) Utopia of place: that is, the utopian quality of the experience is mainly or largely based on the physical situation in which the central figure finds himself.

It is based on a true story, of one Alexander Selkirk, who ran away to sea, in 1703. He joined a ship captained by William Dampier, who was not much different from a pirate; Selkirk, after a quarrel, insisted on being put ashore, alone, on a truly desert island, Juan Fernandez. He remained there, solitary, for five years, when he was rescued. Cowper wrote a poem, which has survived: "I am monarch of all I survey...", and the irony is meant.

But there is a greater irony. Crusoe, like Selkirk, is alone, and has to forage for himself; Defoe gives a lively description of Crusoe's efforts in making a shelter, finding and catching food, examining the island. But one day he sees a footprint in the sand, and realises that he is not alone. His solitude is broken, however, by a man worse off than he is; if he is caught by the tribe he has escaped from he will be cooked and eaten. Man Friday becomes his servant (note the class distinction even in such *extremis*), but his utopian loneliness has ended. Defoe must have realised that there is a sterility at the heart of the story: Man Friday is not enough. But is self-sufficiency enough?

In a very different vein, there is Superman, a child's dream of goodness. It should not be ignored or dismissed as unworthy of examination. The figure has the lineaments of the *deus ex machina*, not least because of his quickchanges between the ordinary Clark Kent and the supernormal cloaked figure, whose utopian tasks are invariably in the form of putting down evil and working for good; it should be remembered that the figure began life as a character in a child's comic paper.

Superman flourished for many years, inculcating his message of upholding the laws – the written and unwritten ones – and defying and overcoming the multifarious villains. Striking testimony to the enduring myth (and every myth that endures must have a core of meaning) is the fact that long after the figure had disappeared from the popular scene, overtaken by other, more modern such heroes, he returned brought up to date, and ready once more to do battle with evil, in a further series of successful, more sophisticated, films.

That leads to the very centre of Science Fiction, and the way that Utopia has used it.

It is difficult, indeed impossible, to say just when real science fiction began, but in their monumental and exhaustive study of the subject, *Trillion Year Spree*, Brian Aldiss and David Wingrove give the honour to Mary Shelley, with *Frankenstein*. Since then, as their 688 pages testify, science fiction has proliferated in an almost infinite number of directions; moreover, Aldiss and Wingrove say at the outset that "Science fiction is one of the major literary success areas of the second half of the twentieth century", and thus make it sensible for seekers of other worlds, however imaginary, to trawl through this genre.

We must tip-toe round *Erewhon* for the moment, but Jules Verne and his ingenious imagination offer amusement and admiration; even he, though, cannot solve our problem. Nor does William Morris exhaust the possibilities. Edward Bellamy, a neglected utopian, places his world in Boston, and offers a musical solution with his *Looking Backward*:

> If we could have devised an arrangement for providing everybody with music in their homes, perfect in quality, unlimited in quantity, suited to every mood and beginning and ceasing at will, we should have considered the limit of human felicity already attained.

After quoting that startlingly innocent passage, Aldiss and Wingrove can hardly be blamed for continuing "Electronics and the Sony Walkman have now brought about just such an enviable situation, and not only to Boston. Yet Bostonians do not claim to have reached the limits of human felicity thereby".

Exploring the realms of science fiction in the search for perfect worlds, however, the explorer comes up against an extraordinary phenomenon – extraordinary, that is, by the standards of all other fields in which utopian thought is to be found flourishing. Throughout the world of science fiction, a very considerable preponderance of imagined worlds are dystopias, worlds where evil reigns, where catastrophe is everywhere, where hope is absent, where all the universes are alike in rejecting harmony, beauty, happiness, virtue, peace, love itself.

The most cursory examination of science fiction's attitudes to Utopia meets words like strange, alien, void, dehumanised, tyranny, dark, reduced, sober, apocalyptic, frightening, brutal, terror, emptiness – until it seems that the entire lexicon has been pressed into service to cry down perfect worlds and revel in wicked ones.

Of course this is not the whole picture, and there are ventures into utopian worlds, but they are few. Lord Dunsany (who, strange to tell, has less than a sentence in Aldiss and Wingrove) wrote copiously in a primitive form of science fiction, and one of his stories might, although tangential, go a little way to redress the balance. In Dunsany's ingenious tale a traveller among the stars alights on a planet where he finds a people far ahead of our own earth; they are beautiful, honourable, selfless, truthful, peaceful – they are the very Houyhnhnms of their world. What, then, holds them back from establishing a perfect world? The traveller finds out quickly, when a huge and hideous creature picks up one of the beautiful people and eats her. They explain that, through the aeons, the creatures have got ahead in evolution, and the humans are, in effect, the equivalent of chickens in a run. Dunsany's voyager stays long enough to break the hold of the creatures, and perfection reigns at last.

But why the general tilt against Utopia in science fiction? Why – for that it must be – the pessimism? The clue is to be found in the chronology of trends in science fiction; as the real world gets darker, so does the writing about the unreal world. The nuclear stand-off must have been paramount in such pessimism; if it was quite likely that the world – the real world – might be destroyed in a flash, gloom was a reasonable response. (And as any collector of genres will understand, the tone of science fiction could not stray very far from the tone of its customers.) Tyranny in the real world, collapse of empires in the real world, war in the real world, this was hardly the stuff of optimism and Utopia. Significantly, science fiction had followed the flag when the first Sputnik went up in 1957. (A better example is the collapse of the Eastern Empire and the liberation of the Helot states. Is science fiction taking note and becoming more optimistic?)

There had been a great deal of pessimistic writing in the genre, and voices had been heard to say that it could be dangerous. C.S. Lewis, who wrote a great deal of science fiction, was in no doubt that it was dangerous, and Thomas Molnar, in his book *Utopia: The Eternal Heresy*, condemned the very idea of imagining a world other than the one we have.

It is worth examining some of his charges; since he writes that "Utopian thinking is itself evil", we may have found the ultimate utopian pessimist. Thus, he says that "...the utopian is convinced that, once we acknowledge the desirability of an ideal state of affairs, we must immediately proceed to bring it about; any hesitation or reckoning with obstacles is an unforgivable scandal in his eyes".

Molnar condemns modern science because it "leads the utopian to believe that the path to perfection has become considerably shorter", and he goes further in saying that "To save both God and the believer from future embarrassment, the religious utopian would like to limit their relationship to a purely moral one...". But "...utopian systems never speak of the individual; they always speak of mankind". And "...Mankind's attempts at total, utopian integration will manage to move forward only on that day when artificial sentiments are torn out by the roots and replaced by false feelings and aspirations...". He sums up:

At Utopia's roots there is defiance of God, pride unlimited, a yearning

139

for enormous power and the assumption of divine attributes with a view to manipulating and shaping mankind's fate. The utopian is not content with pressing men into a mould of his own manufacture; he is not a mere despot...His real vice is, first, the desire to dismantle human individuality through the dissolution of individual conscience and consciousness, and then to replace these with the collectivity and coalesced consciousness...Caligula wished that mankind had only one head, so that he might chop it off with one blow. So, too, the utopian; he wants to deal with one entity so as to simplify his own task of transforming indomitable human nature into a slave...the utopian, in his speculation, ignores human nature, the rhythm of change, the fact that change involves not only gain but loss as well, the reality of time and the essential freedom of the soul...Almighty God created man with a free will, the utopian makes the human condition so rigid that freedom is excluded from Utopia. He replaces the concept of divine providence with unchangeable determinism.

A fearsome indictment; it will take more than *Close Encounters* and *E.T.* to avoid a verdict of guilty. Still, there are witnesses for the defence; one of the most highly regarded is Arthur C. Clarke. He is no pessimist, and he never loses sight of the divine spark that is in all mankind. But the weightiest of all those who can testify on Utopia's side is Tolkien. He knows that life, and for that matter death, is struggle; there is no guarantee that right will conquer, there is only a belief in individual, flawed, uncertain man. In Tolkien's quest the questors have great allies, the greatest of all being Gandalf the wizard, but it is the ordinary folk from the Shire who finally achieve the great task, despite failures, back-sliding, corruption and – above all – the terrible temptation to use the Ring, not to destroy it. No one who touches such terrible pitch escapes without scars, which is another utopian truth of mankind, but Bilbo Baggins and his friends win through – win, that is, by holding fast to the mightiest truth of all: that no one is perfect, but all have some perfection.

But there is more to be said about Tolkien and his work, much more. Whether he would have been pleased to find it coupled here with that of Wagner is another matter. Yet there are great affinities.

Geometrical perfection is the circle; that is why the problem of "squaring the circle" (used as a cliché meaning attempting the impossible) has so tantalised mathematicians and many outside the confines of mathematics.

But the circle has always had an immense power, as a symbol, as a token, as a portent, as a heavenly body, as a source of legend, as infinity, and as a profoundly utopian symbol.

Its most obvious quality is its infinite shape; it has no resting-place, and no point on it is superior to any other. Wherever it is touched, it is sure to be exactly the same distance from its centre as any other point on it. It is almost a definition of geometry.

It defies exhaustion; however many times a seeker of its mystery goes round it, he always comes back to where he started from. No wonder its role in myth is more central and significant than any other shape, as calling it a ring will immediately show; it has the central place in countless ceremonies and other significant situations, from the wedding-ring that binds a love, to the token that shows a messenger's news is true. And so potent and so deep a symbol is it, that it is inevitably to be found in religion and in art (which, after all, centuries ago were one). From the aborigine drawing a circle in the dust, to the stone circles and their still unravelled meaning, the circle in its form as ring has been so tenacious in its hold on us that it is impossible to ignore it.

Two men, one in the previous century and the other in the present one, have seized on this mighty utopian metaphor, and both have made a huge artistic creation out of it, each deliberately sinking himself as deeply as possible in the myth from which it sprang. Of course, there have been hundreds of creations based on that same symbol, but these fall so far short compared to the two which predominate that comparison would be wasted. One of these enterprises is a work of music which demands of the listener four nights to hear; the other is a work of literature which demands of the reader three massive volumes to get through.

Richard Wagner's *Ring des Nibelungen*, and J.R.R. Tolkien's *The Fellowship of the Ring*, have many qualities and even themes in common, but one of the similarities is so striking, and so obviously meaningful, that it may begin this examination of the two works. What they share in this curious corner of their achievements is an intense hatred for their compositions by others; Wagner's music, and Tolkien's words, are – the word is not too strong – detested by many who respectively listen or read.

This extraordinary state of affairs is worth studying. In the arts, we enjoy some things and dislike others; those we dislike we take care not to meet again, but that is *all* we do; we certainly do not work ourselves up into a fury of hate. Yet these two artistic creations are singled out for such treatment.

We hate what we fear; an obvious truism. But why – indeed how – can we hate a work of music or a book, especially when we cannot be compelled to savour either of them? Only, surely, in this way: they touch depths in us that we would prefer to be left untouched; they open doors we struggle to keep shut; they throw back curtains we do not want drawn.

Here, the two works part company; the fear that insidiously infects our feelings when we are listening to Wagner's *Ring* is very different from those we experience in reading Tolkien's *Ring*. The first sounds depths in which lurk damnable things: murder, incest, betrayal; it also sounds depths in which shine noble things: love, unselfishness, courage. And these opposites he parades before us, two by two, insisting that they are not two but one, that damnation and nobility are inextricably entwined, that they are Siamese twins, joined for ever in weal or woe. Wagner, in the *Ring*, denies us the comfort of shutting out of our minds the darkness that is in every human being, and without which no human being can be complete. But we *want* that comfort, and we *want* that shutting out, because what is happening to us is discovering the underside of Utopia. Even if we flee, the demons he has uncaged will travel behind us wherever we go, until we nerve ourselves to turn and face them. For steeped in these flawed utopian beliefs, no wonder we recoil from what the music is telling us.

But what, meanwhile, of Tolkien?

There is certainly mystery, betrayal, violence and the rest of the Wagnerian catalogue in *The Lord of the Rings*; much more than the parallels with the Ring itself. But nobody hates Tolkien for reasons like that. The clue will be found in the *form* of the dislike of him and his elves and orcs and Gollums and wizards, to say nothing of battles and hordes and battering down walls. Whenever a Tolkien-hater is interrogated as to his phobia, the patient claims that he is sickened by the childishness, the King Arthurish uprightness, the carefully circumscribed bloodshed, the certainty from the first paragraph that the "good" will win and the "bad" will lose in the end (as indeed is the case); it is all summed up in the odious word, which designates the reason for the odium: twee.

There is a case to be heard here. In many ways, Tolkien *is* twee; some who can look on Wagner unafraid shudder at the thought of Tolkien's limp and bloodless figures. But – the same question arises – why not shut the book, throw it aside, and forget it forever? There is no power that can command anyone to read it, any more than there is a power to compel anyone to listen to Wagner's music, yet in both cases their enemies behave as though there *is* such a power, and that it is being utilised incessantly, ruthlessly and despite pleas to stop.

Just as the heavy scent of Wagner's *olla podrida*, with its unearthly – literally unearthly – passions gets up many noses, so the sweetness of the scent that Tolkien exudes makes many a reader sneeze uncontrollably. Believe it or not, it is the certainty of goodness that is hated, for goodness is just as terrifying as wickedness. St Augustine would hardly be thought to fear goodness; but in his early years he did precisely that, as the *Confessions* make clear.

It is the gulf between complete goodness in reality, and the simulacrum of it in a work of fiction, that deeply disturbs the readers of Tolkien's inescapable didactic charge. To start with, we hear almost at once of the *Fellowship* of the Ring; but fellowship is a dangerous word. There are Christian echoes in it, for one thing (Tolkien's saga, though deliberately set in pre-history, is strewn with unmistakable Christian traces); a fellowship here is not just a group of friends, but a promise unto death.

Then again, take the ring-symbolism in the book, and compare it with the musical version. At the end of the four operas, Wotan's ring has been indelibly tarnished, by his broken oath; as Valhalla and the gods burn, the ring returns to its original owners, now cleansed from the taint by fire.

And what is the decision made early in Tolkien's story, when the Fellowship are discussing *their* ring? It must be destroyed; even Bombadil, the holy innocent, is not worthy of guarding it for ever, for in his innocence he might lose it or throw it away. No, there can be only one decision: "The ring must go to the fire". Perfection, alias Utopia, is being sought here. When, but only when, the fatal ring is destroyed (and it cannot be destroyed other than by fire) perfection will have been achieved: or the ring has come full circle, as every ring must and does.

The Lord of the Nazguls must be destroyed in the fire that consumes the ring. Here is the Christian message made plain: evil exists, and it must be conquered first. St George killed a dragon, the Fellowship of the ring killed Sauron, and Christ killed the evil in anyone who was willing to do what was necessary for such a transformation.

But very many are not willing. Somewhere in Tolkien's parable a hesitant reader is faced with the kind of choice the Fellowship lived by. It is an uncomfortable meeting, for it is a demanding one. The demand takes the form of reminding the reader in question that if evil is to be conquered, somebody must be found to do the conquering. It is the gulf between the realised necessity and the failure to engage it which disturbs so many readers of *The Lord of the Rings,* or for that matter of the New Testament, and provides, as a shield against reality evaded, the condemnation of Tolkien's book. If that interpretation is a correct one, or even partly correct, it will be obvious that of all the words chosen to reject Tolkien and his mighty epic, the one furthest from the truth is "twee".

12

Eureka!

O F ALL OPTIMISTS of Utopia, Leibniz is the greatest. A gentle, reasonable scientist, he was also the most indefatigable utopianiser; the only man to match Fourier in his certainty that Utopia was just round the corner. As Fourier bombarded any influential figure to promote his scheme for perfection (or at least to put up the money), Leibniz, on a much more elevated plane, engaged in correspondence with countless crowned heads, from Louis XIV to Peter the Great, but the Utopia he wanted them to help bring to birth was no ramshackle Phalanstery or idealised Republic, it was the idea of Europe as one Christian enclave, which would in due course bring about the Christianisation even of China, and ultimately of the remotest and most savage lands.

Many scientists have put their trust in science; Leibniz was the most extreme of them all. Though his vast knowledge spread throughout most of science, his own genius (he invented the calculus in Hannover at much the same time as Newton was doing so in London) was largely algebraic, which led to his obsession with the belief that all discourse could be reduced to number, whereupon disagreement would disappear, and all languages would become one. To the last, Leibniz sought a Utopia in God's goodness and wisdom; for this peaceful soul, the familiar phrase is truly apposite: he wouldn't hurt a fly. None the less, he unwittingly left behind a time-bomb which would go off in our century. It was he who said "The present is pregnant with the future", and the midwives of that delivery have included the greatest monsters ever born. Determinism has always played a part in the search for Utopia, and it could hardly be left out. But it has been made the excuse for anything, saying as it does that the future can be predicted, or even *has been* predicted, so that there is nothing to do but await the future's arrival and applaud when it appears.

There could hardly be a greater difference between Leibniz and the philosopher who now takes the stage. Jeremy Bentham (dubbed, not altogether without reason, "the wisest fool in Christendom") is an odd fish for the utopian slab, yet he fits more than one aspect. His most famous words, "...this sacred truth – that the greatest happiness of the greatest number is the foundation of morals and legislation", have not worn well over the years, not least because he could not foretell modern totalitarianism (who could?), but even more because the principles of utility on which his reputation rests have been long discarded as flawed and inadequate. Moreover, Bentham took those principles to an unacceptable though utopian length: when he insisted that "pushpin is as good as poetry", he had to mean it.

But the case rests on his position as one of the founding fathers of the Enlightenment. It was in France, of course, that the movement came to full fruition, but the seeds had been sown in England (and Edinburgh). If the *Encyclopédie* was the flag under which the *Eclaircissement* marched, its baggage-train was full of Bentham's utilitarian logic. Discarded as it may be now, it was revered then, and the *philosophes* had been indoctrinated by it, whether they knew it or not.

Bentham was, and in effigy still is, the apostle of pure reason, and many have been – are – his acolytes. Certainty, even as the twentieth century moves towards its close, is not yet dead. To be fair to him, it must be said that Bentham was not always several feet above the ground. Economics as we know it ("the dismal science") today, must pay homage to those who devised it, starting (somewhat arbitrarily) with Ricardo, and made complete by Adam Smith. But there were a number of footprints that could only have been Bentham's. A utopian economy would be a very strange phenomenon, at least if it tried to work in the real world, but some of the most modern and ruthless economic systems have more than a whiff of utopianism about them.

There *are* monetary and financial Utopias, too. What else is the monetarism philosophy, expounded by F. A. Hayek (Hayek acknowledges his debt to von Mieses) and, on the other side of the Atlantic, Milton Friedman? Their thesis is pure utopianism: if "the market" is left alone, free of all governmental restraints and interference, prices will settle themselves in the optimum form, employment and wages will watch the arc of the pendulum swinging more and more slowly until it stops entirely at the optimum bargain between capital and labour.

But governments will not let well alone. Regulatory mechanisms, artificially fixed interest rates, minimum-wage laws, unemployment payments (it was Friedman who said that "if you pay a man when he is not working and tax him when he is, it is not surprising that you get unemployment") and the huge, matted wonderland of "benefits" that no government, however monetarist, dare touch – these and many more reins, artificially attached to a system which would work perfectly if it were left perfectly alone, prevent the ideal, the utopian ideal, of a world in which every aspect of finance is in perfect equilibrium.

Few Utopias have managed to come to terms with the problems it poses, but the general consensus is that it will not be needed, because the utopian state will take care of all its citizens' needs, so there will be no need for buying and selling. We smile at the naïveté, but we might stop smiling when we learn that some two or three years ago, a British member of parliament, in no utopian or metaphorical meaning, proposed that all citizens should be provided by the state with employment, housing, food, transport, and everything else needed, leaving the citizen to spend his money on entertainment, pleasure-travel and the other decorations of life.

Why not? That was the question on many lips, too many to go without the answer. It is because such a utopian state would be – would have to be – the master of every citizen, who would be under the direction of those who provided everything necessary. Such a Utopia would be a nightmare of power; the alarming fact in the argument was that practically nobody felt that such a proposition should be rejected out of hand.

There had been, many years before, an even more dramatic demonstration of the power of the market, though nobody noticed it at the time, and there has been remarkably little examination of it since. At the end of the Second World War, Hong Kong reverted to British rule. It had been a very impoverished colony before the war, and was much more so after the years of Japanese occupation, and there was nothing to spare from the no less impoverished British economy to put Hong Kong on its feet.

With no overall plan, no regulatory mechanisms, no zoning rules, and no "benefits" of any kind, Hong Kong created one of the most thriving centres of economic excellence and continuing expansion ever seen. The "German miracle" has been studied and commended, and certainly deserves the accolades it has had for the reconstruction of a country entirely ruined in every sense, but the "Hong Kong miracle" was, if anything, a greater miracle still.

It remains to be seen what Hong Kong becomes after 1997, when it is finally returned to Chinese rule.

★

There are masters of worlds not necessarily ruled by mighty potentates, let alone God. The great cosmographers and geographers recreated the universe with their understanding and their daring; Ptolemy, Newton, Copernicus, Galileo, Einstein and the Greeks – these explored the heavens and the earth for no recognisable gain – not even, for the most part, immortality. From the first sub-man who noticed that the heavenly lights changed their places, and one of them even its shape, to the moment when men stood upon the moon, that restless tribe, humanity, had been assiduously demanding more knowledge of the skies, as if mankind had already discovered, examined and solved all the problems of the earth. One by one the citadels fell; starting with the news that the world was not flat, and going on to the scandalous suggestion that the heavenly bodies rotated not only on their own axes but around other worlds, followed by the even more terrible thought that there might be many more civilisations to be found amid the restless stars.

Nor did the temptations stop there. There was much of the earth itself to be visited, explored and mapped.

Not only were the heaven and the earth examined under torture to reveal their secrets; later torturers, having given up the vastness of the skies and the variety of the earth, dug into the secret of what matter itself is made of, and began to examine smaller and smaller slivers of it, until they were not only dealing with items invisible to the most powerful microscopes, and next with particles so small that the scientists could not find any way of measuring them, finally beginning to hint, and then to announce, and then to cry from the housetops, that there was nothing there and never had been, and that everything, and all of us, were figments of the universe's imagination.

That was a far cry from the terror of Columbus's crew that they would get to the edge of the world and fall off. But it points to the infinite utopian longing in mankind, the longing to know everything that can be known. It is one of the most deeply embedded yearnings in humanity's nature, and it was put some two thousand years ago by Virgil: *Felix qui potuit rerum cognoscere causas*, or "Happy the man who can find out the causes of things". And the yearning never ceases; there are people who are genuinely troubled by the likelihood that they will die before they know whether there are other forms of advanced life. The feeling can easily be distinguished from mere inquisitiveness, for in most of the knowledge we seek in vain there is nothing conceivable from which we could gain other than the knowledge itself.

This yearning is probably a measure of the briefness of our lives, which makes it impossible for us to know everything that is already known, or indeed one thousandth of it; but to know that there is a much vaster universe of knowledge that *nobody* knows sets off utopian aches that cannot be assuaged.

Of *course* they cannot be assuaged, because they are touching the hem of the garment of the puzzle; if we star-gaze long enough we shall be driven to the question that ultimately encompasses all the lesser questions. And the last utopian yearning is the most painful, because we are convinced, perhaps rightly, that however many millions of years the world will survive, and however many of the mysteries now closed to us will be revealed, that one will keep its secret till the end of time.

Restless men throughout the ages have sought new worlds, for riches, territory or fame. The wisest have travelled for none of these things, but for wisdom, understanding and knowledge; all, however, are in some sense utopians. Yet the very idea of travelling to unknown lands is strange. No one seems to know how the concept of other places arose, though presumably it began when men could *see* other territories; the English Channel is narrow enough to make out what became Europe, and the most intrepid cave-men left their caves and embarked in whatever form of boat they were capable of making. But what about the continents, with thousands of miles of empty ocean between them? The explorations of Thor Heyerdahl have proved his point; drifting on a raft with no more means of propulsion than the capricious currents, man can, and certainly did, find lands they could hardly have imagined. But that does not answer the most important question: *why* would men embark on such a journey without knowing if there was anything on the other side – particularly when the idea of a side would have been unimaginably strange?

Is it simply daring, this wanderlust that seems to be buried deeply in all mankind, the daring to do something that others do not dare to? If so, it persists, as witness the modern anthropologist, who thinks nothing of making his life for years on end in some almost impenetrable jungle or desert to study (in centuries gone by, it would of course have been to rob) the lives and customs of the inhabitants, for no more reward than the respect from other anthropologists when the book based on the years-long study is published in an edition of perhaps 750 copies. (The author once asked an anthropologist who had recently returned from a long sojourn among the people of the interior of the Amazon jungle whether the people had any idea of their geography. The answer was "Ten miles all round".)

Presumably, every expedition to a land which turns out, for good or ill, very different from the land the voyagers have left, has its meed of approbation; there is a very powerful propensity in the West to envy the quality of life elsewhere, the elsewhere almost invariably being a state with a governing system that allows no dissent.

There is, of course, an immense literature of *imagined* travels, of which Montesquieu's *Lettres Persanes* is one of the most charming, and even Shakespeare admitted the "anthropophagi, and men whose heads do grow beneath their shoulders". Again, he leaped the centuries, as he did and does again and to this day; the anagrammatic Caliban is portrayed *both* as an ineducable savage and as a deeply wronged creature: "You taught me language, and the profit on't, is I know how to curse".

Nowadays travel has become an enormous world-wide industry, with very little that is utopian about it. Yet there are still places to lift the heart of the least informed tourist, and there are even mysteries which no one can unravel. No wonder Caliban is so ambiguous a figure.

But in what tongue could the original explorers of old speak to the people they found? (To say nothing of the explorers of today with their blue-rinsed hair and their implacable determination to speak no language but their own.) One of the most persistent utopian beliefs is that if the nations could speak to each other fluently and without misunderstanding there could be no more wars, or even disputes. But that would mean that all the peoples of all countries would have to be able to speak all the other languages of the earth, an inverted Babel so absurd as to be not even worth the stuff of science fiction. After all, are there no dissensions among the British, the French, the Polynesian, just because they speak the same language, if indeed they do?

Never mind; the dream is at hand; a language that all can, and should, speak, *together with their own*. There have been many such attempts; but only one has survived, and that one only tenuously.

Esperanto is an ingenious blend of many Anglo-Saxon and romance languages; English (ill-disguised) predominates. Its vocabulary is limited, and two fluent Esperantists, with not a word of each other's native languages, could have a real, though very dull, conversation. But the question comes: why should they? Real languages can be learned; for those who cannot master other tongues there are guide-books and phrase-books (it is said that the monoglot Englishman abroad needs only one sentence to be safe: "the gentleman over *there* will pay"), and if all fails there is sign-language.

And sign-language is far more powerful than is widely realised. Pointing, waving, moving the body in scores of ways, facial changes, acting out wishes (to eat, for instance) – these versions of communication have a huge vocabulary, which lays dormant until needed. The author demonstrated as much when he visited Easter Island, which is literally the most remote place in the world; but sign-language was found to be wholly adequate.

Another utopian aspect of language has arisen in Israel. Hebrew is the official language, and indeed the authorities frown on those who do not speak it, but use whatever the language they were brought up with. But although Hebrew is the language of scripture, there are no references in the Old Testament to vacuum-cleaners, submarines, hay fever, television or sliced bread (unless that was manna). All these things and many more are being turned into Hebrew by Israeli scholars, and very comical many of them must be, though not as comical as the languages now being created in which it is hoped that we shall be able to communicate with extra-terrestrial beings when they come to our earth or we to theirs.

So powerful is this utopian propensity that individuals have created entire languages, and though of course many of these language-makers are eccentrics (or utopians), some have been serious scientific endeavours, such as *Interglossa*, created by Lancelot Hogben. Yet none has ever succeeded in convincing any substantial number of linguists and scientists, let alone ordinary people with a single language to their name, that the effort would be worthwhile. Annually, there is an Esperanto convention (in a different country each time, no doubt) in which the delegates presumably speak only in Esperanto. These gatherings are reported, but less and less interest is shown, and although the devotion to this bastard language shows no sign of waning, it shows also no sign of recruiting any substantial number of new adherents. *Requiescat in pace.*

13

The lame and the halt and the doctor

A ND NOW we come to Utopia's Utopia; the Idea of Progress. It is sometimes argued that the undoubted technological advances in modern times (say from near the end of the nineteenth century) and their equally undoubted exponential march into the future (especially from the end of the Second World War and the introduction of the computer) do not point to the progress the world has made, but insist that these advances *are* the progress. That is an exclusively mechanistic view, but it has a good deal of weight behind it. When we look, however, at the condition of mankind away from his technology, the story changes dramatically. We see hunger, epidemic disease (notably now Aids), oppression and the steadily diminishing numbers in countries – advanced and backward alike – who feel no need of anything other than what can be understood by the five senses.

Closely allied to this last expulsion of the numinous is the emptiness of the lives of increasing numbers of people who have as many modern labour-saving devices as anyone could require, yet feel (or, worse, do not feel) that their lives are meaningless to them.

A case, then, can be made out for rejection of the mechanistic form of progress, and for an insistence on the claim that we have not progressed in, say, the last half century, and that indeed we have actually regressed. Surely, if man is steadily climbing the stony path, and as he turns every bend sees a view finer than the last, he cannot proclaim the news of eternal progress if behind a bush on the miraculous climb there lurk villains who, just as he is about to tell the world his news, pounce on him and kill him.

But that argument will never be finished; indeed it cannot be, because there will always be differences among individuals as to what things are good, useful and beneficial. The argument should be not whether progress has always proceeded and is still doing so, but why it *should* have done, and should have continued in its generous course. For even the most thankful believer in an eternal progress must admit that there is no logical reason for it to continue, even though we do not have to go so far as David Hume, who argued that if he put a match to a piece of paper and it burned, as he had always found that it did, the test is nevertheless no proof that the next piece of paper and match will not behave in a significantly different manner.

Wherever we want to go, we are wasting our time in enlisting prophecy as our guide, for prophecy, by its nature, has never been there before. All closed systems are prophetical; Sir Karl Popper has spent most of his immense life combating the poisoned belief that destiny is already in the womb and that the midwife of certainty is hastening to the accouchement.

The gap in the logic, however, has never been an obstacle. The idea of an indefinite advance of mankind is one of the most tenacious beliefs mankind has ever grasped, and there is still no sign of its being cast aside. It must be rooted in a profound though unconscious utopian optimism, and when science joins hands with a pseudo-scientific system, Utopia reigns. The very words "scientific socialism" immediately make clear that we are not dealing with the real world. When, a few slogans later, we hear of the "withering away of the state", we can be sure that whichever state is meant it will not wither away. Nor, when we call upon "historical inevitability", shall we need to pause and wonder whether there is such a thing.

But Great Science herself is not entirely blameless. She can, and does, say that she gives us the tools and it is no concern of hers what we do with them. Perhaps; but too many scientists have fallen into the utopian propensity, and the consequences have been most ungiftlike. To start with, they have not remained in their laboratories, but have come out clad in the mantle of philosophy. Bacon's *New Atlantis* hovers between the two, but there is nothing ambiguous about Comenius and his *General Consultation of the Improvement of all Things Human*. Science has given us the computer, automation, the microchip, and many another boon, but she also gave us tranquillisers, in her innocent arrogance.

Here we may pause for an explanation from science, and explanation of one of science's wickedest actions, which involved an arrogance far from innocent. It is science's task to search the universe and the atom alike, and the search, as science repeatedly says, must be, and is, treated to the most rigorous testing before it can be pronounced worthy of science. Then how did so many scientists, many of them among those of the greatest renown, reject any such examination when it was most sorely needed? (The dupes discussed earlier had some excuse; these had none.) With no attempt at enquiry, many of the greatest scientists in the world – Joliot-Curie, Haldane, Bernal, Levy, Julian Huxley – these betrayed their calling, their intellect and their countries; they went a-whoring after strange gods, and pretended that those gods were benign and all-knowing instead of the demons they actually were.

This is the arrogance not of physical power but of mind. The minds of those scientists were in a world that lesser men and women could not enter; they could not understand half a dozen words of the language spoken by the scientists. But although the ordinary people could not speak in tongues as the geniuses could, they knew the difference between right and wrong, evil and good, sense and absurdity. The scientists' utopian contempt for all outside the magic circle of knowledge led to a *trahison des clercs*, and the reason consisted of forgetting that knowledge is not enough: wisdom is also essential. The ordinary men and women who could not understand the knowledge could and did understand the wisdom; alas, they were not in time to pass it on.

Perhaps even more to the point is the career of Werner von Braun, which should be a lesson to all those who believe either that science is neutral or that its practitioners take heed to make it so. Having spent the Second World War in the Nazi interest, perfecting the then most destructive and dreadful armaments existing, in the form of rockets crammed with high-explosives, he was invited to create a rocket that would be sufficiently powerful to take men to the moon – invited, that is, by the United States government, all passion spent.

★

We can smile at Leibniz's claim that everything can be reduced to algebra: Bertrand Russell (who, near the end of his life, made a fool of himself more spectacular, though less dangerous, than any dupe among the ranks of the *trahisonistes*) asked of the universe a memorable question: "Why does number hold sway above the flux?" No one has yet answered it; but then, no one has yet reduced everything to algebra.

Yet it cannot be denied that science is regarded by the laity as a magic wand with which the scientist-conjuror brings forth his prodigies. When the moon-visit project was under way, there was science-fiction talk of permanent space-stations in fixed orbits, gravity-free. Well, before men stood on the moon, such endeavours were commonplace, and real science was seeking fresh worlds to conquer. To start with, if human beings can be gravity-free, why should they not be disease-free, pain-free, anxiety-free, sorrow-free? To go on with, genetic engineering, again originally to be found only in science fiction, has already taken giant steps, and there is talk of perfect beings achieved by reassembling the chromosomes of the imperfect present.

The utopianism that runs through the scientific world is inevitable; we return to the point at which science gives us what we want from it (though, unfortunately, also what we do not need and even should not have from it) and we are then responsible for the use we put it to. There is a conspiracy between science and its beneficiaries; the latter egg on the former to proclaim the imminent perfect Utopia of total knowledge. Nor is this an entirely megalomaniac concept; there is a simple but powerful symbol of reality to hand, which strengthens the claim. Long before all the planets we can now see were located, science predicted where they would eventually be found, and they were right.

The science of eugenics has fallen into desuetude; it became tangled in matters concerning race, and dabbled in theories of superior and inferior races. Purged of such notions, it could be a powerfully utopian weapon; Shaw, in *Back to Methuselah*, his most didactic (and most costive) play, argued that the human race would never solve its problems until it lived much longer than at present, for the brief span we have now is not sufficient to acquire the necessary knowledge and understanding.

The wheel comes full circle; Darwin's *Origin of Species* outraged Victorian society, accused as they were of being descended from apes. That was a misunderstanding, but in their indignation they missed the good news that Darwin was bringing them. If the human race has evolved as he believed, it has climbed step by step upwards, through the unseen and impartial test of natural selection. But if that was so, there was no reason to believe that the process had stopped when Homo Sapiens appeared on the scene. When the Victorians calmed down, they presumably agreed that they were a part of a never-ending chain of improvement, possibly taking in such concepts as Shaw's demand for greater longevity. But if that was so, the idea of an inevitable progress was back, however fallacious it might be, and however unprovable it certainly is.

Still the search, the hunt, for completeness, wholeness, perfection, goes on. It goes into some odd corners, shining a torch in the hope of seeing the gleam of the great treasure, the secret of encompassing *everything*, when at last we can all lay down our spades and rest forever. Yet, who but a convinced utopian would dare to claim that it is possible for all sentient creatures to be classified and docketed in an orderly and logical manner, from *homo sapiens* to the amoeba, from the elephant to the ladybird, from the ravenous crocodile to the comforting koala, from the weird orang-utan to the familiar cat? And who, not content with such an endeavour, insists that even the non-sentient phenomena of the earth can equally be lined up in columns of species, from the mighty oak to the lowly pebble, from the pond to the ocean, from the sands of the shore to the snows of the mountain?

Was it some madman, some charlatan, imposing his absurd utopian dreams on anyone who would listen, while he fingered a crumpled sheet of paper on which the cabalistic runes were inscribed? No, it was one of history's greatest naturalists, Georges-Louis, Comte de Buffon, whose dog-eared scrap of scribbled-on waste paper turned into an unfinished work comprising, at Buffon's death, 44 volumes, and which went a very long way towards just such a classification, which still commands reverence from today's naturalists, with their infinitely more powerful and extensive knowledge and means of gathering it.

But, it may be said, Buffon dealt in *things*, whether the rhinoceros of the lake or the berry of the hedgerow. They could be seen, heard, even examined in detail, from the circulation of the blood in hyenas to the wing-speed of the may-fly. How, though, can such a universal classification of *ideas* be accomplished? The answer comes: it cannot, and it is as great a waste of time to search for it as it would be to chase after the elixir of life or the alchemical means of changing base metal into gold.

Nevertheless, that too has been done, and the whole literate world has its progenitor to thank for simplifying its life, while within that world librarians are not content merely to thank him, but go down on their knees at his memory. For he was the man who invented (at the age of twenty-two) the library decimal classification that rightly bears his name: Melvil Dewey. He took 10 sections of knowledge, and each of the 10 spawned, under his guidance, 100 sub-divisions, and from each of those he extracted another

100, and – but it is obvious that the system is capable not only of encompassing all the knowledge mankind is heir to, but also an infinitely extendable hospitality to knowledge that has not yet been discovered.

Equipped with a mighty throng of decimals, he went out to sow his system, which was simplicity itself to operate, once the hardly less simple principle was understood. Music, say, has a section to itself, as befits so great a body of learning and example; let us give it the number 200. There are very many aspects of music, so some of these will fall under the number 210. But in that part of music there are further, smaller aspects to be classified, so our grand number is now 215. But music is by no means finished, so the decimal point is called in, and beyond it, there are more sub-divisions which, so many numbers ago, amounted to "Music". (If you are reading this book, and got it from a public library – a practice authors cannot but deplore, greatly preferring purchase – you will find, normally on the spine, the number 321.07. That is the Dewey classification number which, several sub-divisions ago, was headed "Sociology".)

There is something almost eerie in the thought of that ingenious youth who, in 1873, enabled the world to classify, as to its subject-matter, every book in the world and every book that will ever be written, and to do so with nothing but a few digits. But it strengthens the search for an all-embracing order, a search deep in so many people, and over so many centuries, that demonstrates the hunger for a utopian comprehensiveness, a certainty that the subject is complete.

The Table of the Elements perhaps illustrates that yearning at its most intense; it does need expert guidance to understand the principle. An element is something found in nature; it is the simplest (that is how we get the word "elementary") item of matter into which matter can be broken without breaking it into its nuclear particles. Each element has a certain number of protons in the nuclei of its atoms, and no two elements have the same number. As each of these substances was discovered, a list was compiled; it was dubbed the Table of the Elements. But since no two are identical in the proton-count, the Table, reasonably enough, lists elements by the number of protons they are heir to. And it turned out that the proton-count goes up in a regular way; that is to say, the gap between any two adjacent elements in the Table is the same as between any other two.

Or rather, it almost is; there are some jumps wider than most, breaking the symmetry, and the scientists attribute the irregularities to elements *which have not yet been discovered.*

"You may chase out nature with a pitchfork, but she will come running back"; even the elements of which everything is made obey nature – and so obedient are they that they are willing to help nature in her course. The discovery that there are elements which have not yet been discovered inevitably intensified the search for the missing ones; gradually, they have been found, but not yet all. They must exist somewhere; nature makes no mistakes. But here is another utopian Grail, which will be sought over the years, until the missing links are found, and there will be no dearth of seekers, so powerful is the lust for perfection, for a world in which all is known, so that Buffon and Dewey alike can cease from their labours. If that world is ever created, and those who sought it so assiduously enter their kingdom at last, they may find cause not for rejoicing but for dismay. If there are no mountains to climb, nor giants to fight, no elements to discover, what will become of the search for the highest mountain, the greatest giant, the last element? Will it be their Utopia, another example of the truth that the worst thing that can happen to us is for us to get what we ask for?

Throughout the centuries, the only certainty in mankind's life has been death. The *meaning* of death still escapes us, though many theories have been tried out, none convincing. We know, then, that we must die, and until modern times – very modern, hardly earlier than the 1960s – that conclusive fact has been embedded in the deepest recesses of our minds and souls. We may wish that nature or God or the frailty of the body (whichever it is) had not laid down the rule, but we know that we cannot evade it, and we should, in our different ways, be poised to accept it when our time comes.

Until, that is, only the other day (only the other second if we use as the measure the time conscious man has been on earth), when we began to believe – we being the western world, and particularly America – that we can, contrary to all the evidence, live for ever.

A number of causes have come together to make the astonishing claim. For instance, the last remnants of what was once a world, based however loosely and naïvely, in which there were religious roots or foundations, have almost disappeared. There is therefore very little spiritual feeling, in whatever shape, to correct the ridiculous error. Again, and paradoxically, modern living conditions have improved greatly, so that we are living longer than our ancestors, even our immediate ancestors. In addition, the Second World War, which had not long ended (a mere fifteen years when the 1960s were upon us), had inured us to the ever-present possibility of violent death without warning; when, abruptly, that threat was withdrawn, the understandable sigh of relief turned into a refusal to believe that other and less dramatic forms of death were still active, and that no armistice or surrender terms had been signed.

The greatest contribution (apart, of course, from plain fear) to the growing belief in immortality was (more irony) the remarkable advances in curative medicine, which very quickly were overwhelmed by surgical and other means that not long before would have been confined to the more lurid forms of science fiction.

Organ transplants, rapidly including lungs and hearts; cloning; *in vitro* conception; the mysterious initials DNA, which did more than anything to persuade the persuadable (almost everyone) that by juggling chromosomes the elixir of life was at hand. In vain were the few voices of reason raised against the stampede for life everlasting (Malcolm Muggeridge went further, and denounced the new-found transplanting, to the bewilderment of most). In no time, there were moves to persuade us all (some wanted it to be compulsory) to carry a card which, if the holder died abruptly, in a car-accident, for instance, would state that he or she was willing to release the body from any form of interment, so that the still useful parts could be rushed to the nearest hospital where a patient who needed a better heart, lung, liver or kidney could be rapidly accommodated. After a time, there was hardly any need for rushing; there were even hospitals which collected such bodily treasure-trove and kept a human spare-parts cold-store, from which a withdrawal could be made whenever necessary.

It had started with blood; when science found out how to take blood from a living body and store it for use, generous people were willing to give a pint of blood, which for most people is in no way dangerous or even disagreeable, to be stored in a hospital "blood-bank" as it was called, for the use of ill or injured patients who needed a blood transfusion. This eliminated the necessity of having the giver of the blood present and side by side with the patient who was to receive the blood.

That is now familiar, of course, but in the familiarity a curious use of metaphor was popularised, and is now firmly embedded in the language; one who gave blood was called a blood-donor, but those whose bodily organs were used, post-mortem, in this form, were also known as donors, though they had not actually donated anything, since a corpse can neither give nor receive. It is a tiny point, but like many tiny points, it is important;

in this case it may signal an unease, carefully stifled and even more carefully buried, in what was being done in the name of modern medicine and its beneficiaries. The word donor, used inappropriately, was there to quiet the unease.

Amid the exchange and mart of bodies, the tide of demanded immortality was steadily rising, and indeed shows no sign of slackening; in the United States doctors whose patient dies, though no error or negligence is involved or even suggested, are finding themselves being sued by the surviving relatives. Nor does the belief that a sufficiently expert doctor can cure death (and in advance, too), exhaust the possibilities of modern medicine. If we can keep the means of conception in a refrigerator, surely we can choose to specify which male or female half of the conjunction (according to the sex of the enquirer)? Can we not mate the brave and the fair without them even meeting? Shall we, in time, pay substantial sums for the precious sperm of the latest genius of science or art? (Or, alas, more likely, the latest pop-singer?) Certainly it is medically possible, and as we have learned over the years, anything that is possible will sooner or later be done. It is a far cry from Hippocrates.*

But there was to come, under the strictest medical auspices, something so far in the future, yet ready to hand, that it was, and is, difficult to believe that it could be anything other than a dream or an implausible novel; or, of course, a claim by Utopia.

Oliver Sacks, in his explorations of schizophrenia and allied disorders, found underground rivers of meaning in what had till then been classified as nothing but madness. Sacks, in particular, opened eyes that had long been shut, and not only because he did so quite literally.

It was generally agreed in the scientific world, and far more in the ordinary non-expert world, that if meticulous and independent observation of what he achieved with his drug L-dopa had not been exercised, he would have been dismissed as a charlatan or a madman far madder than any of his patients. For instance, in a single dose of his potion, a woman who had been totally silent and immobile, in the most profound catatonic trance, for forty years without the slightest break, got out of her chair and ran down the ward, talking quite coherently as she did so.

That was only one of Sacks's dozens of "miracles", many of which were more remarkable than that. But one of his achievements not only beggars

*As this book closed for press, all those questions were being answered in the affirmative.

belief, though perfectly true, it points a utopian moral "deeper than did ever plummet sound". (Indeed, the moral not only goes deep, but puts in question the entire utopian thesis. It is said that "God is not mocked", but this must come closer to mocking him than anything in his experience. For it proclaims that the search for Utopia is, and always will be, a chimerical waste of time. A fine thing to discover so far into this book!)

Another of his patients was a man who had been paralysed in every muscle and every part of his body, but one: he could move his right big toe. Long before Sacks appeared on the scene, he had trained himself, with the help of the hospital staff, to operate a letter-board on which he could, with the one toe that was available to him, spell out his wants.

And not only his wants. Letter by letter, word by word, he tapped out a massive autobiography, some 50,000 words long, describing his life (such as it was), his feelings, his rage against the universe that had destroyed his body. Sacks injected the appropriate dose of L-dopa into him, and lo! a miracle, for which Sacks might well have said to the patient "Go, pick up thy bed and walk", for walk he could, and talk, too.

After a time, however, taking the drug regularly now, the man began to show the symptoms of schizophrenia, and also began to be violent. Sacks reduced the dose, whereupon the man's original paralysis began to set in again. Sacks increased the dose again, whereupon the violence returned. Little by little, as the pendulum swung between the two states, Sacks (and, presumably, his patient) realised what was happening: the arc of the pendulum was getting smaller all the time, and soon it would stop. It did stop; but it stopped – and would not stop anywhere else – exactly where the man got up off his bed, cured. He was back, paralysed, dumb and totally immobile apart from his right big toe.

The story does not stop there; if it did, it would teach us no lesson in the world of the innermost utopian soul. The twice-stricken man, just as before, began to write, and this time wrote another autobiography, even longer than the first. But this time, as he made clear, he had realised that his destiny had all along been to suffer, and to learn through his suffering. His miraculous cure had been a mirage, real though it was, and he was doomed to be the same man, in the same condition, that he had been at first, though now he had found that inner peace, which before had been a rage against earth and sky. Content at last, he had accepted his fate. *Nunc dimittis.*

In contemplating the heroic life of the paralysed man, it is almost impossible to avoid comparisons; how would we face such a life, would we be able to reconcile ourselves to our fate, would we yearn for death? Then we scale down the comparisons; we have a toothache, and just as we are about to complain we remember the man with his one big toe. We go out into the rain, and find ourselves cursing our forgetfulness in not taking an umbrella; then we see a blind man, just as wet, but also sightless.

There are scales everywhere, are there not? But those scales have, in one strange particular, been put aside. Instead of weighing one great misfortune against one trivial one, the trivial one has been elevated to rule, with no elective authority. What would the paralysed man say, in his second autobiography, all passion spent, about this extraordinary happening; assuredly he would see a vast discrepancy at work.

★

Suddenly, but from what source no one has discovered, a wave of utopian cleanliness swept over the advanced world. This cleanliness was by no means a general cleaning-up – of littered streets, say, or neglected paintwork on houses, or of the crisis of drug-abuse, or the nation's apparently eternal precarious economy, or the inexorably rising tide of crime. No, it was quite startlingly specific, confined to the single issue of smoking, which almost overnight was proclaimed the greatest evil in the world, so that those who practised the unspeakable vice were to be judged as outcasts, *hostis humani generis*, creatures that any man's hand could be lifted against without penalty – indeed with acclamation.

The use of tobacco was, of course, many centuries old, but only recently – hardly more than a decade before the outlawry of smokers began – it was established beyond argument (though arguments did break out) that there was a direct and inevitable connection between the practice and a number of serious diseases, including severe and often fatal cancers. This led, rightly, to a massive campaign of enlightenment; smokers were not to be left in ignorance of the danger they were running. The result was a satisfactory reduction in the numbers of smokers (a decline which continues), and there was no doubt that the message had been heard and understood; there could have been, and *a fortiori* can be, no one in the land who does not know the dangers of smoking.

Many smokers shrugged off the warnings; there could be no certainty of infection (true), and the risk was felt to be less than the loss of the pleasures of tobacco. In addition, many smokers found it difficult to break the smoking habit; it was a genuine addiction, from which they wished to be delivered, but presumably did not have the will-power to break the chains.

Then the persecution – the word is not too grave – began. In the sure and certain belief that the Tobacco Menace had to be eradicated, the eradicators plunged into an *auto-da-fé* of heretics who professed the devil's creed: "We smoke".

The United States has a murder rate of approximately 32,000 a year, which works out at one person in 6250; there is no fully civilised and democratic country anywhere else in the world with a rate more than one in roughly 660, roughly one-eleventh of the American slaughter. The crashing of beams and the outpouring of motes might be thought, then, to be a familiar sound in that country, but no; the shame is directed not against the bestial slaughter, which is almost entirely ignored, but against those who smoke, doing themselves, not innocents, their own harm. (The persecution there goes so far as, for instance, the dismissal of an employee for smoking not at his smoking-banned place of employment but *in his own home*.) Could there be a more extravagant definition of the utopian purging required to change mankind, whether mankind liked it or not?

This purging, and the extravagant fanaticism employed on it, cannot be, and plainly is not, a matter of health. (Very frequently, there are claims that smokers cost the nation billions of pounds in hospital care; the figures are all arbitrary and manifestly absurd, yet they are widely accepted, so far has the abandonment of reason gone.) Somehow, a reasonable health warning has turned into a demand for a demented utopian perfection, and has grown into a menace to civilised and free nations, a menace, moreover, that has singled out one section of society to be the pariah. What is the meaning of this witch-hunt, a hunt so virulent, impeccable, self-righteous, convinced and ignorant, that its like has not been seen in Britain since the Popish Plot (which, it should be remembered, was also entirely spurious)? And did no one in the United States remember Prohibition, and the horrors and murders that came with it?

Why must this danger, and *only* this danger, be singled out for what is a truly totalitarian cleansing? Images of crazy purification-rites, Aztecs with their obsidian knives sacrificing to a bloodthirsty god, mad prohibitions on Jews or Freemasons, books like *Brave New World* or *Nineteen Eighty-Four*, indeed the most extravagant scenarios of science fiction – these absurd comparisons rise unbidden into this rage for sterilisation, this rush for doing good at the point of the bayonet, this – for it is truly the heart of the mystery – this choosing one dirty thing among a thousand things just as dirty and another thousand actually much dirtier.

Utopian thinking has done much harm over the centuries, and the hounding of the smokers in countries like the United States and Britain (the plague has not gone so far in most of the rest of Europe) is small beer beside some of the effects of it. But this one is unique in its inexplicability.

14

I'll burn my book

THE FIRST QUESTION, when considering Swift and his book, must be: did he write a book about Utopia? True, we can learn much from the anti-Utopias, but can satire alone bear the weight of a utopian theme?

We can start with Swift's genuine adulation of More, whom he called "a person of the greatest virtue this kingdom ever produced". Then again, the merest acquaintance with *Gulliver's Travels* reveals the influence of More, or at least the influence of More's *Utopia*. Yet Swift was not just a satirist; he was a misanthrope, one of the profoundest in history, and that is demonstrated most clearly with Gulliver's account, in talking to the King of Brobdingnag about England. It is possible to take what Swift says about his country at its face value, but only in ignorance of Swift's mind and most of his writing. Swift paints a picture of England that would indeed characterise a Utopia, but he has his paintbox as well as his tongue in his cheek.

Gulliver explains that the House of Commons is filled by upright and selfless gentlemen, who are "freely picked and culled out by the people themselves, for their great abilities and love of their country, to represent the wisdom of the whole nation". As for the House of Lords, the members are indeed, all of them, grave and reverend seigneurs, brought up in the understanding that they are to bear the entire burden of wisdom, responsibility and guidance for the nation. The Lords are pictured as beings hardly below the angels, "the ornament and bulwark of the kingdom, worthy followers of their most renowned ancestors, whose honour has been the reward of their virtue, from which their posterity was never once known to degenerate". And when Gulliver has extolled in equally passionate terms England's religious and legal elders, he has indeed portrayed Utopia. He must have winked at some point in his eulogy, for the King concludes that the reality is "The most pernicious Race of little odious Vermin that Nature ever suffered to crawl upon the Surface of the Earth".

And Swift lays all doubt when Gulliver gets to Lagado. Here, he visits a university in which he discovers (or his misanthropy does) that all the professors are mad. They must be, because

> These unhappy people were proposing schemes for persuading monarchs to choose favourites upon the score of their wisdom, capacity and virtue; of teaching ministers to consult the public good; of rewarding merit, great abilities and eminent services; of instructing princes to know their true interest by placing it on the same foundation with that of their people; of choosing for employment persons qualified to exercise them; with many other wild impossible chimeras, that never entered before into the heart of man.

But it is Gulliver's voyage to the Houyhnhnms (it is said that nobody, since the book was written, has ever been able to spell the word correctly without recourse to the text) that poses the greatest difficulty for the true understanding of Swift. In these all-wise and perfected horses, he describes what is, on the face of it, a pure and consistent Utopia; we all know that the Houyhnhnms have no word for "lie", since lying is a concept that they are unable to understand. In addition, though, they cannot be insincere, they need no government set over them, they have no laws (since they could not do anything that a law would have to deal with), they have no idea of what compulsion might be, they have few wants and no covetousness; in addition, girls have the same education as boys. Gulliver has no doubt that he has found Utopia.

> I had no Occasion of bribing, flattering or pimping, to procure the Favour of any great Man, or his Minion. I wanted no Fence against Fraud or Oppression: Here was neither Physician to destroy my Body, nor Lawyer to ruin my Fortune: No Informer to watch my Words and Actions, or forge Accusations against me for Hire: Here were no Gibers, Censurers, Backbiters, Pickpockets, Highwaymen, Housebreakers,

Attorneys, Bawds, Buffoons, Gamesters, Politicians, Wits, Spleneticks, tedious Talkers, Controversists, Ravishers, Murderers, Robbers, Virtuosos; no Leaders of Followers of Party and Faction; no Encouragers to Vice, by Seducement or Examples: No Dungeon, Axes, Gibbets, Whipping-posts, or Pillories.

Who would not want such a world? But the misanthropy reeks from the page; he is not commending the Houyhnhnms, but denouncing human beings, and it is important to remember that even before the Yahoos (he invented the word, and it has remained in the dictionary and in common use ever since) are introduced. These, of course, are the bestial forms of humankind. They are hideous, covered in hair, filthy, treacherous, cunning, impervious to any attempt at improvement, savage (they wage war), avaricious (they prize shining stones – i.e. coins), and, in short, they are everything that the Houyhnhnms are not.

If we dig a little deeper, we find that that is not exactly true. The casting out of all evil in all its forms has been achieved, but the baby of some important qualities has been thrown out with the bathwater of blemish. The Houyhnhnms are guided by reason only; there are no *innocent* passions among them. Families are patriarchal, but there is no real bond between parents and children. Time has long since stopped; there is no attempt at improvement, or understanding what improvement might be, so there is no inquisitiveness, no explorative impulse and no reason to change anything. They have no history; in addition, they have nothing that can be compared with human warmth, and they have nothing that could be recognised as love. In short, the land of the Houyhnhnms is permanently static – an affliction which strikes the great majority of Utopias. A moment's thought will show that it could hardly be otherwise: when everything is perfect why – *how* – could anyone seek to improve anything?

Gulliver, when he returns home, prefers to seek the company of his horse rather than his family; one more nail in the human race, knocked in with the hammer of misanthropy. Yet, when the reader looks back on Gulliver's experiences, there is just room enough to build a Utopia out of the scraps of benevolence in some of Gulliver's travels, together with the yearning for a world like the one the Houyhnhnms inhabit, warts and all.

To the fury of utopianism, the principle has been used as satire. Swift is the most powerful of these, but there are many more. Samuel Butler's *Erewhon* (not quite "nowhere spelt backwards") took the knife to Victorian society, and struck some deep and painful gashes. The "musical banks", for instance, from which a feeble kind of money, useless for buying anything worthwhile, can be drawn. These banks, it is clear, are the Victorian churches, their vaults stocked with the shadow money that bought nothing, not even comfort. A parallel transfiguration exchanges sickness and crime; the narrator, hoping for sympathy from a kind lady, says that he is ill with a fever, whereupon she turns on him in rage at such flaunting of his wickedness. Threatened with prosecution for catching measles, he thereafter takes care to announce that he feels a touch of crime coming on, whereupon the utmost solicitude is shown to him from all sides. Similarly, the country is ruled by wise ancients, philosophers and men with prophetic powers; these, of course, are contemporary politicians, and the narrator realises that these sages are ignorant charlatans. Butler wrote a sequel to *Erewhon*, purporting to be an account by the original narrator's son of how England is now faring. Badly, it seems; religion is now in the hands of two more inverted holy men, called respectively Hanky and Panky. (Butler was an atheist; also, he believed that the *Odyssey* and the *Iliad* were written by a woman.)

Aldous Huxley's *Brave New World* is a satirical Utopia far more savage; birth has been dispensed with, and human beings are hatched in incubators, which makes it possible to order the whole of society, allocating the appropriate number of higher and lower capacities, as required. The theme of the individual who gains or retains his personality and rejects the ordered state, sometimes defeating it, is a powerful one; it restores Utopia to its rightful place. There is such a non-conformist in *Brave New World*, but he is, significantly, a figure wholly antithetical to the surrounding ethos – indeed, he has no other name than "the Savage". (Huxley later wrote *Island*, a Utopia of benevolence rather than of horror, but it is a pallid exercise beside the earlier book, which may say something about Utopia, or at least disillusion. Or even Huxley.)

Orwell's two nightmare Utopias have deeply depressing outcomes, though the truly satirical one, *Animal Farm*, is written in an elegiac form shot through with black humour. A savage portrait of Stalin and his system, it spawned its own interior satire, when it came up against the British censorship regulations which had remained in force until the end of the Second World War; publication was due in 1945, but the war had not yet quite ended, and it was therefore still impossible to criticise our Soviet ally. Orwell, with a straight face, persuaded the censor that the novel was nothing but a children's story about pigs and horses, as witness the names of the leading characters – Snowball, Boxer and Napoleon.

The subjects of utopian lands, as we have seen, need not be human; pigs, horses, Yahoos, *in vitro* manufactures, miniature men and gigantic ones – sooner or later, it had to be penguins. In Anatole France's *Penguin Island* satire and Utopia join hands once more. Very much as Butler satirised Victorian society at the turn of the century, France savaged the same kind of *bien-pensants*. Its centrepiece is a massive and excoriating parody of the Dreyfus case, arraigning his country at the bar of the civilised world. (It is unlikely that the book is widely read today outside France, or inside either; the *roman à clef* dies when the key is lost. *Erewhon* has had a somewhat different fate; few now would read it, because the reality of today far surpasses anything that Butler invented.)

Other Utopias include E.M. Forster's *The Machine Stops*, a short story set in an absolutely static self-correcting universe, where nobody goes anywhere, because everywhere else is exactly the same. The system, as the title makes clear, begins to crumble, and eventually it collapses entirely; panic ensues, but in the last moments of the destruction that follows, a group of dissident pioneers have survived, infused as they have been with values contrary to those of the system.

There are bad Utopias with happy endings; a bad Utopia with an unhappy ending could hardly be called by the name, though of course there are Utopias, usually with a didactic purpose, which claim that if the lesson is learnt the utopians may be miserable without claiming that their Utopia has failed them.

There is a powerful tale from nineteenth-century Russia, by the minor comic novelist Saltykov-Shchedrin. (He may be classified as minor, in the shadow of Gogol, but Saltykov's satire is even more deadly, and his imagination no less wild.) The book, called *The History of a Town*, is a record of life in Glupov (stupid-town), and consists of an account of all the 21 governors who have ruled over the town, whether repressing them, flogging them, debauching them or ignoring them.

The governors themselves, in Saltykov's catalogue, include one with a musical-box in his head, another with a head stuffed with forcemeat (revealed when it was noticed that he smelt of truffles), another who claimed descent from a bell-tower in Moscow and broke in half in the great gale of 1761, and another who wrote a book called *A Description of the Lives of the Most Notable Monkeys*. Ugryum-Burcheev, the last but one governor of Glupov, whose regency ends the book with the imminent arrival of the last of them all, is possessed of a monomania for regularity, and it is the picture of what happens to the town and to him when he gives full reign to his obsession.

> In each house there would be two elderly people, two adults, two adolescents and two infants…People equal in age would also be equal in size…There would be no schools and no provision for literacy; mathematics would be taught on the fingers. There would be no past and no future, and the calendar would be abolished…Work would be done to words of command. The inhabitants would bend and straighten in time together; scythe-blades would flash, hay-forks toss, picks tap and ploughs turn the earth – all by orders…there would be no passions, enthusiasms or attachments…The whole world would move in straight lines to the beat of a drum…

Then Saltykov, through the mad governor's voice, offers a prophecy for Glupov; remember this is a novel, and the author has the last word. This, *he* tells us, is what is going to happen to the town when the last governor arrives:

> For him there is no lesson to be learned from the futility or patent harmfulness of these misdeeds. He is not concerned with the results of his actions, since they affect not him (he is too lost to feeling to be affected by anything), but some other object, with which he has no organic connection. If through the concentrated efforts of his idiocy the whole world were turned into a desert, even that would not daunt the idiot. Who knows, perhaps a desert is what he regards as the ideal setting for the communal life of man.

It seems, as the book finishes, that the powers of darkness have triumphed; where is the utopian *deus ex machina* to turn the black tide?

It comes from the most humble and patient quarter of all; a river. The more the all-powerful idiot tries to make it flow in his regulated channels, the more it escapes and wanders away, while his maps solemnly record the course it should be pursuing. He cannot dam it, he cannot divert it, he cannot drain it, he cannot stop it. How many real tyrannies have been defied with no weapon other than something as simple and symbolic

(Glupov turned out to be not quite as stupid a town after all), as this wayward, unforeseeable, maddening, triumphant waterway?

★

Surely Don Quixote is the most utopian figure in history, albeit fictional history? His very name has turned into a word (few have achieved that honour) and a word, moreover, with a profoundly utopian meaning: "quixotic" is a word not easy to define exactly, but the sense of it can be felt without the aid of etymology. But he goes further; what would we have done without the expression "tilting at windmills", signalling a fruitless but admirable endeavour? For remember that the Don charged the windmills in the belief that they were mighty knights, taller than any earthly warrior; heedless of the odds, he went into battle, for he believed that the lady Dulcinea had been captured by this nefarious band. All he got for his chivalry were the bruises he sustained from the blows of the sails of the windmills, but he was not at all cast down, except literally; in an extremity of utopianism he refused, even after the battle, to accept that his adversaries were not the sinister army he had thought them. And as for the bruises, he wore them as badges of triumph.

The sad truth is that Don Quixote is a danger to himself and a greater danger to those who have to look after him. Yet we do not wash our hands of him; on the contrary, we put up with his notions *only because he is mad*. In his own inward Utopia, a metaphor for madness, he upholds the cause of the impossible, the rejection of the obvious, the refusal to be reasonable, the indispensability of the nuisance, the absolute certainty that it is the world which is upside down, not the madman standing on his head.

In many cultures, madness has been respected rather than feared; indeed it has frequently been venerated, though presumably the guardians of the holy lunatic still have to minister to him bodily as well as reverently. Don Quixote becomes a vast metaphor, and the Knight of the Woeful Countenance is the salt without which the meal cannot be complete. The truth is that all utopians are mad, not just the crazed Don. What *is* madness, if it is not crying for the moon? (In Ibsen's *Ghosts*, the young man concludes the play and the metaphor at once, by revealing that his brain is diseased, ravaged by the spirochetes of syphilis; he signals the end by demanding that his mother should give him the sun.)

171

Crying for the moon indeed. How Cervantes makes his own madman lovable is a puzzle; the modern world has no trouble in doing so, but half a millennium ago attitudes must have been rather different. Or perhaps not. If genius is great enough, it can leap circumstances and centuries alike; did not Shakespeare have to put up with squeaky youths to represent his most glorious women, from Rosalind to Imogen, because the idea of actresses had not then been broached? But undoubtedly he saw them in his all-seeing eye. So let it be with Cervantes. Meanwhile, we laugh at Don Quixote, as his wild fancies wander through his book, with his faithful steward-cum-guardian at his heels. What does Sancho Panza think of his master? It is he, after all, who tries to make the Don see that giant knights are only windmills, and it is he who fails every time to convince his master.

Cervantes took part in the battle of Lepanto – the second Lepanto, the battle which, had it been lost, would have made Europe part of Islam; it was John of Austria who rallied the faithful, gathered, equipped and led an army, arrived just in time to raise the siege of Vienna, routed the forces of the Crescent, and in doing so ensured that Europe would remain Christian. G.K. Chesterton wrote a poem (an epic poem – who would dare to try such a thing today?), called simply *Lepanto*. He envisaged Cervantes doing great deeds of valour that day, and at the same time being stirred by an idea for a novel which he would write when he got home. Chesterton's poem ended with these lines:

> Cervantes on his galley puts his sword back in the sheath
> (Don John of Austria rides homeward with a wreath),
> And he sees as in a vision, a dusty road in Spain,
> Up which a lean and foolish knight for ever rides in vain,
> And he smiles, but not as Sultans smile, and settles back the blade,
> (But Don John of Austria rides home from the crusade.)

*

As we took the mad knight's name and turned it into an adjective, so we have taken another such; from Rabelais we have rabelaisian, and with the word there poured forth the greatest of all of the Utopias of enjoyment.

Rabelais, and particularly because of Chapters 52 to 58 of his first book of Gargantua and Pantagruel, must have a substantial claim to the title of the First Citizen of Utopia. The Abbey of Thelema was built as a thank-offering for the monk, Friar John, who had done noble service in the mighty war waged on the peaceable Grandgousier, Gargantua's father, by the cruel King Pichrocole; offered the choice of either of two abbotries, he declined both, saying frankly that he could hardly be an abbot and govern others when he could not govern himself. Gargantua then gave the monk more than enough land for a new abbey; whence Thelema. It is worth touching on Friar John's service in the war, which will show that he was by no means the most orthodox of friars. When the abbey was being sacked, his greatest concern was to harvest the grapes, which the enemy were pillaging, in case there would be nothing to drink next year; taking his cross, he rushed at the spoilers, and

he beat out the brains of some, broke the arms and legs of others, disjointed the neck-bones, demolished the kidneys, slit the noses, blackened the eyes, smashed the jaws, knocked the teeth down the throats, shattered the shoulder-blades, crushed the shins, dislocated the thigh-bones, and cracked the fore-arms of yet others...If one of them tried to save himself by flight, he knocked his head into pieces along the lamboidal suture. If one of them climbed into a tree, thinking he would be safe there, Friar John impaled him up the arse with his staff.

The specifications of the Abbey of Thelema begin with Gargantua's suggestion that there should be no walls round it. Friar John readily agrees, and then lays down that there should be no bells or clocks, and that no women should be allowed in unless they are beautiful, well-built and sweet-natured, and no men if they are not handsome, well-built, and of pleasant nature. In addition, because the rules of the ordinary monastery forbid any monk, who has taken the vows, to leave the order, they must remain there to the end of their lives. In Thelema, therefore, they may leave at any time, and because the vows decree chastity, poverty and obedience, Thelema insists that any in the order may marry, get rich and live at liberty.

Gargantua put up the money for the building, which came to 2,700,831 gold crowns, and guaranteed an annual "refresher" of 1,669,000 crowns. In addition, Gargantua granted, for the building's upkeep, 2,369,000 payable yearly. Nor could the dwellers in the Abbey of Thelema complain of cramped quarters; it contained 900,332 spacious apartments. Nor would they run out of reading-matter; there were whole libraries in Greek, Latin, Hebrew, French, Italian and Spanish.

Above the Great Gate was a mighty inscription, making clear – very clear – the kind of people who would not be welcome, including, among others, hypocrites, bigots, snivellers, Ostrogoths, flagellants, beggars, of course lawyers and judges, office-holders, scribes and pharisees, usurers, gluttons and lechers, swindlers, misers and anyone with the pox.

But those who pass the test can look forward to unalloyed happiness, merriment, serenity, companionship, beautiful high-born ladies, and – somewhat surprisingly after all that – God's Holy Writ and the preaching of it. There were in the Abbey pleasure-gardens, a tilt-yard, a theatre, a swimming-pool, tennis-courts, orchards of fruit for the plucking, a park full of game, butts, a falconry, stables, barbers and perfumiers.

Of course there were no directives to regulate or confine the inhabitants, there were no statutes or timetables; they got up and went to bed whenever they felt like it; and there were no meal-times – everyone could eat and drink according to their wishes. In all the life of the Abbey of Thelema there was only one rule, one precept, one guiding line: it was "Do what you wish is the whole of the law".

Of course, there had been Utopias of pleasure and freedom before; but Rabelais, with the meticulously detailed plan of his Utopia, and his freedom from all constraints, as in the Abbey's motto, makes so ravishing a world out of Thelema (for all those who live there can play a variety of musical instruments, speak half a dozen languages in all of which they can write in both verse and prose, and exhibit the most noble and knightly characteristics, the most demure and loving womanhood) that it virtually eclipses the dream-worlds of the entire genre. And the Abbey of Thelema hardly begins to exhaust Rabelais' belief in freeing the individual. Surely the way his name has become an adjective is not a coincidence; he is indeed *rabelaisian*, as he demonstrates in his very frequent use of excretory language. No doubt such coarseness was more acceptable in his time than in ours, but in both the intention is the same: to free those who are trammelled by the conventions. Rabelais would gape as well as laugh if he could see any of our most demotic and earthy newspapers, filled with stories of the most lascivious behaviour, pictures and all, yet thinking it best to reproduce the rabelaisian terms in the form of sh**, p***, f*** or even b****r. "Damn braces – bless releases", said Blake, but we have a very long way to go to catch up with Blake, and even further with Rabelais. The

Abbey of Thelema is within us all, but we still cannot find the key that will let it out. Perhaps we build our kind of Utopia just because we cannot break the imaginary chains that we put on our own wrists, while Friar John weeps for our cowardice.

Incidentally, it is said – there is no reliable documentary proof – that Rabelais' will read (in full): "I have nothing; I owe much; the rest I leave to the poor". No utopian he.

But a utopian world need not be so tumultuous, so earthy, so torrential; we have one, and have had it long, which has all the utopian virtues and none of the noise and breaking crockery of Rabelais. Surely there is room for a Utopia of humour?

If Utopia is a world of perfect bliss, harmony and happiness; of purity, chivalry, and friendship; of laughter, imagination and justice; if Utopia is made of these qualities, then there is a startling omission in the ranks of utopian worlds. For the world that P.G. Wodehouse created is an Arcadian idyll which is built on a profoundly utopian plan. The world he made, he peopled with his idea of human beings, and although these did not and could not be *found* in his Eden, they could be instantly *recognised*. One of his short stories is titled *Young Men in Spats*, and it sums up the image that Wodehouse must have in some way envisaged. True, when he was a young man (he was born in 1881 and died at the age of ninety-three), young men, or at least young men of means, welcomed in society, *did* wear spats, but apart from the fact that Wodehouse was hardly welcomed in society (he was first a bank clerk and then a journalist), the story of *Young Men in Spats* was not about the spats but about the young men.

Wodehouse himself said that "I believe there are two ways of writing novels. One is mine, making a sort of musical comedy without music and ignoring real life altogether; the other is going right deep down into life and not caring a damn".

That is what he said; but in a sense, a strange sense, it was not true. He did create "musical comedy without music", but he did not "ignore real life altogether". What he did was to make an entirely separate world in which everything looks the same as the things in the world we are used to, but is changed in every particular. His characters are not waxwork figures – on the contrary, they leave the reader with a most meticulous knowledge and understanding of them – they have been transformed. But into what?

They have been transformed into utopian beings, who also show clearly the lineaments of human beings. And there is an immediately available test of both halves of these strange creatures.

In many of the stories – a substantial proportion of Wodehouse's oeuvre – young men and women meet, unchaperoned, and often fall in love; at the very least find each other's company romantically agreeable. There are also recognisable Wodehouse characters, these all male, who are constantly being bowled over by the local or visiting beauty. The girls are invariably shapely and, it is implied, they are buxom too. But nowhere in any of Wodehouse's 90-odd books is there any reference, even an oblique one, to a seduction, to a sexual liaison however innocent, to a lascivious word, to petting, to a *double-entendre* issuing in coarseness, to, in short, any indication that human beings mate.

But human beings do mate; how – if none of his characters give any indication of knowing that single fact – can the stories carry any verisimilitude, how can they, indeed, even be understood? Because they have been transformed into so many citizens of Utopia, where "all is understood and all forgiven". The young men in spats do not boast of their conquests, because they have made no conquests, nor even attempted any, and throughout the whole Wodehouse world such standards of utopian rectitude prevail. (They do get married, but almost always "off-stage".)

And of course that utopian rectitude obtains throughout the Wodehouse world. For instance, young men in his stories do get drunk (usually on Boat Race Night) and cause themselves and others great embarrassment, but look what happens when the tongue-tied Gussie Fink-Nottle, desperately nervous at having to give out the prizes at the Market Snodbury Grammar School, breaks his strict teetotal promise and fortifies himself with "Oh, about ten swallows. Twelve, maybe. Or fourteen. Say sixteen medium-sized gulps" of whisky, all unknowing that his friend Bertie and Bertie's man had each already independently laced his jug of orange-juice with huge quantities of gin. There is, to be sure, great embarrassment, but Gussie does not fall down, nor does he vomit, nor swear, nor stagger about, nor indeed do anything in any way vulgar or unpleasant. We know that people who have had vastly too much to drink are not amusing, but disgusting, but we are not utopian beings, and what Gussie does under the influence amuses us and everybody else, precisely because he, and all the characters in the story, have undergone that sea-change. (The tongue-tied Gussie also manages, with the help of the drink, to propose to the lady he loves, and is instantly accepted, whereas before she would not consider such a milk-sop.)

Yet there is nothing artificial in Wodehouse's cosmogony. There is no sense of purging or censoring. Wodehouse claimed to "ignore real life altogether", but real life would not let him. He did something much more significant and difficult. He did not make life unreal, but he made it timeless. No young man today goes about in spats; it is unlikely that spats are worn anywhere at all other than in films or plays set in bygone years. Not even a Bishop today would refrain from saying something more vigorous than "Golly" if someone dropped a very heavy suitcase on his gouty foot. Wodehouse stopped the clocks; it was notable that when he took up the pen again, following the painful pause thought necessary after the end of the Second World War, his attempts to bring his world up-to-date with contemporary language not only failed, but drained the life out of the new stories. He was, of course, growing older, and his powers were declining, but it was not that that made it look as though he was struggling to regain his early strength; it was the jar of the new.

Wodehouse made a world, and the world stopped for him, as it would not for any other world-maker. That was because, whether he realised it consciously or not, he had fed (and he continues to feed) one of mankind's deepest needs; it is the belief in perfection, completeness, the whole. There is danger in that yearning, and too much of it can breed not only disappointment but a terrible reckoning. That is why Wodehouse drew back from genius, saying that he would ignore real life altogether, and in doing so demonstrated the genius he denied.

15

The territorial imperative

A T THE HEIGHT of the Roman Empire's power, its rulers must have thought that mankind had reached its ultimate plateau. To rule most of the known world, and to be at home with most of its culture, must have presented an inescapable triumphalism. In such a world, to have sway over so much and so many would inevitably have portrayed that world as perfection, by whatever name it went. Many nations, many individuals, have been mistaken in their belief that they had attained the highest order in existence.

In this case, there is a paradox. Much of what the Romans knew had come from the Greeks. The Romans had absorbed the Hellenic culture and gained immeasurably from it, but there is no evidence that they acknowledged what they had gained – not from pride, but from a lack of recognition. Yet, Athens truly does have a claim on the title of the world's greatest Utopia; at its height, in little more than a century, with a freeman population of only a few thousands, an architecture, a polity, a pride and a democracy which had never in all known history been matched and which has never been matched since.

How could Rome have failed to absorb something so enormous, deep and abiding? She could not, whence ultimately fructifying combination of the two. But the utopian nature of Athenian culture did not, of course, disappear when the Roman Empire did, and for that matter when Athens did. We, in the last decade of the twentieth century, have still not understood that tiny city state's achievements. Utopia, as we have seen, does not exist, and for good reasons cannot. Tiny communities can, it is true, live

178

something like a utopian existence; and bravely they have done so, over the years. Many of the pseudo-Utopias, as we have also seen, have turned into, or even started with, a hellish inversion of the world of bliss, harmony and fulfilment that the utopians were expecting, and many more have had to make do with a rusty simulacrum of the promised land. Wiser heads have found a way round both the yearning and the disappointment.

All human endeavour is imperfect, but some endeavours are closer to perfection than others, and the wiser heads have been satisfied by studying the one human enterprise which managed to get much further up the foothills of Mount Utopia than many sturdier climbers. How was the trick done? It was done first by limiting the possibilities (no one can scale the summit), and second by picking the route.

The route leads to Periclean Athens, which must surely come closest to what utopians seek. Fifth-century Athens was, like all human states, imperfect; but nothing in the then known world (and indeed nothing in the world for a very long time afterwards, and perhaps not even yet) came closer to a utopian perfection. Let us get the worst out of the way at once: Periclean Athens tolerated slavery. True, there was no society in the world that did not do so, and it would have taken a giant leap in imagination to have thought about the practice, much less thought that it was degrading and unfair. True, also, slavery in Athens then was of the mildest sort (contrast it with the way the Helots of neighbouring Sparta were used). True, again, that before the decline of the Athenian state, the unthinkable was being thought; the nature of slavery was at last discussed. Nevertheless, it was there; human beings treated human beings as though they were not human. But the argument for Athens was that the long-sought quasi-Utopia came with a warning on the label; it was not Utopia, nor did its citizens think it was. They suffered the hubris (and it was *hubris* that helped to bring the city down), but they had a great deal to boast of.

Solon, Cleisthenes, Pericles; these men, it can be said (recognising a very substantial over-simplification), not only turned a poor and backward city into one of the most important centres of the Aegean and in doing so laid down not just a system of laws and civil relations that was a model of the known world, but also built the stage on which the glories of Greece would be displayed, and on which they were displayed to such advantage that the world even today gasps at what Greece created.

The very idea of the 'polis' was, in its Athenian form, a master-stroke of the imagination. It was not quite pride, not quite justice, not quite neighbourliness, not quite honour, not quite duty, not quite enfranchisement, but it was all those things, and in every one of those aspects the Athenian, consciously or unconsciously, revelled. A modern parallel may give an idea of the Athenian's relation to the polis. In all genuinely democratic states, voting is a right and of course one of the most valuable of all rights. (Indeed, in one democratic state, Australia, the right is taken so seriously that, by law, all potential voters must make an appearance at the polling station, whether they want to cast a ballot or not. Failure to appear and have their name ticked off on the electoral roll is an offence, and they can be prosecuted and fined for it.) But in every democratic state, a proportion of those who have the right to vote do not exercise it. The proportion of non-voters varies from country to country; for instance, in Britain it is usually around 25 per cent and in the Scandinavian countries fewer than 20 per cent. The highest proportion is always that of the United States, which rarely gets half its voters to the polls.

The point of this psychology is to make clear what the polis meant to an Athenian citizen. To have a vote and not to cast it would be the sign of madness, so intertwined was the free citizen with the entire workings of the state. Scarcely less strange to an Athenian would have been the idea of a parliament, which debated and passed laws. The whole state was a parliament, as the whole state was a law-court, too.

Of course, with an adult male electorate of some 3000 (the franchise did not extend to the female sex – the other great stain on the Athenian democracy), such close involvement in "politics" was possible in a way that today, with great nation states comprising many millions of citizens, is impossible. Nevertheless, it was the utopian idea of a state in which every citizen is not just equal before the law, but part of it. For that matter, there was nothing called an "army". Every adult male was automatically part of the defence of the realm, and like the Swiss today (the modern Swiss has a good many Athenian attributes), he kept his sword and shield at home, ready for the call.

And from this tiny scrap of land, small enough for a healthy man to walk across in a couple of days, there was given to the world not just the principles of democracy, law, citizenship, public service – in a word, the polis – but an outpouring of genius such as the world had never seen, and in all the centuries that have passed has still not seen. Think of some of the great achieving times – sixteenth and seventeenth-century England, sixteenth-century Holland and Germany, Lorenzo di Medici's court, the whole of the Renaissance, composers from Mozart to Brahms, the nineteenth-century novel in England and Russia; contemplate the great lands that brought forth those marvels, almost all of them sustained by a great patron-prince; share out the strengths of the catalogue, so that we see in which countries and in which eras which art predominates, as Elizabethan England bred playwrights while the Dutch gave the world paintings. Put it all together and wonder again at how this minuscule nation, which flourished for not much more than 150 years, poured out the fruits of a titanic genius (residing as it must have been, in the Greek people), in philosophy, medicine, astronomy, architecture, sculpture, drama, poetry, literature, physics, rhetoric, education, sport, mathematics, warfare, ritual, social relations, diplomacy, history, legend, gods, liberty, equality and fraternity, and all without taking Homer into account, as too early to be included.

A selection from only the more notable figures in Athens would include Anaxagoras, Anaximenes, Aeschylus, Aristides, Aristophanes, Aristotle, Cimon, Critias, Democritus, Demosthenes, Diogenes, Epaminondas, Gorgias, Isocrates, Pericles, Phidias, Plato, Praxiteles, Protagoras, Pythagoras, Sophocles, Thucydides, Xenophon. And these were all born in a space of only 146 years. Remember yet again how tiny the place was; that meant – must have meant – that very many Athenians with no such eminence but with education and understanding would have seen and heard these great ones; the general level of culture, therefore, must have been higher than any state in all of history.

The books, the poems, the scientific and mathematical discoveries, the philosophy that is relevant today, the plays that will be seen over and over again until time itself ends, the architecture that still stands on the Acropolis as witness of the truth below – are these not signs and sounds and stones and words and meanings and truth that say Utopia was here? Well, if it was, it suffered the fate of all Utopias; it fell asleep on its laurels. Athens wandered, unseeing, under the curse of hubris; she began to think herself immortal, and if not immortal then invincible. She was destroyed in disastrous wars, and although she was revived later, so that there was still an Athens, the life-blood had gone out of her. (And as for today…but today, it is safe to say that no one could imagine that Athens now had even the slightest manifestation of Utopia, and the Acropolis stands over the dreadful city below to emphasise that truth.)

Athens v. Sparta; the Pelopponese football match will never be finished.

For modern man (assuming that modern man has enough education to have heard of either), Athens is culture, Sparta is nurture. Modern man (who is even more unlikely to have heard of *hubris* and the Sicilian Expedition) marvels at the outpouring of genius in that tiny place in that tiny space of time, as well he might. He will be puzzled, indeed uneasy, at the putting to death of Socrates, and if he delves more deeply he will come upon the degradation of Pericles, but the enormous credit balance will soothe his conscience. Surely, Athens at her height was the greatest Utopia of thought ever seen in the world? Now turn to Sparta. Where is her Aristotle, her Sophocles, her Parthenon? What is this we hear, that youths of both sexes exercised in the nude? Is it true that every citizen is appointed to some position in the state, and none can choose a profession? Why do they all have to wear the same clothes? How is it that Sparta was at all times ready for war, and was waging it much of the time, with the import of luxuries banned? Why was no individuality permitted, and no privacy either? What about their strange marital habits? And meals taken in common? If you have tears, regard the Helots, an entire race of beings, so rigorously treated as sub-human that the very slaves of Athens might weep at their fate. And newborn babies are inspected for blemishes, deformities or sickliness, by officials who, if they find such stigmata, are empowered to kill the children. And have we not all heard, however little we have dabbled in these matters, of the boy who hid a fox under his tunic, and rather than own up and be shamed, allowed the animal to disembowel him?

Yet Sparta has been thought a Utopia, not only in our contemporary centuries, but at the time. She was admired for her inculcation of national pride, for the hardihood of her young manhood, for the bold stroke of King Lycurgus (some say a mythical figure), who abolished gold and silver coinage, using instead lengths of iron bars for the mechanism of exchange, in order to cut down the tall poppies of grossly uneven wealth. Unlike most of Greece, women were not simply assigned to a husband; love-matches of almost modern form were rife, and although girls were trained in hardihood rather than sewing, it is said they were beautiful. (In the *Lysistrata* Aristophanes pokes fun at their muscles.) Youths of both sexes were brought up to respect their elders, and their musical accomplishments were the envy of much bigger and more sophisticated Greek nation-states.

And anyway, who could withhold truly utopian admiration from the Spartans, the immortal heroes of Thermopylae? Though locked in almost perpetual rivalry with Athens, Sparta joined forces with her ancient enemy to face a greater joint threat, and when, in that war with the Persians, the Greek forces looked like being cut to pieces, the Spartan rearguard kept the pass of Thermopylae open long enough to enable the Greeks to withdraw in safety. When the day was over, every one of the Spartan regiment lay dead on the field.

> Go tell the Spartans, thou who passeth by,
> That here, obedient to their word, they lie.

Has it ever happened since Athens? That is, is there in history, as opposed to mythology, a country, a regime, a place, a state, of which it could be said that its people live in a truly utopian community? Surprisingly, there are several candidates for the elusive but tangible no-place.

Once did she hold the gorgeous east in fee... The modern traveller to Venice certainly thinks that this is Utopia itself; how could he fail to? The unique beauty of the place captivates every visitor (well, not every visitor – D.H. Lawrence took one look at it, called it, shuddering, "slimy", and fled, never to return); it really is unique, with nothing at all with which to compare it; this city – not only *of* water, but *in* – for the whole place stands on stilts.

Let us, for a moment, think about those stilts. The piles were made, shaped and put in place many centuries ago, long before the internal combustion engine was thought of, and before the precious ichor that feeds the engine had been discovered. The original inhabitants, it is true, threw their household rubbish into the canals, heedless of the ecological consequences, but their rubbish was not as modern man's rubbish is; the ancient kind was almost entirely organic, and even a corpse found floating from time to time would disintegrate in a reasonably hygienic manner. Not so today; it is not only the ubiquitous plastic bag and the residue of millions of gallons of detergent that are destroying the earth's rivers and the piles on which Venice stands; it is the waves that thud against those piles as the motor-boats go by.

Venice is dying, of pollution and modernity; but she will be killed long before those poisons can finish their work; a far more efficacious murderer lurks in and around the city. Not long ago, the causeway that connects Venice to the mainland had to be closed; Venice, for a day, was once more an island. The reason was that 36,000 people, in nearly 1000 coaches, joined by another 30,000 arriving by water, had decided to visit the city; this flood of humanity was poised to drown the place five fathoms deep.

That was the worst day; but something approaching those numbers now debouch every day in the tourist season, which in any case now stretches from the middle of March to well into October. The term "tourist pollution" has been admitted to polite society (and soon the dictionaries); it is significant as well as symbolic that it was coined by the Mayor of Venice himself.

Why all this lament, then? However lamentable, where does it touch the utopian ideal? It touches it in three places. First, though it is difficult to believe, the people who built the glorious city in the waves did not set out to make an everlasting jewel of urban beauty; they were looking for somewhere to live, and thought they had found a promising spot. Only later was that spot utopianised, and only much later did it become a beckoning beacon, a city in which, surely, peace, brotherhood, love, justice, harmony, wisdom, art and prosperity reign in utopian glory for ever more.

It is true that Venice even today has a lower crime-rate than the average for Italian cities, and a much lower murder-rate, but that exhausts the catalogue of utopian traces; disappointment is the lot of the visitor to Venice today who seeks the ancient community in which King Utopus has been co-opted as a permanent Doge. The beauty remains, of course, however accidental it was, but even the beauty is frequently invisible over, between, or through those monstrous crowds.

The second relevance that Venice has for Utopia is also a disappointment; through the centuries, right up to the beginning of the eighteenth, Venice's law and government, though clear, ordered, codified and rarely abused, could not be the utopian state of which utopians dream. Ideally, of course, utopians dream of a world without any law or government at all, because the world envisaged has no need of such things, being already perfect, but even in Venice the world must be less deeply utopian than that. There was, then, law and government in ancient Venice. But it was not a polity that a modern utopian would recognise as his longed-for rule. Democracy was hundreds of years away, and harsh punishments were meted out not only for crimes such as theft, but for being on the losing side of a factional struggle for power. (The remote governing Council was ruthless with dissenters; even a Doge, falling under the Council's mistrust, was executed.)

The third connection is the most obvious; it is the entry of the serpent. What treacherous iconoclasts are prowling about in the unconscious, drawing poisoned wine from the vats of disillusion? Why can mankind not make a perfect world, even if it is only a tiny perfect world perched on piles and surrounded by water?

The Medici court does not seem, at first glance, an obvious candidate for elevation to the company of utopian elysian fields. There were, after all, an exceptionally large number of assassinations in the long history of the family, though perhaps not really outstanding by the standards of the times (roughly from the middle of the fourteenth century to the end of the sixteenth). Conspiracies, treacheries, abrupt changes of sides, banishments, fratricides, avengings, forced abdications – these were part of the daily round in Florence when the Medicis ruled, or so it seems to us at the end of the twentieth century. (The eyebrows rose to their highest when one of the assassinations took place in a church, and not only in church but during Mass, the already exciting day concluding with the summary hanging of the Archbishop, believed – rightly – to have been in the murder plot.)

Nor was anything like democracy found under the Medicis; the furthest they would go in tempering an almost absolute rule was to uphold republican principles. Yet again, though we shudder at such concentrated power, the Medici world was one of the least arbitrary or savage, compared to other Italian states, including Venice. If the Medicis practised tyranny, it was a benign version.

Perhaps we can stand back a little, and see the family whole. The Medicis gave the world four Popes, two Queens, innumerable dynasties of Grand Dukes and the like; they built up their stupendous fortune by shrewd calculation rather than rapine; they avoided war as much as they could; they rationalised laws; their taxation policy was merciful; their justice was neither haphazard nor savage.

But it is not for these achievements, actions and qualities that Medici Florence can aspire to utopiahood. It is, of course, for the rulers' passion for architecture, letters and the fine arts. "Passion" is not too strong; indeed, it may not be strong enough. These rulers were nothing like most of today's patrons, endowing an Oxford college in order to enshrine the patron's name, or bequeathing an art collection to a state gallery, or distributing bursaries to promising art-students. The Medicis sought out and found the painters, the sculptors, the poets, the philosophers, the architects who were to be the unending glory of art in all its forms. And they were able to seek out genius because they were themselves steeped in art and the love of it. Nor were their searches confined to artists who would adorn a palace; they instituted searches for ancient manuscripts of no intrinsic beauty but great historical record; they created libraries greater by far than those of the classical world; they formed circles in which the leading figures of the intellectual day would discuss art and philosophy; they recreated Plato's academy and revelled in the lectures of Marsilio Ficino; the artists they enticed or supported or encouraged were not their prizes, to be lionised before the world, but treated as friends and colleagues, nothing like the now familiar figure of the "court painter". Was not that riot of art and its makers a utopian scene? At least, although there had of course been significant artists and art before Cimabue freed art from the stiff formalities of the Byzantine, there had been nothing comparable to this explosion of genius since Periclean Athens.

Such movements do not announce themselves, if only because they do not experience themselves in the same way that those who come after can see the shape and totality. If a friend of Cosimo the Elder (justifiably called Pater Patriae) asked what project Cosimo was working on, Cosimo would not have replied "I am ushering in the Renaissance", not least because the word had not been coined. But that, nevertheless, was what he was doing.

Cosimo was said to be the wealthiest man in Europe, but he was no *nouveau riche*, let alone a M. Jourdain. His father must have known Petrarch, and for sure the teachings of St Francis would not have fallen on barren ground. What is more, the patrons vied with one another to offer artists their patronage. Renaissance Man, in the shape of Cosimo, was real, and he understood much more deeply than other patrons that art was not adornment, even though it did wonderfully adorn. It is true that in the fourteenth century and for a considerable time after it virtually all art was produced for a patron, but how else could it have come into being?

Cosimo was such a patron. He may have felt that his collections honoured Florence and his family, and he would have been more than human if he had not felt satisfaction at the thought of what his patronage had brought him. But his passion for the arts drove him, not the thought of what posterity would say. His first love was architecture, and he called Brunelleschi to his side. The result was S. Lorenzo, the Sagreta Vecchia and Sta Maria degli Angeli. These were followed by the Convent of S. Marco, the Medici Chapel at Sta Croce, and the chapel at S. Miniato.

But his love of architecture did not mean that he had less feeling for painting and sculpture. He commissioned Ghiberti, Donatello, Gozzoli, Fra Angelico, Fra Filippo Lippi, and he did more than commission them – he made friends of them. Nor was the search for manuscripts forgotten;

indeed, it went further than Christian texts, and his agents were soon finding treasures in the East. And towering over even these triumphs was the incomparable library he collected, which remains today under the name of the Laurentian Library. (While all this artistic stir was going on, Cosimo was not neglecting his regular attendance at the Greek lectures he had established, and he even had time and energy to attend to his administrative and financial labours.)

Of course, this remarkable family was not entirely composed of philosopher-kings presided over by the incarnation of Maecenas; almost all of the leading figures of the Medici, however, had a deep feeling for art, and until the line begins to run out with Pietro the Unfortunate (also known as Pietro the Fatuous), the name was synonymous with a love and understanding of art. Even Lorenzino di Medici, who lived only thirty-four years, and was not patron or collector, wrote plays and poetry.

There were more Medicis to keep the flame alight; Cosimo, Duke of Florence, took under his wing Pontormo, Bronzino, Benevenuto Cellini and Vasari, and laid the foundations for the housing of the Medici collections in the Uffizi.

But it was the court of Lorenzo the Magnificent that gave Florence a utopian air. It was he who beckoned to his friendship and patronage Botticelli, Verrochio, Leonardo da Vinci, Pico della Marindola and a fifteen-year-old boy whose youthful drawings impressed Lorenzo, as well they might, considering that the boy was Michelangelo. Not since the fourth century BC has such genius been so wide, so deep, so tended, so lasting. These Medici were not just patrons; they were the most wise, understanding, generous patrons in all history. First Florence, then Italy, then Europe, then the world, were and are uplifted by this astonishing bloodline that poured art wherever it was cut. The paintings, the sculptures, the illuminated manuscripts, the churches, the palaces, the poetry (to say nothing of Vespucci and Galileo), all these have survived in huge quantities, bearing witness everywhere, even to the furthermost ends of the earth, that once upon a time, in a space of hardly two centuries, one family made their home city one of the wonders of the world; such a wonder, indeed, that it is difficult to believe it did happen, and that it was only a dream, only a vision, only a Utopia of art.

San Francisco is the most European of American cities, as Bombay is the most British of Indian cities; both are in consequence suspect by their fellow-cities of being not wholly patriotic, or at least not sufficiently imbued with the ideals, the mores and the tastes of the mother country. However, San Francisco and Bombay, far from hanging their tainted heads in shame, make the differences into a badge of nonconformity, and positively glory in the sight of a finger wagged in reproof.

Such is San Francisco, many of whose inhabitants refuse to believe that the American continent continues eastward for a considerable distance beyond the City on the Bay. (The charge of eccentricity it gladly embraces; the hint of parochialism is less welcome.) A perspicacious visitor from another country, particularly after seeing a good deal of the rest of the United States, will at once sense the difference, and the difference has sometimes been substantial. San Francisco is a relaxed place (the very opposite of New York), and it takes few things very seriously, but the unfazed atmosphere is noticeable in some contexts. During the McCarthy witch-hunts, for instance, San Francisco could be seen as an island of tolerance, and in other ways she has demonstrated her power to resist bullying. (For that matter she demonstrates her reluctance to hurry.)

A utopian city? *The* utopian city? It has its claims, and certainly has many who would see it thus. Even in trouble, she keeps her head. It was in San Francisco that, when the Aids epidemic was growing, the first serious action for the support of those infected was started; San Francisco pioneered the mutual-help groups which could and did give psychological and social uplift.

A modern city as a candidate for Utopia? The idea is strange, but not absurd. Such a claim would not, it is true, escape the scrutiny of immediate examination, an ordeal largely evaded by those historical utopian centres of which it can be safely assured that at the least the tiny blots or pimples have become invisible over the years. And after all, the City of Saint Francis ought to stand out from the run, with a patron like that. So why not cast our ballot for San Francisco, and have done with it? Because there is a grim irony in the very thought of such promotion. Long before Aids was heard of, the serpent visited San Francisco and left his calling-card. No one noticed his arrival or his departure, but long after his brief sojourn in the city its effects began to be felt.

Consider. The westernmost land of the United States is the coast on which San Francisco sits and basks. Beyond is nothing but the sea; the Pacific Ocean. From all over the country, even from the eastern seaboard, the trek westwards goes on. Many of the trekkers, perhaps most, have dreamed of a world elsewhere, a perfect world, a world without the blemishes, the disappointments, the broken lives, the unemployment, the mysterious inward pain. They need not have heard of Utopia; for that matter, they hardly need to have heard of California. Nor do they all journey to leave sorrows behind; there are almost as many who take the trek in buoyant hopes of success and happiness.

Many find a place on the way; the country is, after all, three thousand miles wide. Some turn back. Some change their minds and stay where they were. But still the column makes its way to the west, and finally they stand where they can look upon the City of Hope, and the mighty ocean beyond it.

And then? What was that calling-card the stranger left behind? Many a man and woman seek a new life, a new outlook, new faces; they go anywhere and everywhere, but with one exception they have everything in common. If they don't like the place they have reached, they can go somewhere else, and they can extend that roaming as far as restlessness will take them. But what if – this is the exception – there is nowhere else to go. Of course, a trekker from the east who arrives at San Francisco's Ultima Thule can also go elsewhere if he is disillusioned, but this lodestar of a city somehow wants and gives everything or nothing. To stand upon the Pacific shore and to realise that the trek was a wasted endeavour, for this place is pleasant and sophisticated and beautiful, but it is not the Shangri-La (they will know what that means even if they have never heard of Utopia) they were searching for.

Can you guess the end of the story? It is to be found in the dry statistics of the San Francisco register of births and deaths: that city has the highest suicide level of any comparable place in the Union. The last hope was the western shore; and when that turned out to be a chimera, too, all hope had gone.

★

Again and again, through the ages, great leaders have attempted to pass on their wisdom to their progeny, only to find that the progeny takes no interest in such matters, or – worse – is hopelessly incapable of continuing in the same, successful, course, or – worse still – is a dissolute monster, interested in nothing but his vices.

To guard against such a decline (though there is in truth no way to guard against it), there is an ingenious plan, frequently put into practice throughout the ages; the plan is to put the heir-apparent to school with a great sage or teacher, so that the throne is ascended by one who has imbibed an infinity of wisdom and understanding, thus ensuring that the succession is safe.

Unfortunately, that does not work either. Again and yet again, the tutor might as well have spent his wisdom on the desert air, for all that there is any sign of his teaching having any effect. There have, of course, been wise sons of wise fathers, but it seems that there is no correlation pattern, not even if the pattern is turned back to front, in search of a wise son with a stupid father.

The real philosopher-king is hard to find; there have been very few throughout history. And the belief that they can be made, by the teaching of a great and wise tutor, is one of the gentlest and most touching beliefs in all Utopia. If we broaden the category of philosopher-kings, we can, to our surprise, find ourselves including, as a utopianiser, Peter the Great, consumed with the need to modernise (which meant westernise) his kingdom, as a step towards making it a Russian heaven. The voracity with which he drank in the civilisation of the western world matched his gargantuan appetite for practically everything, from punishments to drink and from modern shipbuilding to battle. To bring an entire nation up-to-date has always involved a mighty and prolonged struggle; we see it currently in many of the southeast Asian territories. In all societies, there are many – perhaps a majority – who defy change, and its functions, which is what those examples describe; he was dragging a vast empire, comprising every kind of people, attitude, experience, history, land, poverty, religion, understanding, race, language and custom, across several centuries, and he was doing it almost entirely single-handed. The transformation he demanded, and ultimately to an astonishing degree achieved, can be likened to a meeting of a Stone Age man with an educated Frenchman of the eighteenth century; all the ranks of Utopia together would hardly suffice to make the miracle happen. Yet Peter lived to see his dream come true in large part, and at least to ensure that his clock would not be put back. The subsequent history of his country would have dismayed him, but he would have been reminded of his own struggle in the sullen ranks of the moujiks rejecting any kind of change, even the change that, in the late nineteenth century, set them free.

For Peter, a throne was a solemn and mysterious thing, though the arcane concepts of royal legitimacy would have meant little to him. The Divine Right of Kings – it was their right to rule – seems both comic and outrageous today, in a world of democracies and constitutional monarchies. But the Divine Right was taken seriously for many centuries, and not only by the rulers who exercised it.

Why not? If a monarchy was the integument that bound a nation, it would not be thought blasphemous that God had ordained a ruler to keep the nation free of attack from without and anarchy from within. Such a doctrine could also be a bulwark against barons and other over-mighty satraps.

Shakespeare, who died only a quarter of a century before the second English Civil War began, and who was born only seventy-nine years after the first one, took no sides (except once, against Richard III), put his ingrained horror of civil war into the mouth of the Bishop of Carlisle, and a most powerful plea against it was the result:

> ...What subject can give sentence on his king?
> And who sits here that is not Richard's subject?...
> And shall the figure of God's majesty,
> His captain, steward, deputy elect,
> Anointed, crowned, planted many years,
> Be judg'd by subject and inferior breath?
> Stirr'd up by God thus...let me prophesy
> The blood of English shall manure the ground
> And future ages groan for this foul act;
> Peace shall go asleep with Turks and infidels,
> And in this seat of peace tumultuous wars
> Shall kin with kin and kind with kind confound;
> Disorder, horror, fear and mutiny
> Shall here inhabit, and this land be call'd
> The fields of Golgotha and dead men's skulls.
> O! If you rear this house against this house,
> It will the woefullest division prove
> That ever fell upon this cursed earth...

Clearly the Divine Right of Kings was embedded deep not only in the kings themselves, but in their subjects.

Internecine struggles tend to be the most bloody; witness the French Revolution and the American Civil War. But the savagery of the English one had an extra dimension, in the ideas that flooded the land: ideas which covered an infinite breadth, but still had, however tenuously, a connection with the seething mass. And the connection was the idea of Utopia.

Just like the present-day fragmentation of left-wing *groupuscules*, no one outside the seething mass of sects could tell one from another, and – again like our time – could not understand why all such lookalikes spent much of their time and energy (though their energy was infinite) denouncing all the others. How Cromwell managed to prosecute the war, let alone win it, with all these foaming doctrinaires tugging at his sleeve is hard to understand.

The names have passed into history, even if their ideas have not. We have only to call the roll – Diggers, Levellers, Ranters, Fifth Monarchy Men, Anabaptists – to conjure up the scene. The scene itself, of course, was awash with pamphlets crying up one group's certainties and crying down all the others'; printers and publishers basked in their good fortune.

A great cleansing was required; despite the differences, visible or invisible, among the "two and seventy warring sects", there was a widespread agreement on that most persistent utopian belief, the Golden Age. The Golden Age in this case was not the Elysian Fields strewn with asphodels and sunshine; it was a world stern in its demand for repentance and the destruction of false religion.

All this, of course, depended on true religion; once again, Scripture was pressed into service everywhere, to strengthen the validity of the particular utopian claim under discussion, except for the sects who rejected the Bible itself and established their own religious structure, no doubt adding texts of their own, supposed to have the force of the discredited holy books.

Nevertheless, Cromwell *did* manage to prosecute the war, though he finally had to proscribe many of the sects, and no doubt wished that the rest would disappear. Many turned against him, others ignored him; the call of Utopia sounded more loudly in the ears of the utopians than what was actually going on in the real England. The notorious solipsism that marks almost all utopian schemes was seen and heard at its most powerful in the inchoate mass of opinions that could be had for asking (and most of the time without asking, so eager was any sectarian to announce his certainties).

Inevitably, a strain of millennarianism ran through the utopian creators;

they were in a hurry, lest the end of the world might find them unprepared. (The Ranters were not only prepared, but invulnerable; they had abolished sin.)

Amid all this, one man quietly got on with the task of devising a Utopia which would require no divine intervention, no overnight transformation of mankind, no total replacement of the existing order. Based on, of all unlikely governments, the Republic of Venice, James Harrington's *Oceana* comes like a refreshing drink from a cool spring, after all the fiery disputations that had for so long held the stage.

The most striking features of Harrington's Utopia is that unlike almost all other Utopias, it could have been adopted, and could have worked. That was to be proved much later, when modern democracy unknowingly borrowed some of Harrington's proposals. His Utopia had, for instance, two houses of parliament; it also had an impenetrably complicated system of voting, but the important thing was not the complications but the ballot. Harrington dedicated *Oceana* to Cromwell, who had more urgent things on his mind; but there are elements in the American Constitution which show the influence of Harrington, whose name and system were known to the makers of that remarkable document.

The English Civil War did more than depose and kill a king; more than let loose a huge menagerie of sects which, though only one was called the Ranters, all did a vast amount of ranting. It demonstrated both the power of the utopian dream and also the danger in that dream. G.K. Chesterton said "When men cease to believe in God, they will not believe in nothing, they will believe in anything". The sectarians of the seventeenth century in England believed in anything; worse still, they believed in *everything*. There was surprisingly little fanatical killing among the banshee denouncings; but they rocked the state to its foundations, and if the Lord Protector had been a man less strong than Cromwell, it might have collapsed. But the torrent dried up with remarkable speed, testimony to its insubstantiality. The sects were incorporated in calmer forms of religion, or died out entirely. Their Utopia was not realised, but that has been the invariable fate of Utopias. What was left was Harrington's harmless trace-elements, and on the morrow of the day which saw the Interregnum end, the people of England woke up and rubbed their eyes, convinced that they had been dreaming. So they had.

Nevertheless, the conquest leaves its mark. It has largely escaped comment in that form, but the idea of conquest is an essentially utopian one. Many a madman demands homage from his conquered subjects, though the subjects are only his unfortunate family. But real conquerors have drunk at the heady spring, and dreamed of ruling the world; some, indeed, have come close to achieving the goal. Alexander did not know of the existence of many lands on the other side of the world; modern would-be conquerors have globes to twirl as they nurse their ambitions.

But there have been other figures who tried to put their dreams into reality; apart from Alexander, there was Charlemagne, Napoleon and Hitler. The first was geographically limited, but the second, for all his genius, must have been deeply imbued with the impossible dream; he had nothing he truly needed from Russia, and his disastrous invasion must have been conquest as part of the dream. As for Hitler, apart from making Napoleon's mistake over Russia, his conquest of all western Europe (with one tiny Swiss lamp in the darkness) was a dream just as megalomaniac as the empire ruled over by an imaginary hegemony and a cowed wife. Unfortunately, it had greater consequences.

16

Don't bless relaxes

WITH THE ADVANCE of technology, Utopia seemed (to utopians anyway) more plausible. A utopian novel lays out a land of the highest happiness for all; its delights include the illumination of the whole country by electric lamps, and the provision of a new kind of bicycle which moves without the passenger having to pedal. The flowering of the modern scientific culture produced many a Utopia that turned into a nightmare. Technology and control in the real world was breeding horrors, and even the most rosy view of Utopia was darkening; conclusions were avoided, let alone morals, and a Utopia without a moral is a sorry sight.

The dawn of the twentieth century was awash with sociological cures for the condition of mankind, but they were tinged with pessimism – could the cure be manufactured in sufficient quantity before mankind's crisis grew terminal? The answer was given by the First World War, and it was no. If there were any serious utopian strivings or literature in the wake of that most unutopian cataclysm they must have vanished without a trace. But as the years went by, and the search for a world order that would make such a conflict impossible for ever, the New Man was born from the embraces of science and historicism, with a drunken midwife claiming to represent common sense. The Thirties abounded in a kind of utopian cleanliness and order – housing developments, New Towns, revolutions in learning, pacifist appeals, the League of Nations, Madam Blavatsky, naturism, seances, Belisha Beacons, Scouts and Girl Guides. Bliss was it in that time; a somewhat uncomfortable bliss, but the best that Utopia could do with such materials. True, in Germany, a madman was preaching total sexual liberation: King Utopus had abdicated, and King Libido had ascended the throne. His name was Wilhelm Reich, and he had discovered a new Utopia, a Utopia of the senses, but based entirely on the pleasure-principle, as distinct from de Sade's version in the form of the pain-pleasure diastole. To invent an entirely new Utopia at this stage of the world's development was a remarkable achievement, but it taught another lesson; not all innovations are welcome to the society in which they are offered. Reich fled from Nazi Germany to the United States, but spent much of the rest of his life in prison for his scandalous doctrine. He was, of course, in good company; many utopians have been imprisoned, some executed and some even burned at the stake for offering a new world to the old one. He died in 1957, just missing the 1960s; it was left to the young to achieve (though sometimes in dubious circumstances) what Reich had preached; proper homage to him was given, not only by their actions, but by the formal elevation of his name as one of those who made the 1960s possible.

If that did not settle Utopia's hash, the Vietnam War must have gone far to doing so. It was said that this war differed from all the wars in all history, in that it could be seen, nightly and immediately, on television; it was even said that so traumatic an experience would mean there could never be another war, for the viewers at home would not permit it. That, perhaps, was the most utopian thought of all those troubled years.

But before that, at the end of the Second World War, scientific optimism disappeared; H.G. Wells, the most indefatigable of the creed of scientism, died at the end of the war, but his last word was a book with a title of *Mind at the End of Its Tether*. The great utopian was defeated at last, no more laying down the law on everything from international relations to the problem of over-population (the remedy was euthanasia), no more brisk solutions to problems that had puzzled mankind for centuries; the atomic bomb had been dropped, its power gradually becoming recognised, and a new attitude not only to war but to the entire concept of security.

Between the Scylla of such frightful weapons and the Charybdis of their necessity, it was inevitable that a utopian solution would be born, and so it was. The Campaign for Unilateral Nuclear Disarmament was an extravagantly utopian idea. Between the two wars there was a suggestion that if war threatened, young women, with no weapons but their beauty, should immediately take up their posts in what would be the firing line, on the ground that no enemy, however hardened or bloodthirsty, would shoot down beautiful young ladies, but the proposal did not attract many adherents. Though CND, as it was known, went almost further, and attracted thousands, particularly on the Aldermaston March, a pilgrimage from the place where the dreadful weapons were believed to be made or stored, to a triumphant rally in Trafalgar Square. It was, perhaps, the last great gathering of utopians for a common purpose, from the followers of Thomas Müntzer in the Middle Ages, through John Ball and Jack Cade, then to the Chartists, and the Voortrekkers in a faraway South Africa. However absurd the pretensions of CND, they put their shoe-leather where their hearts were. The next such massive march, thousands upon thousands, had no such utopian vision; it was by and for those who did not wish to pay a newly enacted law, the Poll Tax. Disappointed utopians must have been even more disappointed to learn that their own selfless marching had had no effect, whereas the Poll Tax demonstrators had achieved their goal almost immediately.

There were other revolutions. The family (the "nuclear" family, as it is called, without irony and indeed without apparent understanding of the implications) was once the utopian centre of the world, the rock upon which the waves beat in vain. The very word "paterfamilias" would steady any imbalance, putting every member of the family in his or her exact and correct position. Metaphors abound: the family listened to readings of the family Bible, the family home and hearth were virtually holy places, of an evening there might be a game of Happy Families, and if one member strayed, he was instantly dubbed the black sheep of the family. It seemed that it would live for ever, this remarkably utopian institution, but it did not. A body of serious scientific studies was built up (one of its leading creators was Dr Ronald Laing), which provided massive evidence that so far from the family being the great and essential stabilising force in all civilised societies, it was accused of being the most disintegrative and damaging centre of all the ills of society. Laing, and others, argued that for the rise in the number of cases of schizophrenia, the family itself was to blame, with its restrictions, its formalities, its rigidity, its mutual secrecies, and its innumerable unsuccessful attempts at revolt.

The next try at Utopia took the form of what came to be called, with some impudence, "the drug culture". There are blind-alley utopian experiences, and our time has seen them in greater profusion than in any other era in history. All the misplaced beliefs, all the false prophets, all the millennarian forces, all the trick mirrors, conjurors' paraphernalia, hypnotists' passes and street-corner thimbleriggers – all these together cannot match, or even come close to matching, the cruelty, wickedness, dementia, falsehood and suicide of an entire generation, involved in the world – almost entirely the young world – of poisonous but temporarily sweet drugs.

There is a vast literature on the subject already, and it grows hourly; the literature is crammed with theories and solutions, no two of them agreeing, and none, having applied one or more nostrums, rewarded by any sign of a useful reaction. The plague is of an extraordinarily short history; it is hardly yet thirty years old, but has claimed many tens of thousands for death, and probably as many millions for irreparable damage.

The aetiology of the plague is simple. The drugs give a brief but immensely powerful feeling of well-being, far beyond any previous pleasure. By the time the user discovers that to repeat the experience in all its joy, an ever-increasing dose is essential, the user is addicted, or "hooked", a word in which a powerful metaphor lies in wait.

Moreover, as the "kick" (another metaphor, even stronger) fades in its force (whence the need to increase the measure), new sensations are promised in new forms and with new but suitable names. At the time of this writing, the leading new sensation is marketed under the name of Ecstasy, a word of great promise, its promise amply fulfilled – for a time.

A Utopia of the senses, indeed. But none of any of that touches the central question: why? Why, that is, did so many predominantly young people find their lives so empty of real pleasure or meaning that they sought out the artificial (and murderous) kind? In what Devil's Cauldron was cooked a meal which offered an end to a life of boredom and triviality, and for the succeeding dishes gave only the terrible property of tasting delicious in the mouth but deadly in the mind?

Utopia pleads not guilty, and there is a fierce struggle in the witness-box. True, the destroyed youth knew the danger, and it is dreadfully clear that the danger itself was part, and a large part, of the attraction. But that could be said of all Utopias, and many a parent has cursed the day that the very word was coined. For the defence, we claim that it was the *lack* of any utopian vision that made a world in which our young chose a hideous death in preference to a meaningless life. "They have made a desert, and called it peace"; our young have concluded that the peace is unreal, and decided that the real desert was a better bargain.

The natural rebellion of the young against their elders has very often been grounded in the idea of money, and in particular the earning of it, and more particularly still, the way their parents got and spent it. But now, the rejection of the parents' affluence was ubiquitous, complete and passionate. If the cannon was to shoot down such living, the match that set it off was a phrase which no one has yet claimed as his or her progeny, but which has certainly earned its place in Utopia's history: the Affluent Society.

In the 1960s society *was* affluent. The cry that rang out in France when Napoleon was finally dispatched – *Enrichissez-vous!* – was everywhere rapidly translated and even more rapidly put into practice. The wretched Fifties were over, and the western world had earned comfort. But that, of course, was precisely what the young rejected with scorn. What *they* wanted was Utopia, and they wanted it at once.

The new age – it was called that, but with capital letters – was dawning, and the confining values that the young had been taught and had rebelled against had no place in that newborn universe. So intent and elegiac were the demands for a new universe, filled with new men and women, that the movement took on the lineaments of a messianic millennium. It was certainly not a coincidence that the longed-for new world was always to be found in the clouds; the word "purity" was one of the cornerstones of the harmonious dwellings in the global village they were making, and of course the higher the purer. To breathe the pure air of the roof of the world, after the choking fumes of the nether regions, can make those who breathe it dizzy.

As the 1960s faded further and further into history, so did much of the furniture of the mind that had accompanied those remarkable years. One of the outposts to which the modern (and young) Voortrekkers repaired was the Indian ashram. By one of those ironies that rear their heads so often and so appositely, that it is most unlikely that they can all be the product of coincidence, it was at a time when the Indian government was endeavouring to become, or at least to seem to become, a modern industrial state, and the sight of the young people – who of all generations might have been the most sympathetic to India's plight and her attempts to alleviate it – streaming along the roads, packs on backs, towards the holy man of their choice, did nothing to endear the young of Europe to those charged in India with modernising their country. The resentment was unjust in two crucial particulars; first, it was India who taught the world that there was inward serenity to be had at the feet of those charismatic Indian figures who dispense it, and second, because many of those young people who did sit at their feet benefited almost unimaginably from what they learned there, so that whatever they failed to do for India, they achieved something real and important for their own cultures and countries, it was surely, on balance, a gain.

The inner Utopia, from which no one is debarred (since it is woven into the fabric of every human being from birth, who needs only to release and face it), was what they were seeking, and in an astonishing number of cases they found it. It may be that, in the end, all Utopias of ideology, of religion, of race, of politics, of art, of literature, of equality, of nation – all those dreams of making mankind perfect by the use of real instruments made in a real world – will have to cede pride of place to the unreal world of the ashram, the still centre in which Candide could cultivate his garden with inner peace, and in which all troubled people, which means all people, can find their own gardens to cultivate in that peace for ever.

That, of course, was what Nechaev thought; society as it is must be destroyed and then remade. Before *he* was destroyed, a good many people had been destroyed by violent means but not, unfortunately, remade. Dostoevsky delineated, down to the tiniest detail, the parlour-revolutionary who loves the bang of a bomb more than the most beautiful music; Peter Verkhovensky was having the time of his life, when from the *événements* in France to the Red Brigades in Italy and the Baader-Meinhof gang in Germany, broken windows gave place to broken lives. And all, remember, in the name of Utopia.

To make something perfect it is not enough to patch it, to make good the wear and tear. No; it must be totally smashed and replaced, phoenix-like, with something vastly better. What, after all, is the hallmark of Utopia? It is perfection. Can even a single blemish be allowed to disturb the smooth body of perfection? Indeed, can any fragment of what has been destroyed be left, a standing reproach to those who think that almost-perfection will be enough?

That is harsh doctrine, but it can get worse. It is only one short step from the belief that destruction must precede construction to the belief that destruction in itself is valuable, even if what is destroyed is not rebuilt, indeed even if there is no intention of replacing it. That is when destruction becomes an end in itself, and mere anarchy is loosed upon the world.

"Damn braces; bless relaxes." Where Blake sowed, others reaped, not always for the better. Man is born free, no doubt, and certainly he should not be everywhere in chains; so far we can agree with Rousseau. But are there any limits, and if there are, who lays them down, and with what authority? Can we do anything at all, provided that we do not hurt another person (or, wantonly, any animal)?

Let us start at a somewhat gruesome point. In 1991, a group of men, in a house near London, met to practise upon one another a wide variety of sadistic homoerotic indignities, many of them truly sickening to read about. In the course of their activities they pierced each other's penises with nails, hung each other up, the better to whip one another, burnt each other with candles, and enjoyed a further variety of such stimuli; throughout, they perused pornographic magazines and photographs.

Police, apparently tipped off, raided the premises and arrested all the participants. They were charged with causing bodily harm, and their defence was that all the participants were of age, that everything done was done with full consent, that the premises on which they were doing these things were entirely private, that nothing in any way improper was done outside the walls, and no disturbance was caused to any neighbour.

All those contentions were accepted at the trial; nevertheless they were convicted and imprisoned, and their conviction was upheld on appeal. Should it have been? (Of course not.)

We may divagate for a moment to consider the human body itself. Once, it was regarded as a sacred receptacle, given by God and not to be abused. God, in his wisdom, did not explain that some bodies were more nearly perfect than others; the ill-favoured had no one to complain to, and the well-favoured were naturally pleased with the state of affairs. But the hideous activities described (whether designated as criminal or not) display an attitude to the body that would once have been regarded as fit only for execution. Eschewing such extreme attitudes, what about the men in the house of horror? Should they be criminally punished? (Of course not.) What does the body say? The human body is not perfect, either in appearance or action. Ideal forms abound in art, but not in reality. The Discobolos and the Venus de Milo, to take two familiar examples, set the standard for their time, which has proved to be a surprisingly long one, considering how many changes in fashion there have been over the years. But the search for perfection is a real need in itself, irrespective of its role in the mating process, and it is not just a fad; it goes very deep, and constitutes a powerful symbol of the yearning for perfection that lies within us all. Leonardo's famous drawing of the perfect human proportions in a circle is a measurement of mankind itself, and clearly meant to be; but long before it was composed, the world had become obsessed with the search for a quality of beauty that was not only in the eyes of the beholder.

Catherine di Medici had a waist measurement of 14 inches; it was achieved by her use of iron corsets, nor is that the most extreme attempt at perfection, for in our own age women have subjected themselves to the torment of having unwanted hairs plucked out one by one, of being baked in mud and clay like any free-range chicken, of dangerous and wholly unnecessary surgery to engineer the notorious face-lift, to "correct" the shape of a nose, or to make the breasts more shapely, of following an infinite variety of diets, each more and more unhealthy and fraudulent than the last, of desperately seeking a way to forget the grim reality of Hamlet's gravedigger: "Now get you to my lady's chamber and tell her, let her paint an inch thick, to this favour she must come: make her laugh at that".

But it is no laughing matter, in two senses. First, even the most beautiful body will, as the gravedigger pointed out, ultimately rot in the grave as inevitably as will that of a blowsy, red-nosed fishwife, and second, the very search for the impossible can only make the seeker unhappy, as the will-o-the-wisp dances round the yearning but never alights upon it.

These observations have been couched in female terms only, but the male gender in its own way is hardly less determined than the other half, as witness the astonishing rise of the male aid to beauty – the vast range of perfumes, after-shave lotions, hair dressings, skin-softeners, pleasingly scented deodorants – all of which have brought untold millions into the coffers of the manufacturers. It is possible that this extraordinary phenomenon has been caused by the significant change in the relations of the sexes, as women, inch by inch, move towards real equality; if the male, who had ruled throughout the centuries until now, is becoming uncertain of his dominance, it may be that he thinks that a rush to grooming will help to shore up his crumbling empire. (And what about the concomitant rise of the "workout" at a "fitness centre", to say nothing of jogging; surely these are also indicative of male uncertainty.)

Nevertheless, the secret of the perfect body has still not been found, and is still avidly sought. The seeking is a long way away from those innocent magazines like *Health and Beauty*, in the days when everything was innocent, which displayed rather unenticing nudes in sylvan surroundings, always with their eyes cast modestly down. Today, the magazines are further from innocence (though not so far as to cross the border of pornography), yet the stereotype, albeit a different one, is there; the uniform gleaming teeth, the uniform substantial bosoms, the uniform provocative pose, above all the absolutely uniform smile, proclaims that the body has now been perfected. True, the "page three girl" has been perfected, but she is an artifact, as is the one in the advertisements, where she is found lolling on the bonnets of expensive motorcars.

However empty or even debased, even the most pitiful attempt at beauty signals the importance attached to the appearance of the body. This is to some extent the mating game moved on a little further, but it cannot be the whole explanation; the style will change soon, and the changed version will in turn be changed, and each time the perfect body will be announced, only to give way to another version. If that is not a form of Utopia, what else can it be? Perhaps it is time, at last, to take de Sade seriously.

★

The *dégringolade* has continued, and at an ever-increasing speed; it is now more than two years since it was revealed that university students in Britain can obtain a degree in English Literature without reading a single line of Shakespeare or Milton. De Sade has posthumously ridden that wave, and the result is that he is taken seriously, and is entered in the files of Utopia under the heading of "Utopia of the senses". Thus, it has been said, he must be classed.

The turn of the eighteenth century saw a loosening of attitudes to sexuality, comparable to that in the years of the English Restoration and the almost worldwide one in the 1960s (de Sade was in the Bastille when the Revolution broke out). Of course, in such a time there were others than de Sade in the field, though only Restif de la Bretonne has endured. Anyway, de Sade's Utopia, as may be imagined, consisted of unenforceable rules by which the "pleasure-principle" may be enjoyed. For complete enjoyment there have to be victims, and de Sade propounds many similarities of less exotic governments and their laws, in arguing that his state is much the same as France's. His logic, too, once unleashed, is perfect; the way to deal with rape and murder is to decriminalise such acts.

Utopia has taken many forms, and will no doubt take many more. Many would not be recognised as such, and some would induce abhorrence. In a sense, the only place for de Sade (apart, perhaps, from the Bastille) is in his Utopia; let him spin his fancies as extravagantly as he pleases, for in doing so we need not take him seriously, and therefore find no need to join the battle of those who would persuade us that he is a significant, even seminal, figure.

Nevertheless, de Sade's fantasy of total sexual licence may be the final holocaust of utopian self-destruction. It is almost impossible to finish any of his books, not because they are so dreadful in what they depict, but because the incessant repetition of the surprisingly limited products of de Sade's imagination is unable to keep the reader's attention. More interesting (though not very much more) is de Sade's influence today.

De Sade's legacy, an astonishing one, can be seen at its most striking in so trivial a form as the pornographic magazine, which flourishes in mainly western nations, and above all in the United States. Very few of these make any pretence of beauty, instruction, meaning or interest; they are for no other purpose (though their proliferation suggests that purpose is recognised by a remarkable number of men) than arousal. To discuss the apparent need of such arousal would be to stray from the remote but enduring role of de Sade, but one aspect of them, which would certainly be familiar to him, is immediately obvious from the merest glance at a few pages. These magazines are one with de Sade in their conviction that woman is and always should be *nothing* but a receptacle, and her *only* nature is one of perfect receptivity and submissiveness.

It is somewhat depressing to realise that, according to the magazines and men who buy them, there has been no advance in the relations between the sexes for more than two centuries, but it seems that in Pornutopia the same standards still apply. That this state of affairs runs side by side with the genuine advances of women which have been won in the matter of equality suggests that de Sade and his progeny are all the more determined not to accept the emancipation now manifest almost everywhere. But that can be easily explained; there always was – and de Sade demonstrates it most thoroughly – a powerful element of fear in men's attitude to women, whence their desperate need to degrade womankind. That fear has certainly not lessened; indeed, it must have multiplied with the growing tide of equality. For it is not very extravagant to think of that fear as the fear of being ejected from Utopia, where *120 days of Sodom* can be enjoyed without any complaint from the infinitely submissive creatures which, to de Sade and his descendants, have no function other than to be enjoyed.

Are there things such as self-restraints? If there are no bonds or bounds, are we truly free, or – a subtle thought may be inserted here – are there some kinds of freedom which are truly unfree? If there were no rules against the use of highly addictive drugs, can the addict who knowingly takes them and is slowly destroyed by them be called free? If not, what is freedom?

Let us be more domestic, and go back to Blake. Many modern psychiatric experts say that repression is harmful. Some argue that we shall never be fully ourselves until we have dispensed with all the shackles that society puts upon us in the guise of religion, morals, rules of all kinds. Explorers of the subconscious mind strive to free us from the chains hung on us in our infancy, but their aim is to give us a balanced and understanding self, not a ticket to, say, debauchery. *The Martyrdom of Man*, by Winwood Reade, is a forgotten book today, but at the end of the nineteenth century it caused a sensation, denouncing, as it did, God, for binding man's hands; ever since, the argument has gone on in one form or another.

Utopians, obviously, must be concerned in this argument. It has been argued that the complete rejection of restraint *is* Utopia, but in the classical utopian texts there is very little evidence to support the view. The great progenitor of Utopias, More, certainly did not advocate licence, even the modest and healthy kind. In very few Utopias are there specific or even hinted provisions for the pleasures of the flesh, or even for the table; there is many a teetotal Utopia, which must be one of the greatest misunderstandings of the idea ever conceived. But we need not confine ourselves to the more obvious pleasures; the question to be asked is "In this Utopia, is the individual restrained by no conventions, whether of man or of God?" The trouble with the question, plain as it is, is that Utopias have mostly refused to answer it. If the longed-for Nirvana is reached, what need of giving it names? This comes back to one of Utopia's greatest problems: when it is achieved, and filled with entirely happy utopians, how do we stave off boredom? But we must here face the real problem: since Utopia has *not* yet been achieved, we must examine these principles in the real world. It can be said that the answer is already at hand; the choice of blessed relaxes has been made. Self-satisfaction runs through our mortal, unutopian world, and gratification is king. We need not discuss it on the level of crime; is what we see about us in the most innocent of hedonisms a danger to societies like ours, or is it the long-awaited health clearance?

17

The Pied Piper comes into his own

O F ALL the problems that irk the utopians, the greatest is the problem of evil. Of course, that problem has existed since mankind began to think about his, and the world's, meaning. All religions have to face the idea of evil, and why we have it, nor is the question by any means easily answered; it may be unanswerable. Even if we think of the universe as meaningless, so that good and evil are alike distributed at random, we cannot escape the thought that it could be eradicated, nor can we readily answer when we come up against the puzzling fact that, by any reckoning, there are far more good people than evil ones; the random distributionists must be alarmed at this assault on what they believe, but they can hardly argue that the balance should be corrected.

Among those who contemplate evil, surely the utopian has the hardest nut to crack. If the world could be perfect, why isn't it? Why have so many plans for Utopia not only come to grief, but in coming there unleashed a vast reservoir of new evil? No wonder that there are extreme utopians who believe that when Utopia is achieved nature herself will take a hand, and there will be no more poisonous insects or plants, and indeed no more weeds. And if that is no wonder, it is doubly no wonder that the utopian, seized of the notion that Utopia can be brought into being, will stop at nothing to help it on its path. It is all the easier to chart the path, what with modern communications technology. Perhaps the computer will usher in Utopia; possibly though, the computers will rule the world, including mankind.

As faith wanes, Utopia gains. Unfortunately, there is no coaching-inn on the road to perfection; we must get there in an instant or not at all. Meanwhile, with neither God nor King Utopus to govern us, the fragmentation of society, thought and comprehension goes on faster and faster; it begins to look as though a great number of people will need remedial counselling (yet another utopian nostrum for our times) before they are fit to mingle with the elect. Actually, the problem is an imaginary one; the whole point of Utopia is that we shall all be exactly the same at the moment we cross the threshold.

Egalitarianism is the first cousin to the essentially utopian belief that no one should earn more than anyone else, whatever the disparities of talents or production. Indeed, the argument goes further; it is widely and publicly argued, particularly in the United States, that there *are* no differences or disparities of talent and to insist that there are is branded as "elitism". (How few years ago it was that "elite" by common consent meant the best!) But these rules can be effective only if there is no independent judge; it is hardly too much to say that, as utopians have dispensed with God, their philosophy would once have been classified as heresy. Indeed, Thomas Molnar here returns to argue his case fiercely:

> At Utopia's roots there is defiance of God, pride unlimited, a yearning for enormous power and the assumption of divine attributes with a view to manipulating and shaping mankind's fate. The utopian is not content with pressing man into a mould of his own manufacture; he is not a mere despot, dictator or totalitarian leader holding all temporal and spiritual power. His real vice is, first, the desire to dismantle human individuality through the dissolution of individual conscience and consciousness, and then to replace these with the collectivity and coalesced consciousness...the utopian...wants to deal with one entity so as to simplify his own task of transforming the indomitable human spirit into a slave...It is noteworthy that while, at least in the world-view of our western religions, Almighty God created man with a free will, the utopian makes the human condition so rigid that freedom is excluded from Utopia. He replaces the concept of divine providence with unchangeable determinism.

That is all very well; buttressed by his own faith, Molnar can – must – denounce heresy as he sees it. But he forgets, in the heat of his indignation, that we are seeking Utopia, not finding it.

Utopia is not self-contained; no Utopia is an island, entire unto itself. We utopianise other lands, other customs, other peoples, most of all other ages. The yearning for a Golden Age, inevitably set in the far past, is only the most obvious of this form of utopification. Distance lends enchantment to the past; it is man's innermost longing, the longing for perfection, that brings about the legends, the "legendariness" of other times, other places. We know that our time is not perfect, and that causes us pain; to assuage the pain we flee to a place that has no pain in it, and we do not mind that the place does not exist, or, if it ever did exist, not in the form we have given it with our envy of the past.

But we do not stop there. We take a rod to our own backs. Despite the fact that we are stuck with our own society, we denounce it with our contemporary feelings for its corruptions, its fallings-off, its indifferences, its hates and angers, as falling short of − well, of what? Surely, of the perfection that no real society can have, but a mythical one, long vanished, can and did have. Many have dreamed of Utopia, of a world without all the ills the flesh is heir to, or even without *any* of them.

Expectation never fulfilled is the hallmark of Utopia, and it is a considerable tribute to the faith of the human race that through disappointments and betrayals, wrong turnings and dead ends, mistakes and failures, false prophets and ventriloquists, we still believe that round the next bend in the road, the next revolution, the next ray of new hope, even the next sunny day, we shall at last inherit the earth.

What exactly is Utopia, or rather, how shall we know it when we see it? There are for instance, in More's own Utopia, punishments; but we seekers of perfect worlds would reject such an idea, and deem the Utopia flawed. How do utopians fill their days, and how stave off boredom? Babeuf was certain that the excitements of Utopia will be enough, though others, no less utopian than he, insist that what faces them is an eternity of peaceful contemplation.

There is a sign. In all the myriad Utopias that we fallible beings have conjured up, it seems that one, and only one, condition is common to them all. As far as the survey of Utopias goes, *in none is there envy*. Perhaps there is nothing to envy in a perfect world, but the idea goes deeper; even in hierarchical Utopias there seems to be no covetousness, for all are contented with their lot. It is a powerful tribute to utopian beings, the banishment of that most corrosive poison. But who said "Utopia lies in rejecting Utopia"?

A striking example of the utopification of ancient lands and peoples can be found in Peter Shaffer's play, *The Royal Hunt of the Sun*, which depicts the meeting of the Inca civilisation and the Spanish. The two worlds seem centuries apart, and their attitudes, mores, ideas of kingship and of fellowship could hardly be more different.

Nevertheless (Shaffer was writing a play, after all), there was a bewildered exchange of civilisations, at the end of which Pizarro's notions of the Incas as sub-human creatures have undergone a startling change. And no wonder, when he learns what qualities lie in these disregarded savages. Hear Atahualpa, the Incas' king, giving his people their instructions:

In the eighth month you will plough. In the ninth, sow maize. In the tenth, mend your roofs…nine years to twelve, protect harvests. Twelve to eighteen, care for herds. Eighteen to twenty-five, warriors for Atahualpa Inca!…At twenty-five all will marry. All will receive one tupu of land…They will never move from there. At birth of a son one more tupu will be given…At fifty all people will leave work for ever and be fed in honour till they die.

On which Pizarro, having understood what he is facing, tells his own people what sort of savages they have fallen among:

Oh…it's not difficult to shame Spain. This shames every country which teaches we are born greedy for possessions. Clearly we're made greedy when we're assured it's natural. But there's a picture for a Spanish eye! There's nothing to covet, so covetousness dies at birth…

A far cry from the absolute? Perhaps; but the very nature of the absolute means that the wind bloweth where it listeth. For instance, mankind seeks symmetry, though there is no gain of any kind in it. Much more important is harmony, which mankind seems to seek even more assiduously, and there is a tremendous symbol in that search in the form of music; a piano cannot be perfectly tempered, however it is tuned, though musicians try again and again, even making special pianos with which to attempt the impossible. The search for a perfect instrument is a most obviously utopian impulse; for that matter, men have gone mad trying to find *pi* recurring, and computer experts have harnessed the greatest mainframes, capable of doing a million sums a second, in the very same search.

An ingenious mathematician wrote a book called *Flatland*, which discussed the impossibility of imagining the extra dimension that we are assured exists in some unimaginable form. Unimaginable, indeed, for in *Flatland* it is impossible for the people who live in an entirely flat existence even to conceive of the meaning of those who have height, and who in turn are unable to understand length. Similarly, it is no use trying to find perfection, because – being imperfect – we cannot imagine what it is or might be.

That might well be graven on Utopia's tombstone; the *Flatland* metaphor is more powerful than it seems. We cannot plumb the depths of perfection; well and good. But we cannot plumb the shallows either, apparently, as witness the history of utopian communities.

The utopian community comes surprisingly late in the long story, at least if we are strict with the definition; the Cave of Adullam is hardly a utopian retreat, and it would stretch the definition dangerously far to include Brigham Young and his Mormons. A case can be made for the monastery, certainly an enclosed community with a single aim, but that is to view it only from the outside; the monks and their order would be horrified to think of their retreat as a long yearned-for island of perfect happiness. No doubt they would aspire to an ultimate Utopia in heaven, but the monastery (and the stricter the rule the more this is true) is only a means of concentrating on the devotions that are to test their worthiness for God.

Virtually all the early communities were inspired by their members' religion; not surprisingly. Today, however, some of these havens have only a mild and super-ecumenical connection with any formal rite. But here we must stop to think about the entire nature and philosophy of the utopian community. Is it, we must ask, only the *Pons Asinorum* of Utopia, or perhaps another instance of the triumph of hope over experience? Since the end of the Second World War, and in particular in the 1960s, there have been countless attempts to found, and o.i firm foundations, a community of like-minded souls which would endure indefinitely.

There is a black mark on humanity's score-sheet, and it seems to have been there almost as long as humanity. It takes the form of an inability to live happily in close proximity with more than a very few other human beings (except for, say, the monastery and other groups bound together by one, and only one, integument). A study of the divorce statistics in advanced countries suggests that the difficulty with groups must be almost insurmountable, to go by what happens where only *two* people are involved. Not only is there an apparent psychological obstacle to overcome, but there is an immense wealth of information on the subject, practically all of it gloomy.

Here, the cloven hoof of Utopia is seen. In a perfect world, any number of people may happily cohabit. But that is because, in a perfect world, the citizens are perfect. In an *im*perfect world, however (which is the only kind available outside Utopia itself), the imperfections in the citizens lead to communal imperfection.

But what then of the enemy? The more perfect Eden, the more determined the snake. One of the strangest obsessions in the long and tragic story of Utopia is the failure of the utopians to allow a margin of error. Again and again they have plunged into a beautifully beckoning paradise without any inspection of the premises. Of course, the beckoning paradise is what they have dreamed of, and a dream so powerful and tenacious is not lightly discarded. Yet no precautions are taken, and the deceived are left to repent at leisure. Many times a week we read in the newspapers of a smooth-talking confidence trickster inducing some hapless householder to sign a document which has no purpose other than to relieve the householder of a sum of money in return for a worthless piece of paper, promising all the delights of a holiday home in the sun. This was called "timeshare"; there were and are perfectly honest timeshare companies, but there are, alas, also dishonest ones, and these feasted so long and so scandalously on the naïve customers that the government had to step in, without invitation, to protect those who made no claim to protection: the piece of paper was pinned to a new law, by the terms of which the piece of paper could not be acted upon until a week had gone by – a week that was used for further and more sensible thought. Good intentions; *but there was no noticeable use of the legislation.*

It is stranger still. Utopias flourish, and Utopias perish; in the very sight of one that is perishing, the progenitors are eagerly hurrying to build a new one, frequently on the ashes of the failure. The utopian propensity, it seems, is so strong in us that no warning, no example, no logic is sufficient to break the golden chain, however many times it is shown to be made entirely of brass.

Have our utopians never heard of original sin? (Let alone the subsequent kind.) The strangeness of the story lies not in the fact that human beings are, and are known to be, imperfect; the mystery is why, when that imperfection is everywhere, do the utopians behave as though it does not exist? The greatest weakness in the utopian psychology is cried up as though it is the greatest strength. Again and again, in the teeth of the evidence, we are told that man is naturally perfect, and only when he is left entirely alone to do what he wishes does he become imperfect.

Harmless utopians, watching their commune fall to pieces, are proper subjects for sympathy. But there are also harmful utopians. Procrustes knew what he was about. If man, born perfect, has become imperfect, he must be made perfect again, at whatever price and irrespective of his own wishes. Men must be made perfect, and nothing else matters. Nor can there be any restrictions on the means by which the perfection is to be achieved.

Men must be made pure, with whatever means of coercion. And if it becomes plain that the re-perfecting of man is difficult, perhaps even getting more difficult as time goes by, it must be that evildoers are obstructing the programme.

The very terminology is significant. Stalin demanded the "liquidation" of his enemies, real or imaginary. The use of that word has largely been overlooked, but it should not be, for a moment's thought would show how strange a word it is for such a meaning. To liquidate, used transitively, means to reduce to a liquid. In that context the word can only mean what it would mean in a modern kitchen with all the labour-saving devices: the enemies were to be crushed so completely that they would be reduced to a liquid.

The road to hell is usually paved with good intentions, but sometimes it is paved with bad ones. The trouble comes when those who follow the road find it increasingly difficult to decide which version they have embarked upon. Unfortunately, history insists that the result is in any case the same, and, tragically enough, there is enough truth in history's claim to make evasion impossible.

The French Revolution was hailed by Charles James Fox with a cry that has gone into history: "How much the greatest event it is that ever happened in the world! And how much the best!" It was not long before the Terror was unleashed, and not much longer before the revolution was devouring its own children – a story that can be repeated again and again through the centuries.

"Come not, Lucifer; I'll burn my book!" But it was too late for Faust to repent; the diabolical bargain had been struck, and Faust, having enjoyed the fruits of his side of it, was now to suffer Lucifer's. Utopians will never believe it, but it is true: *the Devil cheats*. Look at Swift's Struldbruggs. They had prayed to live forever, and their prayer was answered. But as they sank deeper into the dreadful infirmities of mind and body, their prayers were all for death, and *those* prayers were not answered.

For that matter, did Karl Marx imagine, let alone want, the gigantic tyrannies that ruled in his name? No; but he cannot shift the responsibility, which was his. And in any case, his doctrine contained already the seeds of its decay, the inevitable fate of all "closed" systems. Yes, but a utopian community can hardly be called a closed system; why do they, too, break down? The answer has been given: communities, like other groups of human beings, are no more perfect than individual ones, and whereas the solitary sinner has no effect on others, the members of the groups – no less sinning as we all are – inevitably impinge.

Yet if we cannot live together, and we cannot live separately, where shall we find that peace of the heart which heralds Utopia? Throughout all history, there has been an answer to that question, and countless millions have given the anwer. Throughout history, there has been a multifarious form of seeking: it is the seeking of a new land. There have been, throughout history, thousands of great migrations; some have been caused by pressure on food resources or the drying-up of vital water-courses; some have been for conquest, some to avoid conquest, some fleeing persecution, some for sheer inquisitiveness, some from changes in age-old professions, some for religious reasons. But always, there have been individuals, families, tribes, even hordes, who have packed up their possessions (usually few) and voyaged into the unknown in order to better their station in the world, to live more comfortably, to rise from the bottom of society to take a place in it.

Yes, but what persuaded these last that they would be able to better themselves, to rise, to leave poverty for, if not wealth, at least a competence? Many, after all, knew nothing about the country they were going to; the grandparents of the present author, for instance, were told that the ship they had boarded was going to England, but that left them none the wiser, because they had never heard of England. They, it is true, were wandering not entirely for betterment, but also for a place where Jews could live peaceably, without fear of pogroms, for they were subjects of the Tsar. But many, very many, had no such fears to remember, and were seeking to use their talents profitably, or if they had no talents that were needed where they were going, to learn a useful trade as quickly as possible.

Disappointment was inevitable; it took two generations for those travellers to find a niche of success and plenty. Some, inevitably, became embittered; where were the streets that were paved in gold?

That, surely, was the utopian question: how had they managed to dream of riches, how had they guessed, wrongly as it happened, that wherever they were going there was comfort, a trade, success, wealth? The Irish expressed their astonished dismay in song: convinced that the streets of London were paved "with silver and gold", and discovering that they had been misled, they concluded that "they might as well be, where the Mountains of Mourne sweep down to the sea". Meanwhile, something similar was happening in New York, where Emma Lazarus held up a torch which invited the streams of those seeking a new life to rely on it: "Give me", she said, "your poor, your ignorant, your huddled masses yearning to breathe free". Again, the huddled masses found that it was not nearly so easy as that, and the same pattern established itself; two generations had to pass before those travellers felt solid ground beneath their feet. (Though when they did, they far outstripped the successes of Europe; many of the greatest fortunes, and many thousands of very substantial ones, were made by the sons and grandsons of the immigrants, who – again in contrast with Britain – felt no need to change their names for others less outlandish.

Utopia calls; and its voice is heard in the remotest corners of the globe, even if what it is saying is unintelligible. The mere lilt of its siren song is enough to bring the hearers streaming out of their homes and villages like the achievements of the Pied Piper.

The Pied Piper, as it happens, is a perfect illustration of Utopia; by magic, the plague of rats was cured with his hypnotic flutings, drowned five fathoms deep, all but one. But every coin has two sides; the burghers of Hamelin, mean and tragic men, refused their deliverer his pay, and "you'll see me pipe in another fashion". Another fashion indeed, as their children vanished for ever in the mountain. Again and again, amid simple folk and learned, old and young, cynical and romantic, the once burned still do not shun the fire; the mirage of Utopia is professed more powerful, which only means more prize-bringing, than the trick it invariably plays.

There was, in America, another and very different form of seeking a better life; just as so many of the immigrant poor were immigrants not only from poverty but also from persecution, so that those who pushed out the frontiers of a land hardly known to most of its citizens ("Go West, young man!") were seeking profit but by no means only profit; a utopian pull towards a world elsewhere drove them on into the boundless, uncharted, empty land. (Later there was another and far more powerful pull, when gold was discovered, and the utopian rush for that eternal poison began; a few made huge fortunes, more made a sizeable pile, most found nothing, and very many were ruined.)

There is a restlessness in mankind, which can be found in even the most placid of mortals. Men and women seem to be born with inquisitiveness in them, and it is well known that restlessness leads to a desire to find out, and probably *vice versa*. And in no area of this restlessness is the desire for a better life, a better world, greater and more rewarding. Is there a utopian gene in mankind, which pulls or pushes us to *get on*, to prosper, to do better than our parents could? For it is not immediately obvious that we need to get on, and indeed there is pain and effort, and often great disillusion, in the striving that is required.

If that gene exists then, it can hardly escape being labelled utopian, for what can be more utopian than the belief that it lies in all of us to climb the greasy pole when all around us there are millions (and the further we look the greater number of millions) who have manifestly failed to rise on it?

Yet few will challenge the assertion that one great march, which took place a century and a half ago, was the strangest and most pitiable. For obstinacy, for courage, for murderous slaughter, for belief in what they were doing, for the conviction that God had sanctioned their resolve, for the millions upon millions they drove into helotry (drove so deeply that only in the late 1980s were they enabled to take the first steps into unfettered manhood), for all these reasons and many more, the Great Trek of the Boers stands out in history, and will continue to do so, as a monument to men who believed in themselves, and acted upon that belief.

When they harnessed their wagons, the place to which they were moving was almost entirely *terra incognita*. Nevertheless, the Boers, a stubborn people, had persuaded themselves that the interior of southern Africa would give them living-space and more land – which would become the great prize. The Voortrekkers – the very word rings with dust, obstinacy, danger and success – were to learn better. African tribesmen, long accustomed to think the land theirs, stalked and killed some of the Voortrekker bands, whose numbers were reduced also by disease. The defensive circle of oxwagons, which became a symbol (the same circle was used by the American pioneers pushing westward), made the journey safer, and gradually a resistance built up against the wide range of maladies. (Later, a more grim response to the slaughter of Boers was devised: retribution. When a substantial Boer column was utterly destroyed, a fearful vengeance was visited upon the Africans; the river on the banks of which the battle took place was re-named Blood River, because so great was the slaughter that the river ran red for three days.)

The British government, in 1843, announced that the territory of Natal was now part of the British Empire; the Boers, in even greater numbers now, rejected the annexation and set out again on the trek, yearning for a place that would be truly and permanently theirs. But that yearning for a magic land in which they could be satisfied at last was not only chimerical: more than a century later their descendants had become another kind of symbol – the symbol of implacable and lasting obstinacy in the face of necessity of change.

For although many decades had passed since African tribesmen had fought (and frequently won) great battles against the usurpers of their land, a different kind of struggle was growing more intense, a struggle over, of all things, the colour of the combatants. And in that struggle, the obstinacy of the Boers, which had never seeped out of their blood, became the great barrier to a settlement of this mad face-to-face battle for supremacy. So intense was the feeling among the Boers that there was even talk of another Great Trek, but it was a dream – the land of South Africa had advanced as European and American states had, and the modern, urban, mechanised society had no time for such dreams.

Yet it is difficult to condemn the Boers utterly. Their obstinacy was rooted in a vile earth: the belief that an equality between the colours would spell the end of the state, and above all the end of the Boer history. What we have we hold; an ancient cry, heard all over the world. It is a perverted utopian claim, but its strength is extraordinary, and the Boers sold up their farms, their homes, their very memories, to go somewhere, anywhere, that those words could be spoken by them, and lived by them. They lost, of course, and deserved to; but that iron resolve cannot but demand admiration. With people like that, what might South Africa have been, had the Boers all been struck colour-blind? And what would the original Voortrekkers think today, as they see a Boer enfranchising the Africans, and realising that the enfranchised must, by sheer force of numbers, be the dominant people, and rule the land?

18

Full circle

THE UTOPIA of loneliness has received little attention, though there have been countless hermits. Ordinary misanthropy contributes something to the genre, but however intense the misanthrope's detestation of the entire human race, in modern societies it must be impossible to avoid all human contact, even if it is no more than a visit to the supermarket where not a word need be spoken. But whether misanthropy can be classified as an aberrant form of Utopia, it is startlingly rare outside the categories mentioned above.

This is in itself powerful evidence of the bonding instinct in human beings. But can an individual be his own Utopia (as opposed to owning it)? Do we need company – need it, that is, so much that we cannot survive without it? There have been many imprisoned in solitary confinement through the ages, but even those had a regular visitor in their jailer.

Is self-sufficiency enough? Probably not. Man is not a solitary being; if he were, there would be no differentiation between the sexes, or need for any. "Leave me alone" is a phrase well-known and well-used; few of us – probably none of us – have had cause to use it in the form of "Leave me alone, for ever". There is a significant line in Orwell's *Nineteen Eighty-Four*, in which the victim says "Leave me alone", and his captor replies "I will leave you alone so long that you will not be able to bear it". St Simeon Stylites took solitude to its furthest possibility, yet even he was within sight and sound of other human beings. Perhaps only those who rely on an inner voice, a different understanding, a god or a goal – perhaps only these can shut themselves up in themselves, where they are not truly alone.

Maybe it is a pity; self-reliance is a noble attribute, and a world of solitary individuals, owing nothing to anyone else, is somehow an enticing prospect. But very soon those individuals would make contact with one another.

There are more pessimistic versions; *Lord of the Flies* argues that human beings, at any rate children, will rapidly disintegrate, or at least the bonds that keep their innate evil in check will. There is an uncomfortable moral for us in it, adults and all. But the fascination of shipwreck solitude is widespread; has anyone a theory about the extraordinary number of cartoons which show a desert island (this almost always being only a tiny mound showing above the water, with a tree in it)? It surely cannot be an accident, but there is no reason to think that cartoonists find desert-island jokes easier to come by.

Utopians, on the whole, do not warm to the modern world, and considering that utopians have been living in a series of modern worlds (for every world is modern in its day) they must by now be very bad-tempered. So they are, but for a better reason than they have ever had before. Nostalgia has always painted the past, even the most recent past, in heroic colours; it is indeed a utopian propensity to forget the dark side of the past and dwell upon the light. Today, however, as our own time not only speeds faster than any earlier era, but continues to go faster in itself, it is not only utopians who are unable to catch their breath. A computerised world is no longer a dream or a nightmare, but a prosaic fact, and one we cannot avoid or evade; moreover, every kind of mechanisation, labour-saving and general simplification, from credit-cards to advanced telephone systems and from 500-seater passenger aircraft to ground facilities almost capable of dealing with them, reinforces the genuine feeling, based on weighty evidence, that life is becoming literally inhuman.

For a long time, the utopian quest sought countries with a settled policy of resisting the dehumanising tendencies. It was not long, however, before it became obvious that such countries were now hastening to join the general advancement, nor could it be said that they did so on a whim, and were sure to regret it; the picturesque Indian or South American village is truly a moving and enviable sight, but it is likely to be inhabited by families who have not enough to eat, and whose average life-span tends to be about one-third of those in the advanced world.

It is pointless to mourn this movement, though many still do; but if the seeker of nostalgia cannot find a place that resists, and promises to continue resisting, there is nowhere for the utopian to take refuge. Except, that is, in the past, and a very dubious past, too.

Throughout almost all of history, and not only history written by utopians, there has figured the Noble Peasant and the Noble Savage. These are archetypes, and are held up to the advanced civilisations; but the holding is done by the latter. Partly from guilt, partly from the tendency to idealisation, partly from a genuine desire to understand, these noble twins have faced us over the centuries, and face us still. The attitude was at its most intense in the Romantic Movement, but it has never disappeared: what is modern anthropology if it is not its own romantic movement?

The idyll of the twin nobles takes many forms; there is the pastoral one, with the shepherd-boy playing his pipe; the naked and scarred warrior one, his cruel appearance belied by his tenderness to children; the artistic one, epitomised of course in Gauguin (to say nothing of the figures he painted); the tragically diseased one, his malady brought from the outsider into a society unable to resist a virus that, being unknown, cannot produce the essential antibodies; the dashing one, like the "Red Indians", who have seen themselves turned by the white man into a creature worth only slaughtering, and have endured to see the same white man sitting at the red man's feet to learn what wisdom the once-despised Apache is willing to impart; and many more besides.

Nor is it safe to dwell upon the more ancient and startling practices of the Noble Savage's ancestors; discussion of the Aztecs' multiple sacrifices, at which living men and women had their hearts cut out of their bodies by chanting priests, is frowned upon. (So much so that when a friend of the present author, travelling in Mexico, was shown the sacrificial stone, his guide, faintly embarrassed, murmured "Er...that was for the, er, cardiectomies".)

So the Noble Peasant and the Noble Savage have embedded them deep in the utopian tradition. It runs in many channels; one of these is hatred, or at least suspicion, of the city. The city is the epitome of the artificial, the man-made, the unromantic. Since Cobbett dubbed London "the Great Wen", it has become a symbol of putridity, though, after all, London and other great cities are not now the cesspits which brought Cobbett's condemnation. It is a metaphor that the city is held in contempt: modern romantics like G.K. Chesterton denounced the city as the centre of plutocracy, usury and Jews. (Such anti-semitism was based on a belief that Jews brought commerce and commerce was man-made and unnatural, as opposed to nature-made, touched by God's hand and no other.)

There is a substantial body of literature hymning nature and speaking of the city only with shudders; one of the best known and best loved, *Lark Rise to Candleford*, was published at the precise moment when such truly pastoral idylls were about to die. But if a country like England, sufficiently small and sufficiently central in the western world, must lose that innocence, there were countries elsewhere which could keep it longer, indeed for ever if legend would take a hand. To this day, many people who live far away from the south seas believe that in those idyllic lands beautiful girls daily rise from the arms of their handsome and virile lovers, and stroll a few yards to pluck a variety of fruit for their breakfast. Anyone who has seen the enormous number of motorcycles on Tahiti, and heard the noise they make, will be disillusioned, but the illusion still lingers, albeit from afar.

Again and again, we see, or think we do, ancient nations with natural people, ruined by conquest, by force or corruption. The Conquistadores, the "Grab for Africa", the Opium Wars, Commander Perry and the opening of Japan – all of these share the stains of slavery, oppression and destruction which have inevitably followed, to feed the cities far away.

And yet it could have been otherwise, at least in the dreams of utopians. If civilisation is the antithesis of feeling, let us get away from civilisation and simply feel. It cannot be difficult; the seasons come round, as they have done for innumerable centuries, and their cycles, signifying completeness, are welcomed. The Noble Peasant, closer to the land, can teach us all to live, while the brittle civilisation that knows nothing of the joys of nature tries to imitate the peace and harmony of the land: and fails.

So does the parent of all this, the Romantic Movement – a manifestly utopian title. It is foolish to dismiss the Romantics as shallow poseurs, well-bred and mostly rich. Such things were said about them in their time, and we should be able to step back from the follies and the preciousness, and see what they contributed. True, the comical side of it was always visible, but its effects were real. In any case, the Romantic Movement was ripe for Utopia, just as it had been ripe for the two Nobles, and the plums could be heard falling from the beginning of the last quarter of the eighteenth century to the end of the first quarter of the nineteenth.

The Romantic Movement did contribute very substantially to literature and the visual arts, and hardly less (though in a different form) to music. Feeling was all; the most interesting (and of course valuable) result of the subjective impulse was a movement which numbered in its literary ranks

Blake, Coleridge, Wordsworth, Shelley and Keats – hardly to be dismissed as a guarded claque. Moreover, the Movement (the capital letter is engrained in any discussion of the subject) was by no means confined to Britain; such European figures as Goethe (*The Sorrows of Young Werther* epitomised the Romantic Movement throughout all Europe), and there were many more, including Schiller, Victor Hugo and Rousseau, an entire Romantic Movement in himself.

In painting, the subjective feeling almost burst the bounds of coherence; there are people today who still think Turner was mad, but even they must fall silent before Constable. Abroad, David, whose portrait of Napoleon in the saddle instantly became an icon, and has remained so, was joined by Géricault, particularly his *The Raft of the Medusa*, but the greatest European representative of the Movement in art was Goya, from naked Mayas to the horrors of war.

Music could not fail to join the dance; Bach would have been astounded by the new, lush, open-necked sounds, and even Mozart, who was astounded by nothing, would have raised his eyebrows. The Romantic Movement in music credits Beethoven with starting it (Benjamin Britten once said "the rot started with Beethoven"), and so he did, though he ploughed his own furrow, and would have moved as he did even if no one else followed.

Utopia and the Romantics never stopped holding hands. After all, "artists are the unacknowledged legislators of the world", or so they preached, and if feeling is all, those who feel the most are the leaders, who called the followers to transcendence through art, and especially poetry. No doubt they would have been horrified if they could have seen what subjective Romanticism eventually became: socially conscious art. Yet even that can be accommodated if the genius is powerful enough: see the work of Diego Rivera.

The legacy of the Romantic Movement was great; a vast amount of truly valuable art was left to the world, and the legacy far, far outweighed the absurdities. And anyway, they were no worse than the *philosophes*, and they left very little.

★

How does Utopia end? Foolish question; if it ever ended it would not be Utopia. An exploration of its innumerable forms, only a tiny number of which have made an appearance in this book, must demonstrate the depth and strength of the beautiful dream – the dream, that is, of a perfect world and the longing to live in it.

All human beings are imperfect. But in every one of them, however deep it is necessary to plumb, is the seed of perfection, and the yearning for it. Who can be unmoved by the story of the first Utopia, the Garden of Eden? Who can fail to grieve at the transgression which ended the idyll? Who would not wish the deed undone, and everlasting bliss accomplished?

Utopia is widely thought of as a daydream, a palliative for the harsh reality of the wakened world. But that is to make a profound mistake. The utopian vista is, for all its elusiveness, solidly real, and it is no exaggeration to say that we cannot do without it.

How could we do without it? Why should we do without it? Answers galore; but let us take just one, for a moment. The idea of a Golden Age – a world in which the utopian promise had come true, rich and full – haunts us all, until we believe most passionately that once it was, *and will be again.* King Arthur, for one, gave a solemn promise that he would return, and the drowned world of Atlantis is as real to many of us as is the next street, and will one day rise from the water, dripping jewels.

Shortly before this book was finished, there was a newspaper story concerning a Polar expedition; the group had crossed the whole of Antarctica, including the Pole itself. They had suffered appalling privations, physical injury, lingering illness, and there was no purpose at all in the journey – not money, not lasting fame, not discoveries, nothing but frostbite. Could there be a better definition of Utopia? If there is, it must be in the form of those explorers who sailed uncharted seas, heedless of the danger that they would come to the edge of the world and fall off.

But there are dangers, and perhaps the dangers are weightier than the yearnings. The great ideologies of the twentieth century, each of them possessed with a vision of pure Utopia, slaughtered tens of millions in their mad but utopian beliefs. More terribly utopian still, each of these slaughter-houses had its throng of vociferous believers. It is salutary to wonder what would have happened if Hitler had won the war and survived to be praised from far away. Some, even many, would surely have effortlessly changed to the new emperor of evil, but only because they would want a perfect, utopian world to worship.

Full circle

"The end of the world is nigh." That, in one form or another (sometimes in the most literal sense), has been repeatedly prophesied. Eschatalogical beliefs abound in Utopia, and this one is the most powerful and frequent of all. Not surprising: when the world ends, Utopia begins. As the millennium approaches, there will, no doubt about it, be the same kind of warnings, threats, reproaches, dooms, terrors that filled the world a thousand years ago; the tenacity of Utopia is astounding.

Utopia is essential; but it cannot be confined in safe channels, and every now and again it breaks its banks and floods the world. It is part of us, and an important part, but it is all too often treated as though it was the whole of us, and that way disillusion lies. Perhaps it is time to put it away from us forever, though knowing well enough that we cannot do so.

And then there comes into view a gentle rebuke; a rebuke for those who would dispense with Utopia and all the centuries through which it has uplifted mankind. It is a poem by A. J. S. Tessimond, and it is titled "Heaven"; just that.

> In the heaven of the god I hope for (call him X)
> There is marriage and giving in marriage and transient sex
> For those who will cast the body's vest aside
> Soon, but are not yet wholly rarefied
> And still embrace. For X is never annoyed
> Or shocked; has read his Jung and knows his Freud,
> He gives you time in heaven to do as you please,
> To climb love's gradual ladder by slow degrees,
> Gently to rise from sense to soul, to ascend
> To a world of timeless joy, world without end.
> Here on the gates of pearl there hangs no sign
> Limiting cakes and ale, forbidding wine.
> No weakness here is hidden, no vice unknown.
> Sin is a sickness to be cured, outgrown.
> With the help of a god who can laugh, an unsolemn god
> Who smiles at old wives' tales of iron rod
> And fiery hell, a god who's more at ease
> With bawds and Falstaffs than with pharisees.
> Here the lame learn to leap, the blind to see.
> Tyrants are taught to be humble, slaves to be free.
> Fools become wise, and wise men cease to be bores,

Here bishops learn from lips of back-street whores,
And white men follow black-faced angels' feet
Through fields of orient and immortal wheat.
Villon, Lautrec and Baudelaire are here.
Here Swift forgets his anger, Poe his fear.
Napoleon rests. Columbus, journey done,
Has reached his new Atlantis, found his sun.
Verlaine and Dylan Thomas drink together,
Marx talks to Plato, Byron wonders whether
There's some mistake. Wordsworth has found a hill
That's home. Here Chopin plays the piano still.
Wren plans ethereal domes; and Renoir paints
Young girls as ripe as fruit but not yet saints.
And X, of whom no coward is afraid,
Who's friend consulted, not fierce king obeyed;
Who hears the unspoken thought, the prayer unprayed;
Who expects not even the learned to understand
His universe, extends a prodigal hand,
Full of forgiveness, over his promised land.

But perhaps A.E. Housman should have the last word, despite the fact, or perhaps because of it, that he was one of the least utopian men who ever lived. His poetry, despite his wit, is steeped in a profound melancholy, shot through with loss; he was a homosexual who regretted his condition, and he made it plain that he wished he had never been born.

He had given a friend, as a present, the gigantic poem (it runs – and unfinished – to some 4000 Latin hexameters) by Manilius. Manilius, who lived and wrote early in the first century AD, stressed, like Lucretius, the providential nature of the world, and the harmony established by the operation of divine reason. His poem was called *Astronomica*, and the poet was indeed obsessed with astronomy and astrology. Throughout the poem he versifies his heavenly calculations, often forcing his lines into grotesque shapes in doing so. In the circumstances, Housman's gift was bizarre, to say the least; there is no record of the recipient's feelings. But Housman, as he handed the book to his friend, wrote four lines of verse, on the fly-leaf.

These lines, melancholy and all, are what we must cling to. The siren call of Utopia has blurred distinctions, mishandled truth, preferred dreams to waking, soothed pain without curing the disease that causes it, believed things that should not be believed, made the world into a beautiful flower but found out too late that in that flower there is always curled a deadly poisonous serpent.

It is time to go.

> Here are the stars, the planets seven,
> And all their fiery train.
> Content you with the mimic heaven,
> And on the earth remain.

Acknowledgments

For an author who has been tinkering with his subject for twenty years, and has at last written the book, the last thing he wants is to thumb through piles of yellowing pages wherewith to construct a complete *apparatus criticus*; in any case, this is not that kind of book. I have therefore eschewed a bibliography, of which there are all too many (and more, no doubt, in the pipeline). But it is a pleasure, as well as a duty, to list some of the books that have, over the years, chimed with my own thoughts or shed light on my path, or even raised my hackles sufficiently for me to gallop off at a tangent.

There are, obviously, many well-known books that are too well known to need listing; no one needs to be told that William Morris's *News From Nowhere* is a touchingly innocent world, much less explain that Rabelais invented one of the most elaborately hedonist societies ever created. And I presume we all know about Thomas More.

I start with one of the most enchanting books I have ever had in my hands: *The Dictionary of Imaginary Places*, by Alberto Manguel and Gianni Guadalupi (Granada). It lists, in detail, some 1,500 imaginary lands, dark ones and sunlit, every one of them plausible. From there, I go to what is perhaps the most widely read book in this entire genre: B.F. Skinner's *Walden Two* (Macmillan), which turns at the end into nightmare, having been benign (at least showing a kind of benignity) throughout.

Any book of philosophy touched by Sir Isaiah Berlin is worth immediate attention, and his *The Crooked Timber of Humanity* (John Murray) is no exception, although he takes a position opposite to my own. After that, I must go to a position opposite absolutely everybody's; Lorraine Stobbart's *Utopia: Fact or Fiction?* (Alan Sutton) opts for Fact, and argues that More's book described a real place. Inevitably, I must list next *Heaven: A History* (Yale University Press), by Colleen McDannell and Bernhard Lang. The authors do not claim to have been there (mind you, Swedenborg claimed to have done so, and had had a most interesting conversation with the angels), but they deserve to go there for their book, which explores the idea of Heaven through the ages with a most felicitous touch.

Peter Marshall's *Demanding the Impossible* (HarperCollins) is a serious plea for Anarchism; clearly, he would never throw a bomb at anybody, so charmingly naïve is his thesis – that governments are unnecessary.

With Krishan Kumar we are back in the full flood of Utopia and its myriad streams, as his title immediately recognises: *Utopia and Anti-Utopia in Modern Times* (Blackwell). Scholarship (to which, incidentally, I do not lay claim) is here somewhat dry but comprehensive. Changing the form, we come to Lionel Davidson's *Under Plum Lake* (Cape), a children's book, but one so powerfully utopian that it must be shelved with the adult works.

Three more books come together, eyeing one another; these are Robert C. Elliott's *The Shape of Utopia* (Chicago University Press), John Ferguson's *Utopias of the Classical World* (Thames and Hudson) and Christopher Hill's *The World Turned Upside Down* (Penguin).

Sooner or later someone had to write a book called *The Politics of Utopia* (Hutchinson), and it has been written, though it took two authors, Barbara Goodwin and Keith Taylor, and no wonder.

Norman Cohn is one of those academics – they are, alas, few – who write in a style so beguiling that the reader begins to forget what the subject of discussion is: Mr Cohn never lets go of his unfolding story, and never lets go of his eloquence. His *The Pursuit of the Millennium* (Secker) is what all scholarship should be like.

Utopian worlds abound in this story, and one kind – science fiction – has been almost too thoroughly recorded. Brian Aldiss and David Wigmore, with their *Trillion Year Spree* (Gollancz), tell us everything we want to know about the subject, but it is so racily done that we go on reading for hundreds of pages without realising it. Of one book, though, no one would want even another single page, and indeed most would want several hundred fewer. That is the book that Sidney and Beatrice Webb (Longman's Green) wrote in hailing Stalin as the greatest democrat alive, even as Stalin was making millions of human beings dead. Their book was called *Soviet*

Communism: A New Civilisation.

Henry Brailsford's *Shelley, Godwin and Their Circle* (Oxford) puts the pacifist case, and Brailsford never ceased to do so, even through the two World Wars. Aldous Huxley's *Brave New World* (Chatto) is too familiar to need comment, and Herbert Read's *Anarchy and Order* (Faber) ought to be. The wonderful poem by A.J.S. Tessimond (Whiteknights Press), which fills the last pages of the book, sums up the utopian ideal in its perfect form.

There remain, among dozens more, two books of great significance. Thomas Molnar's *Utopia: The Perennial Heresy* (Tom Stacey) is a thunderous and merciless attack on the whole idea of Utopia, arguing that it takes away individual choice, and for that matter defies God. Anyone embarking upon yet another book about Utopia would be wise to put it in the last chapter, though I have not heeded my own advice.

Finally, there is *Utopian Thought in the Western World* (Harvard University Press), by Frank and Fritzie Manuel. This majestic study of Utopia, obviously complete, profoundly researched, eloquently written, a spring that anyone seeking the idea of Utopia should drink from, the Manuels' book is, in its comprehensiveness and insights a credit to scholarship. Or rather, it would be, if it had not stained scholarship with an index so scandalously useless that it mars the great enterprise. O reform it altogether!

But I owe a great debt to the friends and helpers who sustained me through the years like Penelope and her loom, and I must call the roll.

Catherine Tye, my cherished and indispensable secretary, did ten people's work; Oula Jones compiled the index without a flaw, as she has done with my past twelve books; Margaret Grant typed it all beautifully and rapidly; Stephen and Penny Ross looked after me impeccably in their Queensberry Hotel in Bath, where I went to write; I found further peace to write in the garden of Michael and Arianna Huffington, under blue skies, on the edge of the Pacific Ocean, and bathed in their hospitality from day to night; everyone at Jonathan Cape (especially Tom Maschler and Jenny Cottom) was encouraging and helpful; Mike Shaw, of Curtis Brown, my literary agent, would hear nothing but good tidings. (Alas, Brian Inglis, with whom I had a pact – we always proof-read each other's books – died before the proofs of this one were ready.) And Liz Anderson undertook that least rewarding and most drudging of tasks; she read the proofs.

Finally, when I was still prevaricating, and getting no further, my old friend Sir John Burgh took me aside and said 'If you don't write the book now, you will never write it.' Well, I have written it; I hope he likes it.

Index

Index

Index

Index